Does God really exist?

That question arises sooner or later in every human mind. It haunts the believer in his hours of doubt, the non-believer no less in his.

Several years ago, a serious illness raised the question in acute form for Thomas E. Powers, a New York advertising man.

Powers had been, in his own phrase, a "liberal-scientific-humanist-atheist-agnostic." He was fairly sure there was nothing to religion, but in desperation he decided to test for himself its assertion that God is, and that his reality can be experienced by anyone who honestly seeks him.

"It worked."

In those two words, from the preface, is the essential message of an extraordinary book by Powers.

This is not a stuffy academic discourse on spiritual life. It is a powerfully-written handbook on how to find God, by a man who did so, to his own vast surprise.

Although the intellectual level of this book is always adult, and at times even scholarly, Powers writes in the breezy, uninhibited language of the advertising man.

He gets down to brass tacks on the first page.

"If you are in trouble or in some sort of crisis — if you seriously and quickly need to satisfy yourself that God exists — it can be done without a lot of skull-cracking or waste of breath.

"Here is how:

"*First* — Avoid like the plague all unnecessary argument and debate. Accept God as a working hypothesis. You can do this without straining your intellectual integrity, whatever your outlook on life may be. Sincerely ask him, if he exists, to help you and steer you.

"*Second* — Find and associate with a group of people who really do believe in God and who are working their belief in daily life. Try to find a group who are really doing this and not just talking about it.

"*Third* — Be open and truthful with these people about your situation, whatever it is, and follow the reasonable suggestions they make to you. Begin to train yourself as they are training and to do the things they are doing.

"*Fourth* — Keep an open mind and watch. The evidence of God's presence and influence will appear in your own life, possibly sooner than you expect."

This is what Powers calls the "emergency" approach to God. And of it, he confidently says:

"I do not merely hope and believe it works. I know it works."

The rest of the book is directed to "those who are not in an acute crisis, and who have time to make a more leisurely and extensive approach to the subject of God's existence than is possible in a tight pinch."

While these pages also are irradiated with the contagious conviction of first-hand experience, Powers does not rely primarily on personal testimony. He has obviously spent much time in recent years studying the classics of religious mysticism, and it is from this rich storehouse that most of the wisdom in his book is admittedly drawn.

Somewhere along his personal religious Odyssey, Powers became a Christian. But the signposts he has erected along the way to God are not all from the Christian workshop; the book also quotes copiously from Hindu, Buddhist, Jewish and Islamic scriptures, and from such "non-religious" sources as the famed psychiatrist Carl Jung.

"Although I am now a professing Christian," says Powers, "I find truth, get help, and take delight in other religions. . . .

"I must say that acquaintance with the teachings and the people of other religions has never lessened, but on the contrary has deepened, my devotion to Jesus Christ."

For those who are already tentatively or securely committed to religious faith, this book offers a guide toward deeper understanding of the spiritual life.

For those who do not believe in God, but who are troubled by what G.K. Chesterton called "the first wild doubts of doubt," it is a compelling invitation to a great experiment.

Louis Cassels
United Press International
July 26, 1959

INVITATION TO A
GREAT EXPERIMENT

INVITATION TO A GREAT EXPERIMENT

Exploring the Possibility
That God Can Be Known

THOMAS E. POWERS

2009
24 Communications, Inc • USA
Hankins, NY

2009
24 Communications • USA
P.O. Box 500, Hankins, NY 12736
Copyright © 1975, 1990, 2009 by The Queen's Work, Inc.

Printed in the United States of America

Library of Congress Cataloging-in-Publication Data

Powers, Thomas E., 1911-2005
    Invitation to a great experiment.
    p.   cm.
    ISBN 978-0-914896-03-6
    1. Spiritual life 2. God — Knowableness.
    I. Title.
    BV4501.2.P6 2009
    616.86'1 — dc20   90-1933
                                             CIP

This is what you start with

This way of life is not something you merely read about and think about. It is something you do . . .

You start by learning a special technique with your alarm clock: You set it one hour earlier than usual, and when it rings you get up.

Do not underestimate (a) the importance and (b) the difficulty of this simple technique. It is important because it enables you to get what you absolutely need in order to get going on a new way of life — that is, *time*. Unless you make time for it, you will go nowhere. And if you are an alcoholic or involved with drugs or sick sex or some other kind of hard hangup, you can't afford through mere carelessness to lose your chance. So listen to this talk about the alarm clock, will you?

You set the clock one hour earlier than usual and get up. It is *hard to do*. Be prepared for that.

You can see why. It is hard because at first you do not set a high value on it. If somebody were to pay you one hundred dollars for every morning that you got up an hour early, you would do it very cheerfully every day. This new way of life gives you something more valuable than a hundred dollars a day, but who is convinced of that in the beginning? Nobody. All you can do is catch a glimpse from somebody else's experience and hang on to that at first.

It is hard to keep the rule of getting up one hour early every morning in order to do the work, *but it can be done*. And after a while your own direct personal experience will show you that there is something even more terrific than money or sex to be had. After that it will be easier to get up in the morning and to do whatever else is necessary, because even in the face of great difficulties it is easy to do what you love.

I am not theorizing or guessing here but reporting to you out of actual practice. If you will hang in there and really use this hour in the morning, a basic change begins to take place in your relationship to yourself, to the people around you, and to God. *If you will merely do it*, something very big begins to happen. This way of life requires an investment of your time, your interest, and yourself. It pays off very large on the investment; but with no investment, nothing is possible. A great deal hangs on that hour in the morning.

What do you do with the hour? There is a lot of room for using your own judgment and following your own tastes, but it helps at the outset to follow some kind of schedule that has been worked out and found effective in actual practice by a number of people who have really been doing this thing. The following is such a schedule:

You divide the time into three periods of twenty minutes each. In the first period you *read*. In the second period you *pray or meditate*. In the third period you *exercise*.

For what to read, see pages 207-230 and 239-247. There is a *great* bunch of stuff to choose from. But remember that you are reading for know-how and not just fun. A lot of this literature is tremendously intriguing and fascinating, but all of it has a desperately serious underlying purpose: to communicate to you the reality of God and give you practical knowledge as to how to live from day to day.

From your reading you can learn how to get started in praying, meditating, and exercising. Soon you will be able to learn from, and also to help, other people, and that will really begin to change your life.

CONTENTS

This Is What You Start With   xi
Introduction   1

PART ONE
God Is an Experimentally
Knowable Reality. True or False?

Chapter One
First Things First   7
    In Case of Emergency   7
    If You Qualify . . .   10
    It Is Very Easy — and Very Hard   20

Chapter Two
Toward Action: The People, the Books, and the Laboratory   23
    Who Are the Right People?   23
    What Are the Right Books?   30
    Where Is the Laboratory?   41

Chapter Three
The Ways to Knowledge   45
    "With All Thy Mind" — the Way of Reason   45
    "With All Thy Strength" — the Way of Faith   53
    "With All Thy Heart and Soul" — the Way of Experience   58

PART TWO
Is the Experiment
a Practical Possibility?

Chapter One
What, Specifically, Do You Do?   77
    The Alternatives   77
    The Rules   80

Chapter Two
The Practical Life Means Practice   87
    The Practice of the Presence of God   88
    The Practice of Ego-reduction or Dying Daily   96
    The Practice of Watching   106

PART THREE
God's Will:
How to Know It and Do It

Chapter One
God's Will Is The Door; Prayer Is The Key   123
    God Speaks Continuously . . .   126
    But Who Can Hear Him?   128

Chapter Two
How To Use The Key   133
    The Practice of Abandonment   140
    The Practice of Penetrating the Cloud   149
    The Practice of Continuous Prayer   163

Bibliography   183

Special Book Listings   207

Appendix A.
Examples of Spiritual Experience in Holy Scripture   227

Appendix B.
The All Addicts Anonymous Way of Life   231

Appendix C.
The Greatest Books   239

Appendix D.
The Relationship of the Higher and Lower Selves   249

Appendix E.
Group Experience Using *Invitation to a Great Experiment* as a
Work Book   253

Index   261

INVITATION TO A
GREAT EXPERIMENT

Introduction

Osokin and the magician are both silent.

"What am I to do then?" says Osokin at last almost in a whisper.

There is a long pause.

"My dear friend," says the magician, breaking the silence, "those are the first sensible words I have heard from you since the beginning of our acquaintance. . . . You come here, you complain, and you ask for a miracle. And, when I can, I do what you ask because I sincerely wish to help you. But nothing comes of it. Try now to understand why nothing comes of it and why I am powerless to help you. Understand that I can carry out only your wishes, only what you ask for. I cannot give you anything on my own initiative. This is the law. Even what I am saying now I am able to say only because you asked me what you are to do. If you had not asked, I could not have spoken."

Ouspensky, *Strange Life of Ivan Osokin*

God can do anything, but "can do" is not "will do." He *will* do certain things, it appears, only in response to certain of man's doings. God evidently waits and watches for particular freely initiated actions on the part of man. One of these actions is the asking of questions.

And therefore questions are important in the search for reality. A smart man who "knows" so much that he has stopped asking questions can get way off base. A stupid or beaten or broken man who happens to be humble enough to ask real questions may be near to real answers.

This is a book of questions. It is not exactly a book of answers. I am concerned with answers, of course, but I do not hope to give them, only to indicate them. The answers to the questions raised here would make a library, not a book. And the library would fall short of the real answers, because they are to be found in life rather than in libraries, and in the power and presence of God rather than in unregenerate "life."

The experiment of finding God is studied in this book under the headings of three key questions: (1) God Is an Experimentally Knowable Reality. True or False? (2) Is the Experiment a Practical Possibility? (3) God's Will: How to Know It and Do It.

Answers to such questions are not cheap; you have to work for them. But if you undertake this work seriously you find yourself being helped. And among the helps are people and books. One of the ways in which the present book may serve you is in suggesting how you can get in touch with people and work with them. Another aspect of this manual's possible usefulness to you is in suggesting other books which may be helpful. Throughout the following discussions of particular questions, related works and authors are indicated.

In a book of this kind the personal element is inescapable, and since responsibility for it should be taken, perhaps it will help for the author to identify himself briefly: I was born in Chadron, Nebraska, in 1911. At the age of twenty-nine I was a liberal-scientific-humanist-atheist-agnostic — a real omelet. I was an agreeable, witty, thin, and nervous fellow. I was doing very well in the advertising business. But at the same time I was suffering from a mentally and physically crippling illness which the doctors at last pronounced incurable. Doctors are a solemn lot anyhow, and these doctors were not fooling. I had to believe them. Much against the grain of my whole outlook at that time, I was persuaded to seek help in the area of "spiritual experience." I didn't know what it was, and it sounded suspiciously like religion, but in desperation finally I was willing to try it.

It worked. The disease was arrested and eventually fully relieved. But the process went much further. Over a period of years, many problems, previously only half-realized, began to come to the surface and be corrected. A lively co-operation was necessary, but a Power greater than myself obviously was doing the job.

Just on the basis of facts in which I was profoundly involved,

I had to drop my prejudices against God and the great cultural and psychological traditions ascending to God. There is no possibility of describing either the joy or the difficulties that came into my life when I saw that God is real and when I began trying to come into actual touch with that Reality. (Everyone and everything is of course in contact with God; the great turning begins to take place when the contact becomes in some degree *conscious*.)

Somewhere along the line I began trying to be a Christian. I am still trying. I am also strongly drawn to the truth in other great religions. I must say that acquaintance with the teachings and the people of other religions has never lessened, but on the contrary has deepened, my devotion to Jesus Christ. All men are children of one Father, and while it is perhaps inevitable that we should differ about his nature and names, it is a planetary shame and scandal that we get into murderous quarrels about such things.

Only one considerable point of disagreement occurred among my associates in the preparation of this work. We were not of one opinion about the advisability of including a wide variety of material pertaining to the many different religious and psychological systems of the world, as opposed to sticking more strictly to Christianity.

I am seriously impressed with the limitations and difficulties of including many diverse sources. One of my counselors posed this question: "If we are to consider Buddhism, Islam, Hinduism, and Christianity in the same view, are we not in danger of confusing and misleading readers? Are we not in for trouble if we begin to look everywhere for our light and push no tradition far enough to do more than confuse the one in which we are at home?"

I was so struck by the reality of these difficulties that I went some way to avoid them in the structure of this book. But I did not go all the way, for the following reason: it seems to me that there are very large numbers of our fellow citizens and fellow truth-seekers who are not at all "at home" in a religious tradition. These not-at-homers I venture, in all honor and with real affection, to call spiritual mongrels. They include many persons of deep spiritual devotion and considerable spiritual experience. I must confess my own position in this regard, for it will color this entire book, and I must briefly indicate my own viewpoint to which I intend to be faithful:

I am a member of the Christian community and cherish its interests, but I started out in the regenerate life as a mongrel, mothered and taught by mongrels. I have an essential kinship with the breed. I cannot disown it, and would not if I could. I am convinced that spiritual mongrels have an important work to do in the world, a work which may even have a certain deep relation to the core of Christianity: the brotherhood of man.

Although now a professing Christian, I am still a mongrel, in that I find truth, get help, and take delight in other religions, past and present, in nonreligious spiritual movements, and in religiously unlabeled spiritually oriented men. I do look everywhere for my light, and I do not find the process confusing but, on the contrary, illuminating and edifying. I believe that it is possible and necessary for many of us today in seeking the face of God to look not only high but low and not only at home but abroad. This outlook is rooted in deep conviction. I am stuck with it, and, if you read further, so are you.

I have written this book, and have suggested other books and sources, not only for my brother Christians but also for my brother mongrels. I am aware of the dangers of a too wide and therefore undisciplined interest in the various spiritual springs and streams of mankind. But I am also aware of what seem to me the even greater dangers of too narrow an interest. I am sure that readers may be misled at either extreme. While respecting the more restricted view, I am frankly on the broad side. Let the reader, if he is an at-home Christian and not a mongrel, beware.

In my own search, many people and many groups have given me help, much of which I am not in a position to acknowledge here. There is one group of spiritual pioneers on the earth at this time to whom I owe the most. They know who they are, and they know how much I owe.

Thomas E. Powers

Hankins, NY
St. Patrick's Day, 1990

PART ONE

God Is
an Experimentally
Knowable Reality.
True or False?

CHAPTER ONE
First Things First

Kindergarten is a strange place for an adult to arrive, as a student. But kindergarten is the only safe place and the only practical place from which to launch the kind of experiment that this book proposes.

There is no way to avoid touching upon matters in the beginning that may seem painfully elementary. A quick plunge into deep waters may produce unnecessary snorting and choking. A bit of prudent wading about in the shallows is indicated as a preliminary.

In Case of Emergency

If you are in trouble or in some sort of crisis — if you seriously and quickly need to satisfy yourself of God's reality — it can be done without a lot of skull-cracking or waste of breath. I know it can be done because I have seen many men and women, in real need, do it. Here is how:

First: avoid like the plague all unnecessary argument and debate. Accept God as a working hypothesis. You can do this without straining your intellectual integrity, whatever your outlook on life may be. Sincerely ask him, if he exists, to help you and steer you. Second: find and associate with a group of people who really do believe in God and who are working their belief in daily life. Try to find a group who are really doing this and not just talking about it. Third: be open and truthful with these people about your situation, whatever it is, and follow the reasonable suggestions they make to you. Begin to train yourself as they are training and do the things they are doing. Fourth: keep an open mind and *watch*. The evidence of God's presence and influence will appear in your own life, possibly sooner than you expect.

"Find and associate with a group" — I realize that this is more easily said than done. Nevertheless, it is possible.

And certain kinds of trouble make it easy. For example, if you are so fortunate as to be an alcoholic or a drug addict, you will find precisely the kind of group I recommend — one where the people are not merely talking about the work but doing it — in Alcoholics Anonymous, Narcotics Anonymous, or All Addicts Anonymous. If your trouble is gambling or neurosis or overeating, you will find the same kind of group opportunity in Gamblers Anonymous, Neurotics Anonymous, or Overeaters Anonymous.

But suppose you are not eligible for one of these communities. In that case I suggest you start looking in religion, your own if you have one, otherwise in other religions. There are churches where intensive, serious group work in search for God is being done — and where people are not merely talking about it but doing it. Granted, you will not find what you need in every church; religion is a very mixed scene today. You just have to look for the real thing until you find it. If you are a lazy looker or easily discouraged, please notice the heading on this section of this book. It reads: In Case of Emergency. Nobody in an emergency can afford to be lazy or easily discouraged.

If for whatever reason you cannot find a group to work with, you can start one. All you need is two or three people who are in the same boat you are in and who are serious enough to meet once a week and do some work on themselves in between meetings.

I don't want to make the problem of groups seem to be easier than it really is. It is relatively easy to start a group. To keep it going over a period of time is another matter, involving in most cases heavy resistance and serious difficulties. Nevertheless, it can be done.

Also I don't want to seem to be saying that you can't get anywhere without working in a group. You can do a lot for yourself by studying and applying what you learn in your own life from day to day. But sooner or later, no matter how successful you are in working on your own, you will come up against the need of working with others. It is one of the laws of the game, and in an emergency it applies early on.

This book does not build up to any kind of climax. We are not sneaking up on anything. We are exploring working principles and experience. Do not, therefore, underestimate the workable possibilities of the suggestion made here at the outset. I have firsthand knowledge of several thousand men and women of widely different ages and conditions who actually have taken this step and achieved radical success in it. I do not merely hope and believe it works; I know it works.

The description given here is bare bones only, but it is enough to make a start, if you are interested in working and not just reading. I write for a living, and I don't want to say anything that is bad for business, but I have to tell you that writing and reading about God's reality are not good unless there is a real solid chunk of work in the picture, too. Read about it all you want, but that is a waste of time unless you also work at it.

If you do make the experiment outlined above, you may find some of the stuff in these pages helpful as you go along. But above all do not become complicated or confused. The following material is intended for those who are *not* in an acute crisis in their development and who have time to make a more leisurely and extensive approach to the question of God's reality than is possible in a tight pinch. If your need for God is in the emergency stage, stay close to your friends who do believe in God and who are working their belief, and pull back to the simple terms of the experiment as indicated. There are never any real grounds for discouragement. In general, the greater your need, the easier it is to make a real contact with God.

(In case of extreme emergency: If you are in a hospital or are otherwise restricted, if you are cut off from ordinary human contacts and maybe even from books, or if perhaps you are so ill that you have nothing to hope for in this world, your situation is particularly favorable. For great things, indeed the greatest things, are possible between the undefended human heart and God. You are, or you can be if you choose, way ahead of most of the rest of us. You have nothing to learn from us. We could learn from you.)

If you really mean business in a critical period you can go a long way with no more knowledge than you get from reading and acting upon the suggestions in this first short section. That is the advantage of a crisis; it builds a fire under us; it gets us off our seats and into action. Crises, however, do not last. They present unusual difficulties and unusual opportunities, but the difficulties and opportunities pass. If you miss the tide one time, you have to wait until the next time, and nobody knows when that will be. But meanwhile you can make progress toward real answers if you want to. The effort is slower and more likely to peter out in normal times than in tough times, but it can be done.

So if you are not in a crisis, cheer up and read on. There is hope for you, too.

If You Qualify . . .

Is there a God? And can I enter into conscious contact with him? Unless the sanest element in the human race is crazy, real answers to these questions are possible. Not just intellectual answers but answers involving the entire man, answers that satisfy the intellect, the emotions, the instincts, and the deepest longings of the human heart. If you qualify, it is possible to reach such answers.

What does it mean, "if you qualify"? It means first of all trying to be honest with yourself and asking yourself some questions. The first question is *"Am* I honest?" And if the answer is a quick yes, you face the unpleasant fact that this answer is probably a lie. For the question of honesty is never that easy. Lying and self-deception are built into us deeply. An impressive majority of men are in some degree liars. This means not just phonies and sad sacks, but solid citizens, good family men, pillars of the community. And so it may include you. Of course only you would know. But *do* you know?

There is no concern at this point with philosophy or morals but only with a cool fact of experience that may be verified by anyone who will take the trouble — say, a week of alert observation — to notice how much plain and fancy lying he and his neighbors are doing. It will be seen more easily and clearly among the neighbors, of course, but with careful attention the same beast will be discovered in one's own back yard, too.

This is not to take a dim view of the human situation but to face a fact that must be faced, or no progress toward knowledge of God is possible. Unrecognized or unadmitted dishonesty obstructs the pursuit of any kind of knowledge. In the pursuit of God knowledge it is a fatal obstacle. Until the problem of honesty is sincerely faced, you are not qualified even to make a start toward finding real answers to questions about God's reality and availability.

Listen to the late Episcopal bishop of Pittsburgh as he cranks up and cracks this particular nail right on the head:

> Any religious movement or denomination that does not constantly seek to lead individuals to face the truth about themselves is not fulfilling its fundamental Christian responsibility. It is entirely possible to be an academic, or intellectual, or ritualistic adherent to the Christian Church and yet not be a Christian at heart. We can go further and say that it is possible to be a cardinal, bishop, dean, priest or minister in the highest ecclesiastical standing and still miss the point of practice of the faith: to "walk humbly before God," which means to be open to the truth about oneself, regardless of how much it hurts.
>
> Austin Pardue

That is a real cooking-type bishop. He understands what the boys in the beet fields are up against. What we are up against is the crude datum that God is truth. He has said so plainly through the mouth of Jesus of Nazareth and through many other mouths, ancient and modern.

God, as the Upanishad says, ". . . is found by veracity. . . . Falsehood turns from the way; truth goes all the way; the way is paved with truth." Every time you turn away from the truth, for whatever reason, you turn away from God. It is that simple. This is not a play with words. It is one of the facts of life. Truth is not only that which is known; it is also *the power to know*; it is the ability to see and understand. Therefore every time you tell a lie you throw sand in your own eyes. This is a law that anyone who wishes to may observe. These are kindergarten spiritual facts that you cannot skate around no matter how fancy a mental figure you may be able to cut.

Are you willing to raise the issue of honesty with yourself, really raise it and keep it raised, and to learn from other people who are also sweating out this elementary discipline? Are you willing, steadily and patiently and relentlessly over a long period of time, to look squarely into your own honesty and dishonesty, even when this involves painful discoveries and hard effort? If so, you are qualified in this area and may proceed. *But if you proceed without this qualification,* your subsequent efforts will lead not to real answers but to confusion, disputation, and high soarings followed by great crashes.

As sure as you are reading this page, unless you are alert to the necessity of rigorous honesty your efforts to study and work toward knowledge of God will run into subtle self-deceit, "holy" imagination, and other forms of pious blah. It is hard to believe when you are first told it, but take my word that this is the way it *always* works. People love to hear this God-seeking tune played soft and sweet on violins with dim lights and flowers, but the initial sound is more like somebody falling into the drums. The fact is that you have to be crudely, brutally, mercilessly honest with yourself even to make a pass at knowledge of God. Every man thinks he is an exception, and no man is. Unless you put yourself on the honesty carpet with the rest of the spiritual small boys, this flight never gets off the ground. (I hear you crying, and I am full of sympathy. In fact I am crying with you. This is my problem, too. The only comfort I can think of is that we have so much company.)

Note, please, that you are not required at first to *become* honest, in any permanent sense. Even a little research will show you that *becoming* honest is stubbornly elusive and probably will remain so for quite a while. No, all that is required is that you take a good hard look at your own honesty problem and go to work on it. You just *try* to be honest and keep trying. The effort is what counts, for a long time. To quickly say, "Now I am honest!" is kid stuff. To expect early results is to walk into an egotistical booby trap; it is to underestimate the problem and overestimate yourself. Progress comes from patiently trying, even in the face of little or no results. Real, practicing honesty is possible, but it is amazingly difficult. The actual accomplishment has to be slow, because when this mountain moves, the whole man and all his affairs move with it. You are working toward a spiritual avalanche here. It is well that you cannot hurry. The secret is to keep trying.

If you flinch from the discomfort of the effort, or get your dignity up, or fall for your own rationalizations (lies in defense of lies), you are defeated at the start. But, once past these initial blocks, the task of dealing effectively with the honesty issue becomes something that nearly anyone can do and do pretty well, with an increasing sense of enjoyment of the game. The only considerable group of noninstitutionalized people who appear incapable of progress in truth-facing and truth-telling is a class known as constitutional psychopathic inferiors, psychopathic personalities, or moral defectives. These folks are not insane in any ordinary sense, but it seems that they just haven't got it and can't get it in the honesty department, a condition which seems at first glance relatively harmless but which is finally more appalling and hopeless than many of the real psychoses.*

Actually, trying to be honest, while not as easy as the uninitiated suppose, is not at all grim slogging either. The attempt to be honest is an exhilarating challenge which, the moment it is accepted, releases powerful energies. There are apt to be explosions of laughter on the way. It is a relief and refreshment to the soul to drop the pose of being "an honest man," to admit kinship with the rest of the human race in this matter of lying and deceiving, and to begin calmly trying to catch the monkey at the monkey business.†

One attractive and plausible diversion that it is well to watch

---

* See *The Mask of Sanity* by Hervey Cleckley, M.D.

† Throughout this book references are made to "the monkey" and "the adversary." It will be clear from the contexts that we are dealing with the element best known historically as the devil. In deference to contemporary sharply split notions about the devil, no theological or morphological view is proposed here. As a matter of practical fact, however, there *is* a force, or congeries of forces, which operates within human psychophysical nature in a tricky, destructive, or malign way. "Monkey" and "adversary" are time-honored terms for designating this entity, whatever his shape, essence, and number may be. It would be much more convenient to ignore him, but nobody yet has succeeded in doing so. All that is achieved by evasive tactics is a change of names. If

for and avoid on the way to honesty runs something like this: "I am now trying to live truthfully. Very well, I have a problem. I have been thinking about it a lot and I feel I *must* find an answer. Suppose I was living under a tyrannical government and my own son was a fugitive and was hiding in my house and the secret police came and asked me point-blank if he was in the house. Should I lie to save him?"

The reply to that one is that you learn by solving real truth problems, not fictitious ones. You can work up a fine moral sweat by dreaming up these imaginary dilemmas or by agonizing over them in novels or on television. But that is not actually your problem, and it may distract seriously from reality by draining off energy and attention into a running moral soap opera. Your problem is to be truthful in the real situations of real life, not in your own or some author's imagination. Sure, you can learn from the experience of others, but you should observe where fiction begins and where it leaves off, and where it is helpful and where it is not.

In everyone's life there are real and powerful tensions between the requirements of truth and the requirements of love. These tensions create painful problems. *But in real life the problems are never insolvable.* Impossible truth-love tensions occur only in books or in imaginations. In real life you never have to choose between being really truthful and being really loving. It is often exceedingly difficult but it is never impossible to be both truthful and loving. In real life, that is. Try it and see.

And skip the imaginary gymnastics. They do more harm than good, even as a workout. Reality provides plenty of exercise. It is unnecessary and nearly always unwise to call upon the imagination in this connection. The reason why is interesting: in real life the factor of the grace of God is always present. In fiction, even good fiction, it is never present in the same way. And in poor fiction, which is what most of our imaginings are, grace is left out of account altogether, and so you create false problems. To exercise yourself with this sort of thing never is very helpful, and

you are more comfortable with the modern labels, you may call him your subconscious, negative thinking, or what you will. The fact is, he's around, and it is a good idea to be aware of it.

it can be a serious distraction from the real life work which is always at hand, awaiting only your attention.

Honesty is important in itself and also for two great by-products: (1) humility, called the queen of the virtues because it mothers all the rest and keeps them from corruption, and (2) the ability to be yourself.

It is practically impossible to achieve these two immensely valuable qualities by direct efforts. Attempts to be humble tend to be self-defeating or to produce caricatures of humility. Likewise with being yourself: if you deliberately set out to do it, you are likely to end up just putting on an act.

But regular work in practicing honesty automatically deflates pride and arrogance and thus produces a marginal increment of real humility. (If you look at the humility too hard, of course, or rejoice in it too much, it is apt to evaporate. Look at it, if you must, out of the corner of your eye.) And finally, a man who is growing genuinely more honest and more humble does not have to struggle to be himself; it begins to come naturally. The relief in returning to oneself is almost incredible and sometimes almost insupportable. I know men who have wept when they felt it for the first time. The blessed, blessed freedom, the release and joy, of not having to maintain a front, not having to curry favor, not having to fool anyone! The clear, unshifting gaze and the steady nerves! This is worth working for!

Individual, personal work on oneself, trying to apply the principles of honesty and responsibility and fair dealing in the regular daily affairs of one's own life — this, of course, is basic. But without the further aid of a specific kind of group activity, the best efforts at self-honesty are likely to become slipshod, ingrown, and curiously blind after a time.

Why is special group work necessary? Because I can't see my own faults clearly, no matter how hard I try. In the right kind of group, I can get a look at myself through the eyes of others in a way that is deeply revealing and deeply releasing.

During the past few years truth-centered groups have become popular all over the country — a curious development with both good and bad aspects. These groups are usually called "encounter" groups or "inventory" groups, or, when they are extended over a day or two, "marathons."

The elemental power of these groups is great, and it comes from a single source: the truth. Unfortunately many of these groups do not adhere to the simple strengths of the process but soon find themselves involved in an increasing maze of devices, techniques, acts, stunts, tricks, and assorted embellishments that plunge the whole enterprise into mere gimmickry.

Your group discovers, let's say, that it seems good to sit around in a circle holding hands. Well, so far so good. Next, somebody suggests that it would go better if all were barefoot. So, okay. But then some cutie wants to hold the proceedings in pajamas, and another wants to add laurel wreaths for everyone, and one of the weightier brains perceives that it would be great with everybody in the nude. And so on. The details are now common and rather dreary knowledge. In this way a powerful and useful thing is turned into a childish game.

But don't let the game fool you. The thing in itself is clean, sane, and profound — and it is one of the essential tools of the spiritual life. It is not, as the gamesters would have you believe, new. It is very old. It is what the early Christians were doing in their meetings. It is what Gautama's people were doing in the sangha. It is what the Essenes did, and the Therapeutae, and the Desert Fathers, and the Hesychasts, and the Benedictines, and indeed every for-real spiritual group that ever existed.

This kind of honesty and openness is what was going on in the Oxford Groups — "absolute honesty" they were simple enough to call it — and this is what the founders of Alcoholics Anonymous picked up in the O.G. and incorporated into the first movement on earth that ever brought recovery to any considerable number of alcoholics.

The idea of rigorous honesty and openness in groups has spread throughout the land and finally become what many popular things become: a fad with a lot of foolishness overlaying its essential validity and power. But I repeat, don't let the fad fool you. There is something of the most fundamental importance in the work of small groups of people who agree to honor rigorously the principles of truth, openness, and responsibility in their lives and in their group work together.

I am talking about groups who work with the simple power of the principles, and without tricks, gimmicks, idiocy, or publicity. Do such groups exist? Indeed they do. They are relatively rare and hard to find, but they do exist. And if you can't find one you can found one.

When you have seen the necessity of trying to become honest with yourself, then another question can be asked: "Are you serious?" Serious, in this regard, does not mean devoid of humor. It means, "Are you in earnest? Are you sincere? Do you really need to get these answers about God, or are you just making talk?"

This God business is not a parlor game. Either, as the atheists think, there is nothing to it, or there is so much to it that it is no place for fooling around. Of course any amount of fooling around is possible. But in this area, of all areas of inquiry, the mere conversationalist is particularly apt to get nowhere.

You can be more or less sincere in your attitude toward the basic God questions, and the deeper degrees of sincerity cannot be summoned by a snap of the fingers. If you are dying of cancer, for example, you are capable of much greater earnestness in facing the questions about God than is a well-fed, well-heeled, healthy, and happy citizen. But you cannot safely postpone your inquiry into the reality of God until the great crises of life and death are upon you. It is necessary to get on with it now, recognizing that the complacency that comes from temporary well-being and the "happiness" gained by separating your life from the life of suffering humanity are not helps but hindrances to sincerity in approaching the truth of God.

So, if your interest is not merely superficial but to some degree sincere, serious, and based on real need, you qualify in a further important respect.

Another question: "Are you willing to learn?" Many of us aren't. Sorry. But we really are not. After we get out of school and have learned our trade or business, we get out of the way of learning. We say we would like to learn about God. Well, maybe so. But also maybe we only want to get into some talk sessions and issue judgments and state preformed opinions on the subject. Maybe what we really want is not to learn, but merely to converse, to entertain and be entertained. This won't do, of course. With such a start there can be only the dreariest of vaporings about the questions of God.

Regardless of our physical age, there must be a certain youthfulness in the mind, an elasticity and eagerness retained or recaptured in spite of the burden of our years and our dignity and importance as men of the world. Otherwise the way to knowledge of God is shut up tight against us. We cannot begin to go through the needle's eye with our usual baggage of fixed ideas. Don't say, "I don't have them." We all do. Observe yourself inwardly for a week and see.

Somehow we must become young in mind and heart at the very beginning of this inquiry. Christ said we could not make the grade unless we turned and became as little children. Who can do that? Willingness to learn is no joke. Again, a quick answer in the affirmative is probably a lie. It is not that easy. But if after some real experimental work on yourself you are able to say, "Yes, I *am* willing to learn," you have added another indispensable qualification.

At this point it may seem that this is a blood, sweat, and tears approach, and to a certain extent so it is. "Are there," you may say, "no joys, no satisfactions?" Yes, there are great joys and great satisfactions. But if you are in such a hurry to get to the joys that you skip over the difficulties and ignore the disciplines, you arrive at no joys and no satisfactions, or worse, false joys and false satisfactions, ending in discouragement and even possibly in spiritual catastrophe.

The next question is: "Are you willing to work hard?"

Everyone understands and accepts the necessity of hard work in acquiring ordinary knowledge. If you want to learn, let's say, chemistry, you do not expect to get anywhere by holding a few conversations on the subject. And you do not just sit. Particularly you do not sit in your living room and expect to develop the laws and techniques of chemistry out of your own ruminations. No. If you really want to learn chemistry you get up off your chair and go to work. And you expect to work hard. You get in touch with people who have studied chemistry and practiced chemistry and submitted to the disciplines of chemistry and who consequently have some knowledge of chemistry. And you try to learn from them. You attend lectures. You take notes and study them. You get hold of the recommended books. Some of them may seem dry and difficult, but you dig into them anyhow because you know you must. You spend regular hours and long hours and lots of hours in the laboratory. And little by little you begin to know chemistry. Your knowledge is not final or complete, but it is real, effective, workable knowledge.

Now, does all this make you a hero? You know it does not. You know that everyone who learns chemistry (a few geniuses excepted) has got to learn it this way, by hard work. Everybody grumbles a little about this state of affairs but nobody seriously questions the fact of it.

And yet when we come to spiritual knowledge, learning about reality, learning about God, a strange conceit and an even stranger sentimentality appear. More often than not the candidate imagines that *this* kind of knowledge can be poured into him like oil into a cruet, with no pain, no strain, no work, and certainly no *hard* work. This attitude, if it exists, is a considerable obstacle. It is based on the common assumption that since God is a loving Father, he must also be a silly old fool who would just as soon raise a brood of spoiled brats as a company of transcendentally competent, strong, gentle, brave, compassionate, free, and triumphant sons.

Whatever God may be, he is not some kind of chucklehead. It is a crude mistake to suppose that we may presume upon his paternity to expect him to suspend the laws of the universe or amend them hastily and miraculously in our favor just because we have lately deigned to become interested in him. Also we can hardly expect to seize the reins of divine power and go off on various kinds of health, wealth, and success drives in the first few years of our apprenticeship. There is a vogue for this sort of thing today, but it never gets anywhere over any period of time, because the Law is stern enough and tender enough to check it before it has gone very far. God is no doubt even more loving and kind and provident than anybody ever said he was. But at the same time, most fortunately for us, he is not a big boob whose leg we can pull for favors or whose pocket we can pick for material or spiritual perquisites.

Knowledge about God, and particularly knowledge *of* God, is not easier to come by than ordinary knowledge; it is harder. How could it be otherwise? Certainly there is such a thing as God's grace. And he does undoubtedly temper the wind to the shorn lamb. And he is the help of the helpless. And we cannot take one step in his direction without his prevenient mercy. And his yoke is easy and his burden is light. But at the same time no man may reasonably hope to come to knowledge of God without working harder than he ever worked in his life, without literally and painfully stretching every nerve, without grunting for it at least as heartily as he grunts for money.

It Is Very Easy — and Very Hard

There is no way around this paradox: the way is very easy and it is very hard. The logical mind wants to know which is true. The answer is that both are true, equally true, deeply true, and that there is no contradiction. Can this be? Yes, it can. One of the first bits of knowledge that our hard work will win for us is this: that while the logical mind has a very high place in the quest, it has not by any means the highest place. Transcendental wisdom, even the kind we encounter in spiritual nursery school, comes from a level at which the logical mind can only stutter and blink like an owl.

And since most of us today are heavily centered and identified in the logical mind, our first hard work will win for us not only a little knowledge but also a little humility, a precious advantage so early in the game.

So this is kindergarten. These are the qualifications you need to invoke and develop before you can go on safely toward real answers. In summary:

1. You've got to try to be *honest.* (Honestly, will you?)
2. You've got to be *willing to learn.* (Honestly, are you willing?)
3. You've got to *work hard.* (Honestly, now, will you?)

Even in this elementary stage, you must find other people who are doing this job and you must associate with them and work with them, helping them and accepting help from them. It is impossible to do it alone. This is no mere opinion; it is knowledge won from hard experience, from trial and error. Some of us have tried it alone. It doesn't work. Solitude is indicated in parts of the way, certainly. But no one yet has gone the whole route alone. Christ himself did not accomplish his assignment without human association, without forming a group, without working with people.

You've got to work with others, and you've got to sink yourself to the neglected level of simple honesty, of elementary truth-telling staying patiently with it and working from there. Certain basic books along these lines may be consulted, the most basic of which is the Bible. Notice that the truth occupies a central position in the New Testament and especially in the Gospel According to St. John. The Fourth Evangelist's view of the truth ranges from the first description of God's appearance in human flesh, "full of grace and truth," to the showdown between the divine verity and the sophisticated ignorance of this world, expressed in Pilate's enigmatic question "What is truth?" See John 1:14, 1:17, 3:21, 4:24, 5:33, 8:40, 8:44, 14:6, 14:17, 15:26, 16:13, 17:17, 17:19, 18:37, 18:38.

In connection with realizing the importance of truth, an acquaintance with M. K. Gandhi is suggested; his book *My Experiments with Truth* is a starting place; Vincent Sheean's *Lead, Kindly Light* is a good follow-up; try also Louis Fischer's biography *The Life of Mahatma Gandhi.*

We necessarily have had to beat the truth and honesty bushes so hard in this first chapter that the writer becomes involved here in a peculiar way. I fully expect to be caught in my own bear trap. Surely some person, wandering through this book, is going to find places where the truth is violated. The person will then say: "Powers, you preach but you do not practice. If you are such a steaming hot character in the truth department, why have you fostered a book with untruths in it?" So I hereby take refuge in a prior disclaimer. Most of the warmth which I experience in attempting to practice truth arises, not from the comforting radiations of success, but from the friction of repeated full-tilt running pratfalls. I cannot promise that the present writing will be devoid of untruth. I can and do promise that such untruth as it contains will be the result of ignorance or incompetence and not of intention.

The problem of finding the people, the books, and the laboratory facilities with which you will actually go to work now presents itself. We turn to that next.

CHAPTER TWO

Toward Action: The People, the Books, and the Laboratory

If you qualify at the kindergarten level already indicated — if you are willing to try humbly and stubbornly to be honest with yourself, if you are willing to swallow your grown-up pride and go to class again in the school of the spirit, if you are willing to give to this enterprise at least as much work as you would give to something important in ordinary life — then you are ready to move toward action. You will need three helps: (1) the right people, (2) the right books, and (3) a suitable laboratory or workplace.

Who Are the Right People?

They are the people who to some extent already know what you are seeking to know and who may be willing to help you and teach you. Do such people exist — people who really know the truth about God, people, further, who have direct knowledge of God?

Yes, they do exist. I testify that they do.

This is not merely a pious hope. It is a statement of fact, based upon my own and others' experience. Just at the point when the powers of darkness are at their strongest, the power of God is more than ever apparent. It has been so in my own case. God knows I've sunk deep enough in this life, into very black areas where I did not believe or see how it could possibly be true that there was any Spirit, any hope, any truth. And in that blackness messengers of light, people, came to me and said, "Look, God *is* true!" They didn't get it out of books; they were talking out of their own experience; they were people who had been in the same kind of darkness I was in.

I see people who have *not* reached into the extremes of despair and nevertheless are awake and alert and have caught this good news and are helping others and being helped. I have great faith not just in the hope of this community but in the actuality of it. This wonderful thing permeates the world much more extensively than is believed by those who are not yet consciously involved in it. It transcends and overwhelms and soaks up the world's misery.

When you seriously set yourself to seek for the truth, the truth brings into your life men and women who have different degrees of authentic knowledge and who are able to pass it on to you, *if you are alert to the opportunity* and willing to receive what is offered. You have to be on the lookout for these people. They do not appear ringing bells and waving flags. Their real nature is hidden from the reach of careless scrutiny. They do not lightly disclose themselves. You might know one of them quite intimately in an ordinary life situation, say that of a business associate or even a brother or sister, and yet not know him at all from a deeper standpoint.

This is not a cloak-and-dagger operation; it is just the way it has to work if it is to occur in this world at all. At intervals and for special reasons a truth-bearing person permits his nature to be seen without veiling and without defense. And then there is apt to be a terrific hue and cry and a great outburst of worshiping and hating. The person so exposed often is injured or killed. So caution is necessary.

It is not that the spiritually awakened are not willing to witness, willing to help, and willing to sacrifice everything to those ends. They are aware of the sayings "Let your light so shine before men" and "He who does not confess me before men, him will I not confess before the Father." But they are also aware that there is danger of a useless and wasteful trampling under foot. They remember the counsel to be as harmless as doves *and* as wise as serpents. And they recall the admonition, repeated so many times, "Tell no man." The awakened, even the slightly awakened, have a keen respect for the ignorance, perversity, and violence latent in unregenerate human nature, and they are unwilling to provoke it except at their Lord's command.

In everyday life, therefore, you bump elbows with people who really know the truth of God, and yet you do not sense the opportunity that lies so close at hand unless your own hunger for real answers has come to life and begun to stir. Indeed, until you are hungry there is no more opportunity in the nearness of these people than if they were on the sun. The physical proximity of God-knowing men and women is more common than you think until you start looking. But their real and effective nearness to you is determined by other than physical laws. It depends upon their level of development (in which there are wide variations), upon the state of your own heart, and upon the sincerity, patience, persistence, and alertness of your search.

The great thing is that these people are available to you, and if you really try you can find them. The following is my own experience:

I started looking for answers about God when I was thirty-one years old. After many false starts, I had finally been working hard for four years and was beginning to get somewhere, when suddenly I had to move from New York to Chicago.

I thought to myself: "This is going to throw everything out of gear. At last I have begun to make real progress; I am in touch with people here in the East who know what the score is and who are giving me practical help; and now I have to go and live out in a new place where there will be nobody to steer me."

For about three months after I arrived in the Middle West, things were almost as bad as I had imagined them. I looked hard and I did find a number of people to work with, but there was nobody to give me the kind of help I needed most: contact with men of greater experience than I in the Way.

One day my wife said, "Look, we are going to have to join a church. The kids in this neighborhood are starting to make fun of our children because they don't go to church. And they are right. We've got to do something about it."

I had been "un-churched" for many years. I was brought up in a Christian home, but I threw it all overboard in my teens. Later in life, even after I came back to an interest in God and began actually working on it, I still had reservations and as a matter of fact a lot of resentments toward formal religion and church. But I could see that my wife was right. Our children weren't babies any longer and they needed some religion in their upbringing. The kids in the neighborhood had done us a favor.

A few days later my wife said, "The minister is coming to call this evening." I said, "The minister?" Then I remembered about our getting back to church, and I said, "Oh, sure, sure. I hope he won't stay long. I have some work to finish up." My wife said, "I hope he won't, too, because I am going to do some shopping with Aunt Kate."

Well, the clergyman came. He was a man about sixty years old. And he hadn't been in the house twenty minutes before I began to realize *that this man really knew something,* and that he could teach me. For a while I was stunned. I had never dreamed that a man of the cloth could help me, never even thought of the possibility. You can see how deeply my prejudice against religion ran.

My wife didn't do her shopping that night and I didn't get my work done. We talked with Father Holt (he was an Anglican priest) until late, and when he was gone I walked around saying to myself, "Well, I'll be damned." Shows how silly language can be. What I meant was, "How could anything so wonderful happen with so little warning?" Because I knew what subsequent months and years proved: that this man could help me.

Looking back on it now, I am still amazed and I still thank God for it. Father Holt not only knew about God; he knew God. He was exactly the man I needed at that point in my life to give me the help and encouragement and discipline and instruction I needed. I know it is easy to be superstitious and believe too much about this sort of thing; but you also can be negatively superstitious and believe too little. The truth, in my opinion, based on a considerable further experience and on the reports of others, is this: Once you really begin to go toward God, *the people you need to help you are brought to you,* often when you least expect them, for example when you've been trying hard and have failed and have almost quit trying.

This is just one man's story, of course, and it has its individual peculiarities, but it is characteristic of many others. It typifies in fact a perfectly reliable law of the way: the great law of A, S, K — *Ask and you shall receive, Seek and you shall find, Knock and it shall be opened.* It is a fact that your teachers and helpers in the path to God knowledge already exist. It remains for you to seek them out.

So you watch for these people. But when you find them they are sometimes not at all what you were looking for. It is by a miracle of grace that our human helpers-in-God come to us at last, because although we must look for them, we very often have wrong notions of what they should be. *The Philokalia,* the great book of wisdom of the Eastern Church, says that no one can know anything real about God unless he is willing to find and take his place in "the chain of saints." We make heavy weather of finding and taking our place because we have such strange ideas of what a saint is. We are looking for someone with folded hands and upturned or downcast eyes. Or if not quite such a plaster-cast image, then someone who is very "healthy" — or very "successful" — or very "good" — or nearly "perfect" — or at the very least a good churchman.

Yet when it really begins to happen we may find ourselves learning about God from a man with pimples and a bad temper who chews his gum too loudly. Indeed, it can be worse than that. We may have to learn from a recovered alcoholic, a reformed criminal, or an ex-whore. This sort of thing is not inevitable, of course; the conventionally outcast have no corner on the knowledge of God. (Some of them think they have and so fall into a kind of inverse snobbery, but it is not truly so.) Our teachers may turn out to be quite ordinary folk: an industrial executive, for example, or a traveling man from Scranton, or a housewife with three children and allergies. But the New Testament should have prepared us for the fact that just about anything can happen here and that the world's social and educational standards are not God's. Christ, you may have observed, often exercised a powerfully indelicate taste in his choice of friends.

A saint in the sense here considered is *anyone who is really looking for the Truth and who has already gotten somewhere on the*

Way. And let us not be deceived anymore by our expectation of words than by our imaginary previews of persons. The saint next to us in the chain, for example, may not use the word "God" very much. Possibly he is one who, with no great gifts otherwise, has somehow been captivated by the practice of truth-telling, who has been following it, and who really knows the ins and outs of this difficult and neglected art. This is not to say that churchmen, clergymen, good pious laymen, and the like may not turn out to be among our helpers and teachers, too. They may. It is only to say that we must be prepared for a few surprises in the kind of people through whom the Truth chooses to speak to us.

This is a serious matter, because all except really sincere and really alert searchers will inevitably be put off, offended, by the people who could and would teach them. "Blessed is he who is not offended in me," said the Truth when he was presenting himself in the rural areas north of Judea in the person of a local carpenter up that way. Of course *now* the carpenter has a gilt-edge reputation. He came out on top in spite of a nasty turn or two, and so a lot of us cheer for him at a safe distance of two thousand years, and we soothe and flatter and tickle ourselves with pictures of how we would have recognized and accepted him if we had been there. And at the same time we freeze as rigidly as any Pharisee of old when the same Truth ventures to address us through a contemporary mouth in which the teeth are not straight or the breath is not sweet.

"But," says a conservative friend, "don't we have to be awfully careful about phonies here? Aren't there a lot of people who pretend to knowledge of God? Aren't there a lot of hypocrites and lunatics working the God pitch?"

Sure there are. But so what? This is only to observe that we are still operating in the human realm. Every human activity, the highest as well as the lowest, is crowded with con artists. Medicine has its quacks. The law has its shysters. Statecraft has its demagogues. Business has its pirates. Education has its crackpots. And so on and on. But still there *are* real doctors, legitimate lawyers, genuine statesmen, good businessmen, and capable educators. Likewise there are real and true knowers of the way to God. Yet here, as in every other concern involving mankind, "let the buyer beware." It cannot be otherwise.

The search for the people who can teach us is exciting, frustrating, bewildering, and immensely rewarding in friendships born of the love that has no price tag and seeks no return. This search requires of us a real hunger for the truth, a refusal to settle for anything but the truth no matter how it is disguised or hidden, and a willingness to suffer any pains for the sake of the truth — the qualities, in brief, of a true scientist.

In addition to our teachers, there are other people whom we need to seek out and associate with: folks who, like ourselves, are newcomers and know very little at first. We need the company of our peers as well as our superiors and elders on the Way. We need the help of those who are approximately in our own position, with whom we can share our experience, strength, and hope.

And there is still another group with whom we must enter into a working relationship. These are the men and women who are younger on the Way than we and whom *we* are able to help and to teach. Is this presumptuous? On the contrary, it would be presumptuous to assume that we could make progress without passing on what we have been given. In order to approach truth, we need not only helpers but those whom we ourselves can help. The relationships are informal and unfixed, of course, and the positions are quite apt to shift. No one need be surprised if his pupil someday becomes capable of teaching him, or if he himself becomes an instrument of instruction to someone who has been his mentor. Here we are dealing with, or rather being dealt with by, the Holy Spirit, and he has made it clear through all true tradition that he cannot be bottled up in our conventions, not even in our religious conventions, much less in our social conventions. So we need — *we just must have and cannot do without* — our teachers, our pupils, and our friends and fellow travelers in God.

"But," you say, "I am the shy and retiring type. All this talk about working with different kinds of people throws me way off. It simply is not the sort of thing I am good at."

Sorry. Objection not sustained. These are not ordinary relationships we have been talking about, and as a matter of experience the shy types do just as well in finding their proper associates in the pursuit of God knowledge as do the friendly and socializing types. This business of coming into contact with the right people, given real willingness and alertness on our part, is a matter that is engineered finally not by us but by guidance, by grace, by the Reality which we, however clumsily, are seeking. And the Reality in its working is not unduly facilitated by extroversion or outgoingness. Neither is it unduly hindered by shyness.

There are no good excuses for ducking this job, but you must observe yourself honestly and see what excuses you actually are making to yourself. There are no real reasons in anybody's temperament or circumstances for being put off, for being "offended." But there are a lot of very plausible phony reasons, and something — the adversary or the monkey or the subconscious or the you-name-it — *something* works very hard to make these poor excuses stick. You need only to look inward steadily for a little while to see the process at work.

The truth is that you can begin to get real answers, and you can begin to find the people who can help you, just as soon as you mean business and are willing to stop lying to yourself and go to work. But you must mean business. Otherwise the whole affair turns into just one more charade, one more thing with a lot of wind and words that go nowhere.

What Are the Right Books?

It is possible to get along without books. Knowledge of God was imparted to man and transmitted from one man to another for a very long time before books were invented. You *may* learn what you need to learn by having another person teach it to you by example and word of mouth only.

But that would be very unusual today. Teachers who can teach that way are now rare, and even they might not wish to eliminate the use of books entirely. In the last three or four thousand years written or printed documents have become such basic adjuncts to learning that if you can read at all it would be rash to overlook them. Books can strengthen understanding and faith, deepen prayer, give basis and structure for meditation, and sometimes even provide the spark that sets off the sunburst of enlightenment, as in the cases of Bucke, Pascal, Augustine,* and others.

There are four kinds of books about God and the path to God. The first kind are *bad* books, ranging from merely indifferent to really bad. They are either useless or harmful. At best they are a waste of time; at worst they may get you mixed up or lead you badly off the track. The second kind are *good* books. There are so many of these that their very number creates a special problem, which we will consider in a moment. The third kind are *great* books. It is necessary to know what these books are and where you may find them, because they are basic tools in the work we are carrying on. Fourth and last (but first in importance) are the *greatest* books. They are in a class by themselves, and you should by all means know them and know how to use them.

When it comes to bad books, we have to face the fact that certain kinds of reading can do us definite and serious harm. There really are bad books and they really can hurt us. The trouble is, there are few hard and fast lines beyond which you can say that any book, as such, is bad. A book that may be useless to one man may be useful to another man. A book that may be harmful to nine hundred and ninety-nine men may be dangerous but still helpful and good for the thousandth man.

It depends on you whether a book is good or bad for you. And here *people* can help you; here the problems of "the right people" and "the right books" overlap. It helps greatly to talk over your current and prospective reading diet with friends who are somewhat ahead of you on the Way. Knowing you and your particular abilities and problems, they can suggest books which can be helpful and they can warn you off books that would be bad for you.

There is another and even more important source of help.

---

* R. M. Bucke, *Cosmic Consciousness*; Pascal, *Pensées*; St. Augustine, *Confessions*.

From the very beginning, and continually as we go along, we should seek the direct influence of the Holy Spirit, the ever-present and all-pervading Spirit of Truth, in selecting and guiding our reading. *This influence is always available,* and only in a state of spiritual sleep or idiocy can we ignore it.

So the first step in seeking knowledge of God by means of books is to learn to smell out and avoid wrong books. A person does not need to be warned, of course, against such obviously bad books as the blind, banal, sentimental, and luxurious trash of all ages and the actual pornography which has become so accepted and so popular today, except as this kind of "literature" may be involved in any struggle he may be having with an actual hangup. Certain books are so clearly out of order that they normally present no problem. The books you have to be on guard against fall into such groups as these:

- books that are over your head;
- books that start with the truth but lead into byways or blind alleys;
- books which may be good in themselves and useful to some people but which are unsuited to your present needs and your present abilities to absorb and apply;
- books which are "smart," "intellectual," "clever," "bright," "scientific," but which really have no root in faith or experience, no heart, no sincerity, no truth.

These are general indications only. You have to develop know-how as you go along. It is quite impossible to make anything like a list of the "hundred worst books" or "five hundred spiritual stinkers." It is impossible in fairness to mention even a few titles and to say that these books always and under any circumstances would be harmful. You will not stub your toe too badly if you will only try to stay reasonably humble, reasonably alert to the actual dangers of the situation, and reasonably close to the sources from which help is available to you. You just have to keep awake, keep in close touch with your more experienced friends-in-God, pray to the Spirit of Truth for guidance, and go ahead cautiously, promptly putting aside books that turn out to be doubtful or definitely off base for you.

One more word of caution while we are doing some necessary negative thinking about books: even good books may be bad for you if you take them in the wrong way or at the wrong time. It is possible, for example, to get a swelled head from reading the Bible. Too much reading also is a bad habit, and in some natures it can become disastrous. It leads to garrulousness, to the confusion of wordiness with wisdom, and finally to pride and its chain of delusions. (The mentally lazy, of course, take cautions against overreading as an excuse not to do the reading they should do. The *shaitan*, the internal adversary who works continually against truth, can turn every truth to his own ends if you permit it.) But reading when it is God's will for you to be doing something else *is* spiritually a very deadly thing. This has been recognized from ancient times: "And further, by these, my son, be admonished: of making many books there is no end; and much study is a weariness of the flesh. Let us hear the conclusion of the whole matter: Fear God, and keep his commandments: for this is the whole duty of man" (Eccles. 12:12-13).

Father de Caussade, the great French Jesuit teacher of abandonment to God, sees the book problem very clearly. In *Self-Abandonment to Divine Providence*, in a chapter entitled "Reading and other exercises of piety only sanctify us in so far as they are channels of the action of God," he has this to say:

> The reading of a book arbitrarily chosen independently of God's Order is harmful to us; the Will of God and his Order give us grace which works in the depth of our hearts through the books we read as through everything else we do. Without God, books are but vain appearances and, deprived with regard to us of the vivifying virtue of his Order, merely empty the heart, through the very satisfaction they cause the mind. . . . A proud man who reads spiritual books from curiosity alone, averting himself in his reading from the Will of God, only receives the dead letter of what he reads in his mind and grows ever drier and more hardened. . . .

If it is the duty of the moment to read, the book will

effect this mysterious fulfillment (sanctification of the soul) in the depths of the heart. If the Divine Will bids us abandon reading for the duty of actual contemplation of God, that duty brings to birth the New Man in the depths of our heart, whereas reading would be injurious and useless.

The following words of wisdom about books were spoken by Sri Ramakrishna, the nineteenth-century Hindu master. They are included in a chapter entitled "Religion is realization and not a matter of philosophical discussion":

> One day the late Keshab Chandra Sen of revered memory visited Sri Ramakrishna in the temple of Dakshineswara and put to him the question: "Many learned men read no end of sacred books; how is it then, that they remain ignorant in spiritual matters?" The reply was, "The kite and the vulture soar high up in the air, but all the time their eyes are fixed on charnel pits in search of putrid carcasses. The minds of the so-called learned scholars are attached to things of the world; hence it is that they cannot acquire true knowledge. What good could the reading of a vast number of sacred works do them?"
>
> Sri Ramakrishna used to say of *granthas* (books) that they were so many *granthis* (knots). In other words, mere reading of books, without discrimination and non-attachment, serves to increase one's arrogance and vanity, i.e., it multiplies the knots in one's mind. . . .
>
> He also said, "In the Hindu almanac it is recorded that the rainfall in Bengal will reach twenty adas. Wring the almanac, so full of rain-predictions, but not a drop of water can be got out of it. So, also, many good sayings are to be found in the sacred books, but the mere reading of them will not make one spiritual. One must go through the practices enjoined in them."

Of course, these very warnings *against* books are solemnly and serenely printed *in* books by the sincere followers of the men who uttered the warnings. Obviously all this speaking against is only against the misuse of books. After everything possible has been said by way of caution, reading remains one of the very great aids, and usually one of the indispensable aids, on the Way.

Books are not the answer, *but they can lead to the answer.* The paradox of the useful uselessness of books in the spiritual quest is apparent in the following two incidents in the life of Ramana Maharshi.

On the one hand: one day a visitor asked the Maharshi, "Should I give up my business and take to reading books on Vedanta?" Replying, Sri Bhagavan said, "As for reading books on Vedanta, you may go on reading any number of them. They can only tell you, 'Realize the Self within you.' The Self cannot be found in books. You have to find it for yourself, in yourself."

On the other hand: describing experiences leading up to Sri Bhagavan's full realization, Arthur Osborne writes:

> The second premonition came soon after. This time it was provoked by a book. Again it was a wave of bewildering joy at perceiving that the Divine can be made manifest on earth. His uncle had borrowed a copy of the Periapuranam, the life-stories of the sixty-three Tamil Saints. Venkataraman (Sri Bhagavan) picked it up and, as he read, was overwhelmed with ecstatic wonder that such faith, such love, such divine fervor was possible, that there had been such beauty in human life. The tales of renunciation leading to Divine Union inspired him with awe and emulation. Something greater than all dreamlands, greater than all ambition, was here proclaimed real and possible, and the revelation thrilled him with blissful gratitude.
>
> From this time on the current of awareness which Sri Bhagavan and his devotees designate "meditation" began to awaken in him. Not awareness of anything by any one, being beyond the duality of subject and object, but a state of blissful consciousness transcending both the

physical and mental plane and yet compatible with full
use of the physical and mental faculties.

Arthur Osborne, *Ramana Maharshi*

There are so many *good* spiritual books that nobody but a librarian can know even the names of a major portion of them.
And those you can know about are still so numerous that it is
easy to become confused. Because which of them is right for you,
now? With only a limited amount of time for reading and with
so many and so many kinds of books to choose among, how can
you make even a start?

Here again you need the help of people who are a little
ahead of you, who are experienced in spiritual reading, and who
can recommend books that will fit your problems, and your particular lines of growth.

Great spiritual books stand out from merely good books by
their profound influence throughout the centuries or by their special power in our own time. Most great books that we are able to
recognize as such are older books; these are easier to identify as
great because they have the witness of many years and much use
and experience behind them. Yet not all of the great books are
old. For example, Thomas Kelly's *Testament of Devotion*, written
by a man who died in 1941, is probably a great spiritual book in
the truest sense. Only future years can confirm its greatness, but
it is possible now so to classify it. Not everyone, of course,
would agree with this classification, and that reminds us that the
line between "good" and "great" is not hard and fixed and there
is room for plenty of difference of view.

Perhaps the best way to indicate what is meant by great
spiritual books is to give a few examples: The works of Philo
Judaeus, the *Enneads* of Plotinus, *The Philokalia* of the Eastern Or-
thodox tradition, the works of Dionysius the Areopagite,
Shankaracharya's *Crest-Jewel of Discrimination*, the *Mathnawí* of
Jalálu'ddín Rúmí, the works of Meister Eckhart, *The Divine Com-
edy*, the works of John of Ruysbroeck, *The Cloud of Unknowing*,
The Imitation of Christ, the *Theologia Germanica*, the works of St.
John of the Cross — such books are properly called great. You
can think of many more offhand, but the whole list of presently

available works is not large and might not exceed three or four hundred.

Every searcher should be on the lookout for great spiritual books and become acquainted with as many as possible. They provide solid food for the journey.

What are the *greatest* spiritual books? They are the sacred scriptures or holy writings of mankind. And they are, as we have said, in a special and peculiar class.

The number of these greatest books is very small. Among all the books of the world, they are a unique phenomenon. All of them are profound, difficult, often obscure and puzzling, not by any means "easy reading." Yet it is one of their strange qualities that they serve spiritual babes as well as they serve spiritual adults, and plain people as well as those who are called to scholarship. The holy scriptures are known, revered, read, studied, cherished, and absorbed at depth by men, women, and children of all kinds and classes in all times. They are the backbone of the spirituality of vast populations over great ages. These books have had an incomparable effect upon the mind and heart of humanity. We cannot afford to be ignorant of them.

No person, nation, or race is big enough to express fully the greatness of a true scripture. Only the passage of millennia and the testimony of countless redeemed lives can begin to bear witness adequately to the power and stature of a genuine sacred book. In the holy scriptures we find a reflection on our level of the *one* great Sacred Book, written in living words that penetrate all levels, by the Father of Lights himself. The *real* Word of God is indiscernible to merely human eyes and unendurable to merely human nervous systems. But we see something of it, and its very power is mediated to us in a strange and marvelous manner, in the greatest books, our sacred writings.

Again, a word of caution is necessary. In spite of their immense value, you can trip over the holy books or get mixed up in unnecessary diversions because of them. People can abuse anything; they do abuse even the best and highest things; and our old friend the adversary is well known to quote scripture in the context of his own highly specialized interests. Therefore, not only in spite of, but often just because of, the power inherent in sacred writings, they are involved in everything from silly personal arguments to miserable and futile doctrinal squabbles. Regardless of clear warnings, the letter of scripture is still preferred to the spirit, the form to the essence, the necessary but deadly husk to the living and life-giving core.

Well, enough of warnings: on with our consideration of the greatest books. What are their names? What are they about? Brief descriptions of six of the greatest scriptures of mankind — the Bible, the Koran, the Upanishads, the Bhagavad Gita, the Book of Tao, and the Buddhist scriptures — are given in Appendix C, page 239. The books described there do not by any means include all the sacred writing available. For example, we have not covered the Persian Zend-Avesta, the Chinese Book of changes, and others which are of very considerable interest and importance; but the ones discussed are outstanding in historical times and the ones most likely to be of practical use to a searcher.

Although holy scripture is in some ways the most difficult of all reading, from another angle it is the easiest of all, the safest of all, and the best of all. Most of us do well to include at least some scripture in our reading from the very beginning and to keep scripture as a kind of backbone to our further study, no matter how widely our interests range.

But note: Some persons cannot read scripture at all at first. It is too strong a dose. I give my own case for example: I got very far from God at one time, and it was several years after I turned toward the Light again before I could bring myself to read the Bible. In the meantime I could and did get great help from other, lesser, but more-to-my-measure books.

Scripture enthusiasts must be careful not to try to ram holy writ down anyone's throat. Some perfectly genuine little ones in Christ can be seriously offended in this way, a development which the Lord does not take lightly (Matt. 18:2-6). The sacred texts are just as wonderful as the keenest enthusiast thinks they are, but at the same time they are not everyone's cup of tea. And in these cases, help *can* come through other channels. The Spirit of God is not, never was, and never will be confined to any words, even the holiest words. If you forget this you may be rewarded with some poor results and with some handsomely deserved rebukes in your attempts to help your brothers-in-God — particularly your puffed-up or beaten-up brothers, your hardboiled-and-aggressive or scared-and-skittish brothers, your undereducated or overeducated brothers. Scripture is great. It is the tool of tools with which to learn about God. But it is also a fine instrument with which to make a fathead of yourself if you are not careful.

Read scripture if you possibly can, and keep on reading it. But you've got to know how. Here again friends can help. Talk over with them your Bible reading and your attempts to practice biblical principles in your life.

There are some basic considerations to be observed. First of all, no one, not even most saints, can read large sections of sacred writing at any one sitting. Really *read* it, that is. Of course, any eager beaver can, and many do, pass big chunks of scripture through their mental alimentary apparatus at one sitting and right out again, practically untouched, as in the case of all hastily ingested and excreted matters, by the assimilative processes. Cramming and bolting are not good practices with scripture. They nearly always lead to psychic indigestion, or, worse, to spiritual flatulence — a kind of gaseous and incontinent pride.

As a serious student you soon find out that in order to get the real good out of Bible reading you must take small pieces at a time and chew them thoroughly. And you don't jump right up and run around afterward. You have had a meal. You sit down and let it settle for a while.

Hit-and-miss, now-and-then scripture reading is better than no scripture reading, but only somewhat better. For best results you should read on a regular daily schedule which you follow as faithfully as brushing your teeth. There are many good printed schedules. The Episcopal Book of Common Prayer has a Bible-reading schedule or lectionary on page x. Certain editions of the Bible itself contain daily reading schedules. Or you may make up your own schedule.

Does holy scripture mean just the Christian Bible? That depends on you. As a Christian you may wish to stick to the Bible exclusively for your scripture, not through any lack of sympathy or interest in other sacred writings or other religions, but because, as Ramakrishna has pointed out, it is better to dig one deep well than many shallow ones. This may be the part of wisdom for you.

On the other hand, most Christian denominations recognize that the Holy Spirit is not restricted to the Judeo-Christian writings, and that the highest Truth may express himself not only outside the Christian canon and Christian apocryphal works but outside the historical and formal Christian tradition entirely (although never of course outside the Christ who is all and in all [Col. 3:11]). So it is possible that you may extend your reading, not only safely but with great profit, to include such books as the Bhagavad Gita, the Tao Te Ching, the Upanishads, and others. Again no general rules can be laid down. These choices have to be made in terms of particular persons and actual circumstances.

Finally, a practical note: decide as you go along what books you need, and get those books. Don't say you can't get them. Borrow them from your friends or from libraries if possible; if not, buy them. "But this is expensive!" So it is. But if you were studying ballet or geology or dog training, you would get the books you need, somehow. A real student always manages to get hold of the books he needs, somehow.

People are funny about books. Even people who are hard up spend whopping big chunks of money on automobiles and television sets, but when it comes to fifty or a hundred dollars for some needed books, suddenly we are confronted with a howling impossibility. Here is an index of where the heart is and where the treasure is.

Get the books you want and need for your spiritual work. Buy them when you have to. If your bookstore doesn't have them, buy them from the publisher. If he is out of stock or the book is out of print, have one of the companies which locate books find what you want (see the *New York Times Book Review* classified advertising section for addresses of some of these companies). Or use the internet to track down hard-to-find titles. Go to

Amazon.com or Alibris.com, or use your search function for "out of print books." One way or another you can find almost any book you're looking for.

One good way to tell if your spiritual quest has the minimum necessary kick and bite and drive is to ask yourself honestly whether or not you are too tight to purchase the essential tools. In a financial pinch it would not be good Christianity to steal the needed books, but it might be an encouraging sign for a Christian to think of the possibility. The point is to get the books, and if that takes money, get it up.

Where Is the Laboratory?

Anyone who starts out to find real answers to questions about God's existence and availability finds himself involved, not in a pleasant pastime, but in hard work. And anyone who does real work needs a workplace, a workshop, in the broadest sense a laboratory.

Fortunately a most amazing situation exists here. *Every man, woman, and child on this earth already has a perfect place in which to pursue the work of finding God.* Unfortunately very few realize that this is the situation, and even fewer take advantage of it. Many people have never heard of such a thing. Others, when they do hear of it, cannot see it or will not believe it. But it is true. You already have the perfect laboratory. It is large but portable; you can and do carry it around with you wherever you go.

This laboratory, this perfectly equipped workshop, is your own life: your body and mind; your exact circumstances, good and bad; your past, present, and future; your advantages and handicaps; your hopes and fears; your heart, lungs, glands, and brains; your hair and skin, hands and feet, warts and moles; your sensations, thoughts, and emotions. Everything that may properly be called you, everything that has gone, now goes, and some day will go to make up your life — this is your workshop, your laboratory. And it is ideally suited to the work of finding God and completely equipped for it.

If this is so, what about your weaknesses and shortcomings,

your faults and failings, your pains and miseries, your depressions and frustrations? All of these are indispensable parts of your equipment. They are just as useful and necessary as your strengths, skills, abilities, successes, pleasures, joys, and attainments. Your bad qualities are no doubt bad enough in themselves, but in this work they are useful — provided you *work with them* and on them.

Good and bad depend on where you are going. On the way to God, part of your light and heat comes from burning your own garbage. Later on and at a higher level it comes from helping to burn the world's garbage. Repudiations, dishonor, disgrace, physical torture, mental agony — the worst things, deserved and undeserved, which you may have to face — all are fuel for this fire. Christ gave us a hair-raising example of how it works. Nothing is lost. The bad things all are turned to good use in this laboratory.

The kingdom of God is within you. Really, now, what can that mean? Well, some of the meaning is not such a hidden matter after all. It can only mean that the answers you are looking for are within you — not in the South Seas or India or Italy or Tibet (unless you happen to go there and make them a part of you). Our Lord's words on this subject are quite explicit and quite clear. The answers — the real answers, the Great Answer himself and his kingdom — are within *you.*

It is of considerable importance, therefore, to understand what is meant by you in this case. Evidently it is not just your physical body. Human bodies have been drawn and quartered and otherwise cut up for centuries before modern autopsy brought some refinement to such procedures. And nobody has ever yet found the kingdom or any real hints to it in that way. The physical body is deeply involved in the search for spiritual answers, but obviously it is not you in the sense Christ means you when he speaks of the location of the kingdom. The pure in heart do not get that way by opening the thorax and sponging it out. And seekers for the kingdom do not physically explore their own viscera. Real clues, vital and essential symbols, can be found in the body, but not the answers themselves.

Well, then, what is meant by *you?*

You are *your whole life,* extended in and beyond time. It is something much greater than you suspect until you seriously begin to look into it. You are your body and mind and soul; you are all your associates and associations, all your experiences, pleasant and unpleasant, remembered and forgotten (but nothing *is* forgotten!). You are in truth a great whole within the Great Whole, of which the ordinary little "you" is only faintly aware at any one time. "You" have to enter *you* and go to work there.

Indeed, when a man asks himself, "Who and what am I?" he has raised the question of questions, and the full and ultimate answers lie not only in the heart of man but in the great heart of God.*

For immediate and practical purposes, however, it is enough to realize that you — the you in which the kingdom of God and the answers to the reality of God are to be found — are your whole self. You are your workshop. It remains only to go to work.

How you work is the next consideration.

---

* The question of one's identity, not just as a philosophical preoccupation but as a practical pursuit of real knowledge, is basic in the spiritual life. For further light on this question see Ramana Maharshi's *Self-Enquiry* and his *Who Am I?* These are in *The Collected Works,* edited by Arthur Osborne. Note also Radhakrishnan's *The Principal Upanishads,* pp. 73-78.

CHAPTER THREE
The Ways to Knowledge

The first of all the commandments is, Hear, O Israel;
The Lord our God is one Lord: And thou shalt love the
Lord thy God with all thy heart, and with all thy soul,
and with all thy mind, and with all thy strength: this is
the first commandment.

Mark 12:29-30

Who can hear this amazing and terrible commandment without a shocked realization of how far we are from being able to
obey it? *And yet we can make a start.* We can make the first movement of love by turning our attention and our *interest* toward
God. And we can do it in the ways he has indicated by enlisting
(1) our minds, (2) our strength, and (3) our hearts and souls in
this work. Let's see how it develops.

"With All Thy Mind" — The Way of Reason

Nearly all men reason about God. The unbeliever reasons
against him, the believer reasons for him, but no one except an
idiot can escape reasoning *about* him. The atheist least of all can
avoid reasoning about God; his whole position depends on it. So
there is no question as to whether we should or should not or
will or will not reason about God. The only question is whether
we will reason well or reason badly.

The ground where reason bears on the question of God is exceedingly well worked over.* Incalculable numbers of hours of
debate have been devoted to the problem. There are mountains

---

* Reasoning about the *existence* of God is a relatively modern phenomenon, occurring during the last two millennia, mostly in the West. The
authors of the Old and New Testaments, for example, are not much
concerned to prove that God exists. There is a reference in Psalm 14 to
atheism, but it is regarded there simply as folly, not as a logical position and certainly not as a philosophical problem. Throughout the Gos-

of books on the subject. The complexities, the difficulties, and the mere mass of material are immense. Would it not be better, therefore, just to skip this section entirely? Is not this whole problem of reasoning about God full of serious limitations at best and full of real booby traps at worst?

Yes, so it is. But we can't skip this section. We can and under some circumstances should postpone it, but we really cannot skip it. A normal man while awake can no more stop reasoning than he can stop breathing. He can stop briefly but not for long. In a few seconds or at most a couple of minutes he is breathing — and rea- soning — again. If we are going to talk about God at all, we must reason. We may hope to get beyond reason, but not around it.

Reason, in the quest of God, is not an ass upon which we can ride and prance as in merely utilitarian pursuits. It is a lion on the path that must be faced. It is a sphinx whose questions we must answer, or go down to spiritual death. Reason is not a luxury with which we may or may not dispense; it is a necessity with which we must deal. If the questions of reason are not an- swered and the legitimate demands of reason are not met, reason will never stand still. And it is only when reason — pointing at last beyond itself — *does* stand still that the deep truth about God can begin to come to us.

Applying the honesty part of the program, could we agree that a large part of our desire to avoid reasoning arises out of la- ziness? Most of us are not yet intelligent enough and not yet

---

pels and Letters unbelief is not a problem of unbelief in God, but of unbelief in Christ's demonstration and teaching (Matt. 13:58, 17:20; Mark 6:6, 9:24, 16:14), unbelief in the promises, oracles, and plain revelations of God (Rom. 3:3, 4:20, 11:20; Heb. 3:19, 4:6), and unbelief in the Chris- tian evangel (Acts 14:2; Rom. 11:30; Heb. 4:11). Only a few passages re- fer possibly to a rejection of God's very existence (Luke 12:46; Heb. 3:12). Not only the Bible but all of the great sacred writings of mankind take for granted the existence of a Supreme Being, either as a Supreme Person or Persons, or as a Supreme State of Being which transcends and includes all states of being, or both. Serious philosophical and theologi- cal efforts to develop "proofs" of God's existence appear in the West in the thought of Plato and Aristotle; they begin to take elaborate form around the time of St. Anselm and of St. Thomas Aquinas. The question of God vs. no-God reaches a kind of climax in the thought of Kant, and it emerges as the key underlying factor in the modern world political crisis.

enough in love with the truth to be afraid of reasoning. We are not put off by the real dangers of reasoning but by the fact that good reasoning involves hard work. (Bad reasoning, of course, is easy, and we do it all the time with no effort.) But good reasoning about any subject is a workout, and good reasoning about the largest of all subjects — God — is a real sweat-producer, inevitably.

So let's buckle into it and let's not mix it up. Remember, we are trying to get real answers to real questions; we are not playing games with words or amusing ourselves with ideas; we are not trying to prove that we personally are right or that some school or viewpoint is right. We are trying to find out what is the truth.*

Three general rules may help us; they are based on the experience of ordinary men like ourselves who have beaten these particular bushes before us:

Rule No. 1: Don't try to think or reason about God in a vacuum. The vacuum here is merely one's personal self. Heavily solitary thinking tends to be ignorant, self-centered, and sick thinking. Naturally we do a lot of thinking when we are alone, and that is fine up to a point. But somewhere along the line we need to mix our lone thinking with other thinking; we need to cook it in the fire of conversation and refine it in the discipline of reading and study.

Again, we need people and we need books.

Try to find a few persons, or at least one, who will take the time and trouble to talk with you. It does take time and it does involve work. And it is better to do it on a regular basis than haphazardly. Thus you will find yourself working with a small

---

* Eugene Exman, in *The World of Albert Schweitzer*, reviewing the great doctor's stress upon the importance of thought, says: "Rational thought is important for its own sake and as it leads to a higher form which Schweitzer calls mystical thought. Pure reason can carry us only so far; to penetrate further, we must quiet the mind and await the insight for which reason has prepared us.

"This higher thought may contradict the expectations of logical, rational thought. Perhaps that is why men have often distrusted it. Actually the new insight may be a premise in support of which rational thought must build a new structure. Moreover, intuitive insight may include a larger whole than sense data can immediately verify — just as complete knowledge of H_2O must include awareness of ice and steam even though water be its present form recognized by the senses."

group or a single friend or several friends individually. You should expose your ideas, questions, and problems freely in these conversations. Your friends should feel equally free to open their minds to you. Together you will be able to make progress toward truth that none of you could make alone.

Your discussions may blow up some storms. Sincere thinking about God touches the deepest part of us, and it is apt to trigger powerful feelings and stubborn prejudices. You will need all the good will, tolerance, forgiveness, and love of truth that you can muster. But if you are fundamentally sincere, if you really are seeking real answers to real questions, you can count on the fact that God's grace is greater than any troubles which can possibly arise during your studies and talks. This is an important promise, and you can prove by actual experiment that it is a true one.

Along with work with people you will want to be doing some reading. It does not make sense to try to think your way through the questions of God's reality without taking a look at what the rest of the human race has thought in the course of the centuries and is thinking today. You can stimulate, nourish, and regulate your own mind, you can save yourself useless sweat, and you can avoid a lot of intellectual blind alleys by means of a well-chosen program of reading — sharing your insights with your friends-in-God as you go. Original thinking is great stuff and most of us assume that we are pretty good at it, but every man who tries to go this route entirely alone tends to repeat in his own thinking all the heresies and confusions that have ever existed. So our original thinking will move straighter toward truth if it is tempered by exposure to the best thinking that has already been done.

Rule No. 2: Don't get in over your head. In reasoning about the deepest things in life, this rule is a very simple but very important consideration. It just means that you take care not to get bogged down in conversations or books that are too complex or too difficult for your present degree of understanding (which you must estimate objectively and humbly).

Of course, there are times when the truth confronting you will require that you stretch your mind to the utmost. Often you will have to make hard efforts to study and digest some very tough material. But, following Rule No. 2, the minute you find yourself really in over your depth, you will cheerfully admit it and back up a bit.

Now and then you may have to back *way* up. One needs occasional vacations from hard efforts at serious thought. Reasoning at its best is cool and disciplined, but it can become a cold and dry process, and then it tends to starve other areas of the soul. Humility, honesty, and a sense of humor in good working order are needed to maintain one's balance. Which brings us to . . .

Rule No. 3: Don't lean exclusively or too heavily upon reason. It is very easy to do so, not only for eggheads but for us squareheads, thickheads, and boneheads, too. Even a modest ability to reason and a limited capacity to think can be giddy stimulants, and of course a really facile thinker may quite easily be led into a dead end by his specialty.

All of us, whether we are "clever thinkers" or not, must recognize the limitations of thinking. Note well, please, that we do not wish to value reason at anything less than its true worth. Let's give it everything it has got coming, which is a great deal. But at the same time may we remember that the spirit of our own times (the past three or four hundred years) has swung heavily toward idolizing reason. Men of today are terribly apt to assume that men, by taking thought can probe the deepest secrets of the universe and call God himself on the carpet to give an account of his being and doing.

In sober truth, it simply is not and cannot be so.

The thinking faculty is limited, and there are places it cannot go. This fact has been recognized not only by saints and mystics but by thinkers and reasoners of every age, from Aristotle, Augustine, Aquinas, Kepler, Leibnitz, and Kant to Poincaré, Planck, Carrel, Eddington, and Whitehead. It is not the real thinkers but the superstitious idolizers of the rational faculty who wander out into the deserts of mechanism, materialism, and positivism.

Reason has been regarded as a veritable goddess, as a divine faculty. It is obviously the distinctively human quality of mind, distinguishing human consciousness from that of the lower kingdoms. There can be no doubt as to its dignity and necessity in the human scheme; when reason is lacking, men quickly sink to bestial or insane levels. And yet this noble function is a curiously limited and finally inadequate instrument for attaining full knowledge of anything at all and especially of God.

You can reason about eating until your head aches, and never come near the kind of knowledge that one good mouthful of potatoes brings you. Reason may help you to eat properly, but it is no substitute for actual eating. Furthermore there are other and sometimes better ways of learning to eat (and to live) properly than reason; the instinctual, sensual, affective, and intuitive faculties must be involved and often given precedence over reason, or we die. And when it comes to knowledge of yet deeper matters — of the spirit of man and of the Supreme Reality — still greater functions must be allowed their due scope: prayer, contemplation, revelation, and unitive or integral cognition. Some worshipers of reason like to pretend that these deeper experiences are unimportant or unreliable or even that they do not exist; but this is very unreasonable.

"Oh," says the monkey, wearing his humble costume, "but these are *high* matters, beyond the concern of unpretentious and unassuming men (of which, of course, we are one)." On the contrary, it is exactly unpretentious and unassuming men (without any phony humility) who often have been most richly endowed and most profoundly exercised in these highest faculties of knowledge.

It is particularly necessary for us hard-pressed men of the twenty-first century to reason clearly as to where we stand historically with respect to reason. A great cycle is coming full turn. In the past three or four hundred years reason has experienced one of its periodic elevations to a position as supreme arbiter of truth and judge of action in the affairs of men, all higher faculties being denied or lip-worshiped and effectively circumvented. And now we are having to realize that reason in the position of supreme Lord is in a false role. Reason is not thereby exalted. In practice it is debased and finally dethroned by the vital forces which it may have the intention to direct but lacks the sanction, the effective virtue and authority, to control.

Something very much like all this has happened before. It happened among our predecessors the Greeks. Hear what Will Durant says:

> The conflict between religion and philosophy had now seen three stages: the attack on religion, as in the pre-Socratics; the endeavour to replace religion with a natural ethic, as in Aristotle and Epicurus; and the return to religion in the Skeptics and Stoics, a movement that culminated in Christianity. A like sequence has occurred more than once in history, and may be taking place today. Thales corresponds to Galileo, Democritus to Hobbes, the Sophists to the Encyclopedists, Protagoras to Voltaire; Aristotle to Spencer, Epicurus to Anatole France; Pyrrho to Pascal, Arcesilaus to Hume, Carneades to Kant, Zeno to Schopenhauer, Plotinus to Bergson. The chronology resists the analogy, but the basic line of development is the same. . . .
>
> When a new religion [Christianity] took form out of the intellectual and moral chaos of the dying Hellenistic world, the way had been prepared for it by a philosophy that acknowledged the necessity of faith, preached an ascetic doctrine of simplicity and self-restraint, and saw all things in God.

In seeking psychological and spiritual truth, the *rational* must be given its full share of attention but the *superrational* no less so, for it is in the latter sphere that the deepest and most practical truths often lie. C. G. Jung has made a disciplined inquiry into these necessities. In his foreword to Richard Wilhelm's translation of the ancient Chinese oracular scripture, the I Ching or Book of Changes, Jung says:

> The I Ching insists upon self-knowledge throughout. The method* by which this is to be achieved is open to every kind of misuse, and is therefore not for the frivo-

---

* The method of the I Ching is irrational, noncausal, in Jung's terminology "synchronistic."

lous-minded and immature; nor is it for intellectualists and rationalists. It is appropriate only for thoughtful and reflective people who like to think about what they do and what happens to them — a predilection not to be confused with the morbid broodings of the hypochondriac. . . . I have no answer to the multitude of problems that arise when we seek to harmonize the oracle of the I Ching with our accepted scientific canons. But needless to say, nothing "occult" is to be inferred. My position in these matters is pragmatic, and the great disciplines that have taught me the practical usefulness of this viewpoint are psychotherapy and medical psychology. Probably in no other field do we have to reckon with so many unknown quantities, and nowhere else do we become more accustomed to adopting methods that work even though for a long time we may not know why they work. Unexpected cures may arise from questionable therapies and unexpected failures from allegedly reliable methods. In the exploration of the unconscious we come upon very strange things, from which a rationalist turns away in horror, claiming afterward that he did not see anything. The irrational fullness of life has taught me never to discard anything, even when it goes against all our theories (so short-lived at best) or otherwise admits of no immediate explanation. It is of course disquieting and one is not certain whether the compass is pointing true or not; but security, certitude, and peace do not lead to discoveries.

Do use your reasoning capacity, but don't force it. If your brains get overheated, fall back on prayer, or take a walk, or both (it's a nice combination). The answers to questions about God, when they come, involve the whole man. Give reason its proper place in your search, no less, but *no more*.

It is a simple matter to sum up the limitations of reason as a God-seeking and truth-seeking faculty: Reason is always too cold, too late, and too external to touch the living truth itself. For example, one of the most skillful reasoners who ever lived was the author of the monumental *Summa Theologia* and *Summa Contra*

Gentiles, the Angelic Doctor of systematic theology, Thomas Aquinas. How amazing and wonderful, considering this man's labor in the field of thought and his mastery of reason, is the experience that came to him near the close of his life (as reported by Reinhold in *The Soul Afire*):

> One day, the 6th of December, 1273, as he was celebrating Mass in the chapel of St. Nicholas, a great change came over him. From that moment onward he ceased to write or to dictate. . . . Reginald ventured to complain. "I can do no more," said his master. Reginald insisted. "Reginald, I can do no more; such things have been revealed to me that everything I have written seems to me rubbish. Now, after the end of my work, I must await the end of my life."

For books that may be helpful in studying the way of reason, *see Special Book Listings; page 207.*

"With All Thy Strength" — The Way of Faith

No one can read the New Testament through seriously even once without realizing that faith is a quality upon which Jesus placed critical stress. He made amazing promises to those who shall have faith, and he spoke with a strange mingling of compassion and sharp rebuke to those without faith or with little of it.

What is this key quality? How may we examine ourselves for its presence or absence in our lives? And, lacking it in some degree, how can we fill our need for it?

Faith first of all clearly is not, repeat *not*, mere belief. It is not just every belief that is well-meaning and firmly or even heroically held. Millions of people during a certain period believed that a man named Hitler was a good leader for Germany. Many of them were entirely sincere, and they backed their belief with sacrificial action. But this belief *never was faith*; it was always delusion, because, as history has shown, it was *belief in falsehood*, and that is what, by definition, delusion is. It is a degeneration or perversion or caricature of faith, but it *is not faith* and indeed may be further from faith than simple unbelief.

Could we agree that *faith is the power to contact the truth, to recognize and accept the truth, and to trust and follow the truth when it is not yet perceptually evident or logically demonstrable.*

Faith is a homing instinct for the truth that transcends the sensual and rational functions. Faith is never blind. On the contrary, it is vision above the relative blindness of the lesser faculties. "Blind faith" is a contradiction in terms; there is no such thing. Blind belief, yes, but never blind faith.

The faculty of faith is used by everyone every day in the most ordinary activities. Without the exercise of faith no man would have the power to get up in the morning, eat his breakfast, and go to work. Indeed, in mental depression, when faith runs very low, a person may literally become unable to perform simple acts, such as eating and working. Note that *faith,* even at the ordinary levels of living, is directly and very practically related to *strength.* Peter (faith) is the brother of Andrew (strength).

Lack of faith or weak faith is a kind of illness. Faith is not a luxury in which "religious" or "spiritual" people indulge. It is a basic function of the human being, and when that function is in default the person eventually becomes unfitted for ordinary life, let alone spiritual life. When ordinary faith runs low, the strength merely to live runs low; when spiritual faith runs low, the strength to seek God runs low. When *faith* runs low, *strength* runs low.

So faith is not hard to understand. Just watch yourself for a few days and see it working in your own life. Everytime you sit down at the table and eat a meal you are exercising ordinary faith. Your wife, you know, may be secretly fed up with your shortcomings and may be planning to poison you. It is perhaps a remote possibility, but still it *is* a possibility, and a sticky one. How to deal with the situation? You could hire a couple of operators to keep an eye on your mate, particularly while she is shopping and cooking. You might also hoist a few samples of the nutriment she is dishing up and send them out for chemical analysis. On the other hand, maybe the best way is just to go on believing in the dear girl's good will and trusting it. So you do this, and over the years her cooking does nothing worse than make you fat. This is *faith.* If, however, someday she does poison you, it will have been *delusion* after all. You see how important the difference is.

Everyone throughout life is sharpening his ability to distinguish between faith and delusion. Every healthy man goes on continually believing and trusting and trying to place his belief more in the true and less in the false.

Real trouble starts if you try to run away. The person who becomes frightened, withdraws from the game, and stops believing and trusting invariably falls into grave disorder of one kind or another; the kinds are legion.

Ordinary faith is easy to observe; it works hand in hand with the reasoning and perceiving faculties, and you use it every day. When you get into your car and drive off, you exercise faith in the manufacturer, in the man who recently changed the tires and relined the brakes, and in the local superintendent of highways. Every time you cross a bridge you demonstrate life-and-death faith in the engineers, builders, and maintenance men. Your whole day, and indeed your whole life, is a parade of acts of faith, spotted occasionally with mishaps which show where your faith has lapsed into delusion.

Spiritual faith is less common. Ordinary faith keeps us sane; spiritual faith leads us to peace and fulfillment. Ordinary faith illuminates ordinary life and keeps it from falling below the level of God's minimum intention for us, which apparently is that we do not become morally rotten or go crazy. Spiritual faith leads toward God's maximum intention for us, of which we see a forecast in the life of Christ. Evidently we really are intended to live in the same radiant freedom and beauty which Jesus demonstrated, transcending all the ills of this world, including the ill of death, and proceeding to states of power and benignity and joy far beyond our present capacities to imagine or desire.

If anyone says he will settle for ordinary faith and that spiritual faith is a bit too rich for his taste thank you, there is a tough answer, rooted in hard experience: if you will not set your sights upon spiritual faith, upon the hope and promise God has put before us in the great religious traditions, you will not be able to remain for long in ordinary faith. Sooner or later you will fall below it into physical or mental illness.

How do you get faith? It is a gift, and you get it in the same way you get any gift. (1) You just find upon examination that you have it, willy-nilly, without asking or knowing where it came from. Or (2) you find upon examination that you have not got it; you recognize your great need for it; you have the elementary common sense to ask for it; and you get it. (Those who have it willy-nilly find that they do not have enough of it, so eventually they have to ask, too.) You get faith by asking for it.

Does anyone ask and not receive? No one. Of course a man may be merely playing with the idea of God in his still-proud mind, and he may "ask" in this mood and not receive, not because God is a slow giver but because evidently he does not enjoy dull games and does not encourage fools.

Anyone, however, who is ready to stop fooling around and really ask, really receives faith. How much? As much as he needs at the time. Usually, in any one dose, only a little bit. But this stuff is dynamite and a little does a big job, *if you use it.* How much more you get and how soon you get it depends on *how you use what you have already been given.* When a man is ready to receive faith, God usually draws him into association with those who already have it, and he catches it by a sort of benign contagion.

Faith and reason are not enemies, not contradictory, not mutually exclusive. It is a widespread modern heresy and superstition to believe that they are opposed and incompatible, and a very implausible and unreasonable superstition it is.

Reason and faith obviously are necessary to each other's health and strength and growth. Reason without faith becomes garrulous and thin and dry and finally cold and deadly. Faith without reason continually slips into delusion, exclusivism, fanaticism, and their attendant illnesses. In *The Supreme Path* "The Ten Errors" are listed; the first two are as follows: "(1) Weakness of faith combined with strength of intellect are apt to lead to the error of talkativeness. (2) Strength of faith combined with weakness of intellect are apt to lead to the error of narrow-minded dogmatism" (Goddard, *A Buddhist Bible*).

In a sound mind, faith and reason complement and correct

and stimulate each other. Let them challenge each other by all means! Let the steel of reason strike sparks from the rock of faith. And let them encourage and support each other, too, as in the lovely, sane words of the old hymn: "Faith, our outward sense befriending, makes our inward vision clear."

Indeed the wholly imaginary "quarrel" between faith and reason occurs only in the minds of men who do not have faith, who do not understand faith, and who do not recognize the nature of the poverty from which they suffer. On the other hand, those who have faith but are weak in the appreciation and exercise of reason are equally unfitted for the pursuit of verity. The balance which alone qualifies one to eat the strong meat of truth is found in the mind in which both reason and faith are well developed and in right relation. *True faith* is never hostile to reason and, although transcending reason, often makes powerful use of it. *True reason* is strongly governed by faith and is to be sharply distinguished from the corrupt and undisciplined "reason" of the merely curious or monkey mind. In the words of Gregory of Sinai:

> True reason, such as man had in the beginning, cannot be had or acquired by any man who has not first been purified and become passionless. . . . None who are wise in words ever had true reason, because, from birth, they let their reasoning powers be corrupted by unseemly thoughts. The sensory and prolix spirit of the wisdom of this age, so rich in words, which creates the illusion of great knowledge but actually fills one with the wildest thoughts, has its stronghold in this prolixity, which deprives man of essential wisdom, true contemplation and the knowledge of the one and indivisible.
>
> The Philokalia

But faith as a spiritual quality — as the sail which we raise to the ever-blowing wind of God's grace, as the means whereby we are able to love God with all our strength — is far more than the capacity to *believe* the truth or even to *know* the truth. Above all, faith is the power to *trust* the truth, to bet our lives on it, to leave all and follow it.

Faith is the world-shaking and world-redeeming power of *loving confidence in God.* It cannot be faked or imitated, and its presence finally is unmistakable: those who have it are simply willing to dare all and lose all for God. And often they *are* heavy losers. But wisdom is justified especially in these children, for they find all in God eventually, and that is so great a thing that this poor old world can hardly bear the dazzling truth to which they witness: the truth that God *is real* and that *he can be known.*

It is no good arguing about God. It is no good trying to persuade persons who don't believe in God to believe in God. Even Christ did not make this effort. It is no great thing after all to believe in God. The devil believes in God. Evidently something more is required. And this is where we all balk.

It is said that God cannot be comprehended, but shall we therefore assume that God cannot be apprehended? Obviously God cannot be comprehended. But what follows? Neither can the ocean be comprehended. But it is still possible to jump into the ocean, to be drenched by the ocean, to swallow mouthfuls of the ocean, to come out dripping with the ocean and smelling of it.

To *merely* believe in God can be a greater disaster than not believing. Much talk about God winds up talking all around God. There is really very little to discuss. If you know enough about God to know that God *is,* you know all you need to know of that kind of knowing. The rest is a plunge.

That plunge takes us beyond reason, beyond faith, into spiritual experience.

For books about the way of faith, see Special Book Listings; page 209.

"With All Thy Heart and Soul"
— The Way of Experience

Have you had any spiritual experience, as yet? Time is flying. Don't waste another moment.

Brahmananda

Now we come to it. This is the key word and the key way: experience. You can tell a key term by the heat it generates, and "spiritual experience" is a hot one.

Let us observe the heat first: a very large group of earnest and learned people today is convinced that spiritual or religious experience has no basis whatsoever in reality. They say that it is all fantasy, hyperbole, poetry, wishful thinking. Another large group believes that spiritual experience is real enough in a way, but that it is also pathological, varying from crackpot to actually insane.

A detached observer could hardly fail to remark that both of these groups, although they are agile rationalizers, are not very valuable witnesses, because they pass judgment upon a kind of experience which they themselves invariably have not had and which they take rather scrupulous care to avoid.

Certainly there is such a thing as psychosis with religious content. Some of the insane do kick up a fuss about religious and spiritual things, but they also fuss about parents, children, politics, food, and sex. Shall anyone really take this fussing as an indication that there is something inherently insane about parents, children, politics, food, sex — or religion? A severely disturbed mind simply is apt to hurl its subject into the areas of deepest human concern, namely: parents, children, politics, food, sex, and religion.

Spiritual experience, more than any other kind of experience, should be open to searching criticism and rigorous evaluation. But to try to dismiss it, without direct contact or participation, as unreal or abnormal is the mark of a mere quibbler in this field. And it is far too important a field for time to be wasted in word-mincing, logic-chopping, and beating around the verbal bushes on the fringes of the subject.

One of the keenest inquiries into these pseudo-intellectual and pseudo-medical objections is to be found in William James's *The Varieties of Religious Experience* (pp. 3-26). But if you wish really to satisfy yourself as to the verity, sanity, and value of spiritual experience, don't brain it around too much in advance, even with William James. Debates in this area are a dissipation of precious energy. First go get instruction and follow the instruction that leads to actually having spiritual experience. Then read the intellectual pro and con books if you will. (They will be more interesting in that case and yet less detaining, because you will be moving on to other and far more interesting books.) The great thing is that *spiritual experience is real, and it is attainable.* Many sources testify to this, the central fact of human life:

> There is a great experiment possible in this life and there is a great crown of the experiment, but in the nature of things it is not to be bought cheaply, for it demands the whole man.
>
> A. E. Waite

> And as he journeyed, he came near Damascus: and suddenly there shined round about him a light from heaven: And he fell to the earth, and heard a voice. . . .
>
> Acts 9:3-4

> There is a man I know who was carried out of himself in Christ, fourteen years since; was his spirit in his body? I cannot tell. Was it apart from his body? I cannot tell; God knows. This man, at least, was carried up into the third heaven. I can only tell you that this man, with his spirit in his body, or with his spirit apart from his body, God knows which, not I, was carried up into Paradise, and heard mysteries which man is not allowed to utter.
>
> II Corinthians 12:2-4

> As regards this state and as regards its gifts, even at the early stages, I testify that the Divine in the universe answers to the Divine in man. . . . A life which is tuned to the keynote of the eternal mode knows of the things that are eternal. It knows very soon that it is not on a false quest. . . . If we say that there is something which is, as it were, ineffable in the world above, we need not think it unattainable in respect of ourselves: it may be an untrodden field of our consciousness. . . . The normal personality does not cognize this supernal part of being, but we must not be deceived by the idea that their sepa-

ration is on account of a distance in space; it is because
of the restriction of self-knowledge in the normal state. . .
. If we be faithful to the aspiration, the realization will be
true to us. It may come like a thief in the night, at a
point where we least expect it: the Gate of Glory opens
and we see that God has his throne in the highest part of
our nature. . . . The records tell us that there is an experience of unity possible to the soul of man. The testimo-
nies concerning it are everywhere; and, when every al-
lowance has been made for the distinction of national
mentality, for modes of metaphysical thought and the diverse helps or hindrances of official religious belief, the
testimony is always the same.

A. E. Waite

At times a man rests on his bed, and it appears to
his family as though he were asleep, but he spends this
hour in solitude with his Creator, blessed be He. That is
a high rung, that he beholds the Creator at all times with
the eye of his insight, as he sees another man. And consider this: if you persevere in a pure thought, then the
Creator also looks at you, as a man looks at you.

Martin Buber

Know for certain that God can be reached — that his
spiritual form can be seen and it is possible to talk to
him.

Brahmananda

This matter of experience is crucial. Very many men and
women are inwardly called to seek the answers about God. Relatively few of them arrive at real answers, full answers, utterly
satisfying answers, undeniable and life-transforming answers. But
these are the only kinds of answers worth having.

Why do so many thus fail?

Because they stop short. They stop short at reason or they stop
short at faith. And neither reason nor faith, nor reason and faith
together, is enough. Reason and faith are means. *God himself is*

the end. And the means, blessed and wonderful in themselves, become deadly obstacles if they are mistaken for ends. People and books can help, but they cannot do the job for you. You will never get the answers you are seeking until God unmistakably gives them to you. And the answers are not words only, not thoughts only, but God himself, directly experienced. All original religion, all scripture, every voice that ever has spoken with authority on this point, agree: in order to know the truth of God one must win through to *one's own experience of God.*

Who has not tasted, does not know. Who has not eaten is not satisfied by conversation with him that has eaten. Who has not drunk, his thirst is not quenched by the narration of him that has drunk. Who has not experienced, the experience of another does not profit.

Bar Hebraeus, *Book of the Dove*

A clear vision of the Reality may be obtained only through our own eyes, when they have been opened by spiritual insight — never through the eyes of some other seer. Through our own eyes we learn what the moon looks like; how could we learn this through the eyes of others?

Erudition, well-articulated speech, a wealth of words, and skill in expounding the scriptures — these give pleasure to the learned, but they do not bring liberation.

A sickness is not cured by saying the word "medicine." You must take the medicine. Liberation does not come by merely saying the word "Brahman." Brahman must be actually experienced.

A buried treasure is not uncovered by merely uttering the words "come forth." You must follow the right directions, dig, remove the stones and earth from above it, and then make it your own. . . . Pure truth . . . can be reached by meditation, contemplation, and other spiritual disciplines such as a knower of Brahman may prescribe — but never by subtle arguments.

Shankara, *Crest-Jewel of Discrimination*

If reason has led you to see that God may indeed be real and available, and if faith has led you to further insight and to putting your conviction into practice, sooner or later you will begin to have spiritual experience. How soon depends on several things: your *need* for it, your *desire* for it, the sincerity and persistence of your *practice*, and the unpredictable and unfathomable action of the grace of God. Nevertheless, if you are faithful, it will come.

Caution: the adversary, the monkey-mind inside each of us which works against man's coming to knowledge of God, plays his cards very adroitly when the question of one's own actual experience arises. The monkey, having failed to keep one out of spiritual life entirely, tries by every possible device to block the issues of direct experience. He works feverishly to keep things on the level of reason and faith. He hates these faculties but greatly prefers them to the (to him) deadly possibility of *experience*.

His arguments run something like this: "Sure, spiritual life is great stuff and we are all for it, of course. But humility is the thing, isn't it, and not getting too big for our britches? We've done a lot of thinking about God, and we should continue to do a lot more. And we *have* got faith; see what a difference it has made in our life! So let's not go overboard on this experience angle. It's all right for saints, no doubt, but we are a good comfortable long way from that. Thinking and believing, and of course lots of good works, are plenty good enough for us. And they have the merit of being safe. Once you get to seeing or feeling or actually experiencing these things, who knows where it will end? People did consider this man Christ to be crazy, you know, and look at the nasty mess he and some of his friends finally got into. . . ." And so forth and so forth and so forth. There is something in each of us which balks hard at our opening ourselves to the direct touch of Reality and will fight cleverly and persistently to prevent it.

In the face of all the false humility, the monkey's chattering, and the coward's whistling, the scripture says, calmly and plainly enough: "Taste and see that the Lord is good," and "Blessed are the pure in heart, for they shall see God." The aim of every great religion is direct experience of the Divine. Such experience is not something tacked on to religion as a bonus for a few honor students. On the contrary, *spiritual experience is the target to which the heart of everyone without exception is directed.* It is recognized that many will miss the mark, but all are called to shoot at it. Furthermore, those who seem to miss do not finally miss. We see very little of the whole human life in the short period between birth and death. Vast possibilities open up at death and beyond.

Everyone, therefore, is encouraged to press forward — as humbly and prudently as you please but at the same time ardently and with high hope — toward the great realms of direct spiritual experience where reason is illuminated and transcended and where faith is transfigured in the living Light of the Divine Reality. That Light is not far removed from ordinary men. Spatially it is not removed at all. We, unknowing, are immersed in it continually. It is our very life. Only a film of hypnotic ignorance prevents our seeing, feeling, *knowing* the Light for what it is. *And the film can be removed.*

As the Light of spiritual experience begins to dawn on the horizon toward which our life is moving, the adversary rushes forward with another stop-the-cruise effort. "Wait," he cries, "this is utterly uncharted sailing. This may be great, but it is the great abyss. This *really is* the unknown!"

Well, "Boo!" right back at him. Again the truth is quite the contrary. The way to God *is* charted. The way of reason is well charted; the way of faith is very well charted; and the way of experience is wonderfully and gloriously charted.

Naturally, you have to know that there *are* charts. You have to know how to find them. And you have to learn how to read them and follow them. Your course in spiritual experience will be guided from three sources: first, books. As experience begins, you find that reading takes on a new and very different character. You are no longer reading for instruction, for correction, for direction — comparing your own data with those of others who have gone this way before you. You use a book now the way a chemist or a doctor or a dietician uses a book — for practical, working reference. Or, even more wonderfully, as you read you may find yourself able to aim not only to know the truth of God but actually to taste it. "When one is reading," says St. Bernard, "let him seek not so much learning as savor." Thus reading can, under grace, become directly related to spiritual experience.

The second source of guidance is people. One of the discoveries that accompanies the beginning of your own spiritual experience is the happy realization of how many other people have had actual experience, too. You ask yourself, "How could I have failed to notice this before?" The answer, of course, is simple enough: People who have had genuine spiritual experience are often reticent about it. If they do not know it at first they soon learn that this kind of experience, as we have said, is a hot potato in our society — widely regarded as at best eccentric, at least fantastic, and at worst pathological. So people of real and sustained and developing spiritual experience are not quick or loose talkers. On the other hand, they are willing to share their knowledge with anyone whom they recognize as a sincere seeker of God and certainly with one who has himself begun to pass into direct experience.

The third source of guidance is the action of the presence of God upon one's own inner mind. ". . . You have by the grace of God, the desire for spiritual knowledge. . . . Now you must strive to win the grace of your minds . . ." (Brahmananda). We may say that at a certain point God himself begins to direct the experiencer into yet deeper and fuller levels of experience, and to encourage and correct him.

> Howbeit when he, the Spirit of truth, is come he will guide you into all truth. . . .
>
> John 16:13

> And all thy children shall be taught of God.
>
> Isaiah 54:13

Naturally an uncooked ego can make a fine mess out of things if it attempts to improvise this condition of inner illumination or to manipulate it after it has genuinely come. All sorts of inflations are possible: "illuminism," silly flights, and paranoid twists. Not pretty! And many seekers become involved, at some time and to some extent, in this kind of aberration. A little sincerity and simple honesty, however, soon break it up, and no real harm is done in most cases. Indeed the subject often is humbled and enlightened and, when he has had his spankings, proceeds onward with better ability to keep his feet on the ground as experience deepens. A real casualty, a prolonged inflammation of the ego, is possible; but it is quite rare and nearly always involves a character which was fundamentally unstable from way back. If you have anything like ordinary common sense you can receive intuitive guidance from God with great benefit and without upset. All you have to do is check your intuitions against what you learn from authentic books and genuinely experienced people, be willing to be corrected at all levels, including the intuitive, and you will find yourself getting along very well.

Spiritual experience is a development in many ways comparable to physical growth. Although some of the factors are inscrutable, the process is an orderly and reliable one. It moves along well-established lines by well-marked stages.* In the spiritual tradition of the Western world these stages are indicated as follows:

1. *Awakening:* This is an experience in which the person for the first time, or at least for the first time in adult life, becomes unmistakably aware of the living presence of God in himself and in the universe. This experience may be gentle and gradual; or it may be abrupt and in the nature of a drastic upheaval. A genuine awakening has a profound effect upon the life, and it leads, except where there are unusual obstructing elements, to the succeeding stages.

---

* The phenomenon of spiritual awakening, sometimes called conversion, is a special consideration in itself. The three "ways" which follow awakening — the purgative, illuminative, and unitive — are a deeply traditional Christian scheme of understanding spiritual experience. The terms go back to Dionysius the Areopagite (Pseudo-Dionysius), that "anonymous, mysterious, monastic genius" who, writing probably in the fifth century A.D., "taught the foremost Christians for ten centuries both in the East and in the West, for nearly every great medieval scholar made use of his writing and his authority came to be almost final" (Introduction to *The Mystical Theology,* Shrine of Wisdom edition).

2. *Purgation:* The person continues to experience the presence of God, it may be strongly or it may be faintly, and usually with many interruptions. The Presence acts upon the man, as St. John of the Cross says, like fire upon a wet log. It "cooks" the spiritual, psychic, and physical natures, exposing and driving out weaknesses and impurities. Conscious awareness of what is happening and cooperation with the action of grace are of great importance, and to a considerable extent they determine the length of time one remains in purgation.

3. *Illumination:* When purgation is well along in its work and the mind and body are beginning to come free of obstacles to the presence of God, the consciousness begins to be illuminated from within by a Light which is both intellectual and affective. The person knows and feels things he could not know or feel before. Difficult and obscure points with which his understanding formerly struggled now are clearly and easily comprehended. There is a considerable ability to know and to carry out God's will and to help others. And the life is increasingly flooded with joy.

These major stages overlap, and there are phenomena of flashback and flash-forward. For example, at the time of awakening a person may spend a few hours or even a few days in an illuminated condition. On the other hand, having won through to illumination as a fairly steady state, one may find oneself dropped back into purgation for a while. These temporary and necessary returns to the purgative condition must be distinguished from a profound purgative state, called the "night of the spirit," through which one passes when the illuminative is developing into the final or unitive phase of experience.

4. *Union:* There comes a time when the experience of God goes beyond the subject-object relationship, and a transforming mergence, marriage, or union occurs. This fulfillment is largely beyond description in our language. It involves relationships so sacred that, in Paul's words, "it is not lawful for a man to utter" the knowledge of them he may have. Certain kinds of music are much more successful than words in giving hints of the triumphant reality of the unitive state. We beginners are well advised not to fash ourselves unduly with such matters; it is easy to be-

come psychically overstimulated and either frightened or ambitious from hearing about them too much.

On the other hand, it is good even for very new beginners to have some realization of the staggering and glory-drenched heights to which God has called man and to which some men and women have already been raised. It is good to know that the invitation to move in this direction is extended to everyone, and that the meanest of us can, if he will, start the journey right here and right now.

To *begin* is the great key. The idea of "heights of glory" is all very well and all very true, but it is true in a sense we cannot well understand in advance. The point to remember, cling to, and never forget is that experience of God begins right here and now, down in the midst of this common, ordinary, everyday life. Sooner or later there will be flights to the heights. But it is wrong to overwork the imagination about them; doing so, we go on miserable pseudo-flights and gravely stunt our true spiritual growth.

The first utterly valid experience of God is the experience of everyday *truth,* of *common honesty* and *common decency.* Cling to this, work at this, be faithful in this, and the gates of glory will swing open — not yet on high, but here, now, on this still frightfully unredeemed earth. Meet God where he meets you — here, now. Don't be concerned about moving up. Sit down in the lowest seat. Have your experience of God in the place where you are. Let him take care of the moving up; then it will be in safe hands; not otherwise. God can be found, experienced, known, wherever you make your bed, even in hell. Find him where you are, today.

It is of critical importance that spiritual experience be not taken in a woolly and thoughtless way. If it is, great confusion can result, particularly right at the point where some actual experience has occurred but has not been understood or has been feebly and improperly understood. A common confusion of this kind arises *when the experience of awakening is assumed to be the whole of the regenerative process.* The man who has just begun the journey thinks he has reached the end of it. Thomas Bromley, in London in 1710, wrote a most helpful comment upon this crucial point (condensed, with italics supplied, from *The Soul's Progress in the Work of the New Birth,* quoted by A. E. Waite in *The Secret Tradition in Alchemy):*

> Regeneration greatly concerns us in its initiation, progress and consummation. The *beginning* of the work implies that first change of the soul when the frame of the will is swayed God and Heavenward. In it is the growth and motion of the soul from the image of the earthly toward the image of the Heavenly. In its *end* it is the bringing forth of the perfect and complete image of God in our humanity. When we attain this we are complete in Christ, wholly new-born, and made fit to see and enjoy that Eternal Kingdom which has been prepared for us from the beginning of the world. Regeneration then in its full latitude is that transforming quickening work of God's Spirit which begins, carries on and completes God's image in us. But in the ordinary acceptation [the term "regeneration"] is used for the first change of the soul toward God in Christ; and I find too much weight laid upon this first work, as though it were the complete new birth. Hence many rest upon and have a continual eye to it, though they feel their chariot-wheels stand still.

We do need guidance in our experience of God, and holy scripture is the best of all written sources. The Bible is a book of God experience from beginning to end — from the experiences of Adam, Enoch, Abraham, Jacob, Moses, Samuel, David, Elias, Isaiah, Daniel, and many other Old Testament seers to the experiences of Jesus Christ, and of Paul, Peter, John, and many other apostles and disciples. (For examples, See Appendix A, page 227.) There is a common obstacle to the application of the Bible in our own quest of God experience. It is the notion that the great meetings with God which happen over and over again in the Bible are confined to remote times or to people who are very different from ourselves. The notion is unfounded. And once this block is removed the Bible becomes a very practical guidebook in the realities we are seeking personally to contact.

Finally: beware. For it is all true, after all. God does exist.

And once there is any sincere seeking, *experience may come at any minute*. And then we may find ourselves reacting like the actor who was supposed to be shot in the second act, and whose line was "Help! I'm shot!" But one night a real bullet somehow was put into the pistol instead of the customary blank, and he delivered his line with new emphasis: "Help! I *am* shot!"

Far from being a dream figure or a merely psychological entity, God is the Reality of reality. And that Reality is vivid, intense, and dangerous. Yes, plainly, dangerous. All scripture is quite blunt on this point, and so is the testimony of God-realized men and women everywhere. God is the most solicitous of Fathers, tenderly aware of the teardrop on the infant's cheek, but he is also Lord of the flaming caldrons of deep heaven. He is love, but he is also law. The heart of his compassion lies between mercy on the right hand and severity on the left.

Let no one who may be attracted to the search for God by the feeble witness of this present book complain, if he is knocked about or burned in the process, that he was not warned. I do not compose the warnings; I merely call attention to them. They are sounded in every age. They are obviously not intended to discourage the timid, who are in fact tirelessly and ingeniously coaxed by God's love. No, but the warnings are there simply to tell the rash, the foolish, and the perverse, if they will hear it, *that God is real*, that it is dangerous and futile to hide from him, but that it is also dangerous to come into his presence without due preparation.*

---

* Let's face it. Contact with God can unhinge a person. That is why preparation is so stressed in every true teaching. The contact may be utterly real, entirely valid, and still throw the mind out of gear. There may be actual psychosis with religious content, *or* the man may be completely sane and yet so altered, so much the vehicle of authentic and powerful spiritual influx, that his associates are frightened and distressed (Jesus, St. Paul, St. Francis of Assisi, Chaitanya, Muhammad, George Fox, Sri Ramakrishna, and the apostles on Pentecost Day are examples of the latter condition). The state of people who are touched by God in this way is traditionally recognized in Islam and in India, where they are protected and honored at all levels of society. This seems more clear-sighted than our handling of the problem in the West, where the God-intoxicated person is simply thrown in with the run of psychotic cases and left to flounder there. This sort of thing happens more often today than you would know if you were not in contact with it. I am intimately acquainted with a number of cases. It happens

Friend, how comest thou in hither not having a wedding garment? . . . Then said the king to the servants,
Bind him hand and foot, and take him away. . . .
                                        Matthew 22:12-13

It is a fearful thing to fall into the hands of the living
God.
                                        Hebrews 10:31

Jung puts it beyond all possible doubt that the experience of God, which brings God home to us as a living
quantity and not merely as an object of faith in the sense

---

right along: these people get a real touch of the Spirit; it knocks them off
their trolley for a while (or, while they remain quite sane, their behavior is
so changed that they are deemed insane); they wind up in psychopathic
wards where doctors, whose philosophy includes no provision however
remote for the realities involved here, fumble around trying to classify
them; and finally they are set loose again when their harmlessness becomes
apparent and they begin to recover their balance, which they nearly always
do spontaneously after a while.

The problem of derangement incidental to spiritual awakening needs
practical study by men who are qualified to make such studies. These
cases, as mankind's birth struggle deepens in the next few years, will probably increase. This is not necessarily a bad sign. Instances which are considered insane but which, like those of Paul, Ramakrishna, etc., turn out to
be genuine awakenings, should be distinguished from cases of out-and-out
psychosis. Genuine insanity, with hatred, suspicion, hostility, and ego-infla-
tion, should not be identified with the condition of God-struck people who
are certainly confused and perhaps psychically shocked and paralyzed, but
in a benign and harmless way, and whose prognosis is one of far better
than normal maturity and scope in this life if they are handled not necessarily skillfully but just without too much blundering. St. Francis, George
Fox, and company, as history abundantly has proved, were *not* psychotics;
they were cases of real or seeming derangement incidental to religious or
spiritual awakening; *psychosis with religious content is something else again*; it
would seem very important to distinguish the two. And even in the latter
cases, not only a great healing but a great advance in the whole life can
take place if they are treated with religious and spiritual insight. (See
Boisen, *Religion in Crisis and Custom*.)

Spiritual experience is real. Sometimes it comes on gently and gradually.
But sometimes it is like grabbing hold of, or being touched by, a high-volt-
age wire. If you are in any way really prepared, all goes well in spite of
the power of the experience. But today this kind of contact is coming closer
and closer to large numbers of people who are not at all prepared. We really should find out what is happening here and learn how to handle it
properly.

that we acknowledge or subordinate ourselves to a traditional dogma, is an extremely dangerous and terrible thing. Psychically, it claims the whole man, and it is a fatality which may land him in greater spiritual distress and disaster than many of the purely outward circumstances we so dramatically call "fate." . . . When the experience of God is a real living thing, it touches us to the quick, and time and strength are needed in order to come to terms with it. In moments like these we feel the perils and ambiguities of life not only in the surrounding world, not only in our bodies, but in our very souls; then they are as close to us as they possibly can be, are as dangerous and terrible as they possibly can be, and in certain circumstances are also as rapturous as they possibly can be.

> Hans Schaer, *Religion and the Cure of Souls*

And not only the unknown depths of reality but outer conditions and men, too, become a menace to the God-seeker: ". . . Yea, the time cometh, that whosoever killeth you will think that he doeth God service" (John 16:2). And yet, at the very same time, if we are willing to develop sincerity, willing to work, and willing to learn: there is nothing to fear. The most broken, the weakest, and the most undefended of persons are exactly those who have the least cause for anxiety in approaching God:

> Blessed are the poor in spirit . . . they that mourn . . . they which are persecuted . . . [Matt. 5:3, 4, 10]. Come unto me, all ye that labour and are heavy laden, and I will give you rest [Matt. 11:28]. Are not five sparrows sold for two farthings, and not one of them is forgotten before God? But even the very hairs of your head are all numbered. Fear not therefore . . . [Luke 12:6-7]. Peace I leave with you, my peace I give unto you . . . [John 14:27]. In the world ye shall have tribulation: but be of good cheer; I have overcome the world [John 16:33].

The sentimental seekers after a soft berth with God and the

angry thunderers of anathemas both can find plenty of references to quote in support of their positions, but both have to quote sharply out of context, for both are very far from the most veritable and most universal descriptions of the Way to God. These truest indications are always paradoxical: the Way is easy and hard, joyful and full of terrors, ecstatic and suffering, sweet in the mouth and bitter in the belly, offering both a cross and a crown.

C. S. Lewis has touched upon this truth in introducing a book of selections from the writings of his teacher George MacDonald. Referring to MacDonald, Lewis says:

> I dare not say that he is never in error; but to speak plainly I know hardly any other writer who seems to be closer, or more continually close, to the Spirit of Christ Himself. Hence his Christ-like union of tenderness and severity. Nowhere else outside the New Testament have I found terror and comfort so intertwined. The title "Inexorable Love" which I have given to several individual extracts would serve for the whole collection. Inexorability — but never the inexorability of anything less than love — rings through it all like a refrain; "escape is hopeless" — "agree quickly with your adversary" — "compulsion waits behind" — "the uttermost farthing will be exacted." Yet this urgency never becomes shrill. All the sermons are suffused with a spirit of love and wonder which prevents it from doing so. MacDonald shows God threatening, but (as Jeremy Taylor says) "He threatens terrible things if we will not be happy."

For books about the way of experience, see Special Book Listings, page 212.

PART TWO

Is the Experiment a Practical Possibility?

CHAPTER ONE
What, Specifically, Do You Do?

Getting down to practical, day-to-day details, how do you follow the ways to God? What, specifically, do you *do?* That depends on you and circumstances.

The Alternatives

If you have latitude in your choice of a way of life, that is, if you are not closely bound by duties, and if you are of a certain temperament and vocation, you may enter one of the several possible situations in which the way to God is mapped out in detail and with the authority of much successful experience.

For example, you may become an Anglican Benedictine monk; or you may become a Roman Catholic Trappist or Carmelite; or you may place yourself under the direction of a Hindu *guru;* or you may become a Buddhist *bhiksu.* There are many such possibilities. If you choose one of them, your procedure, inwardly and outwardly, is clearly explained to you. Your task is to find your way upon a plainly marked and well-trodden path. Directors, techniques, books, and associates — all are provided. The problem of your relationship with the world and its duties is largely solved at the outset, or the manner of its solution is definitely indicated. A wealth of appropriate material is at your disposal as you set about the practice of the spiritual life in earnest.

But there are many men and women who sincerely want to seek God who would say that none of the above kinds of ways is practical for them. By which they mean that they cannot discharge the duties of a householder, a father or mother of a family, and at the same time follow the established ascetic, monastic, or yogic ways to God.

What then? Must the householder give up the idea of finding God or put off the quest until circumstances change? Not at all.

As a householder, particularly in this day and age, you *can* find your way to God right in the midst of your immediate surroundings, however "unspiritual" these may be at the start. Perhaps as you go along you will alter your circumstances considerably, but it is not necessary to abandon the life and duties of a family man or woman; these are not barriers to real spiritual progress.

There is authority for this conclusion. Christ himself founded no monasteries, ordained no priests, and called most of his immediate servants from among laymen and householders. And he said that not only common people but whores and politicians would enter the kingdom of God, and that they would get in before the professed religious unless the latter stopped playing big shot and got down to earth with the rest of the human race. You, as a family man or woman, with all the duties and limitations inevitable in that state, have as good a chance as anyone to receive the *charisma* — holy, saving power and wisdom — and to go on to full regeneration. All you have to do is abandon yourself before God, ask for the gift, and act in its light.

And this evidently is a universal offer. If your outlook is receptive to Eastern spiritual teachings, you will find the same point emphasized there. Among the great Hindu teachers, for example, our near-contemporary Sri Ramakrishna repeatedly assured those who consulted him that the life of the householder is not incompatible with God-realization; see *The Gospel of Sri Ramakrishna*, particularly Chapter 4, "Advice to Householders"; Chapter 20, "Rules for Householders and Monks"; Chapter 22, "Advice to an Actor"; and Chapter 31, "Advice to Ishan."

Founding figures in our main spiritual traditions — Jesus, Buddha, Muhammad, Lao Tse, Sri Rama — were laymen who lived and taught in the world; three of the above were married. The Christian tradition, prolific in ecclesiastic and monastic developments, at the same time is full of laymen who faithfully and successfully have followed the way to God, from Simon Bar-Jona through Francis of Assisi to Therese Neumann.

St. Francis de Sales, himself a priest and Doctor of the Church, was deeply concerned with the spiritual direction of men and women who were devoted to giving their lives to God in the midst of worldly duties and occupations. His book *Introduction to the Devout Life,* a masterpiece of counsel for just such people, grew out of casual notes of instruction and advice which he wrote to Mme. de Chamoisy, a cousin by marriage who had placed herself under his spiritual care. Another great churchman who was a specialist in the direction of God-seeking men and women in the world was Fénelon, Archbishop of Cambrai; his wonderfully sane, practical, and loving letters are as alive and helpful today as when they were written and first read in seventeenth-century France.

Among the Eastern teachings which are of value to householders seeking God, none is more helpful than the Bhagavad Gita. The Gita teaches karma yoga, i.e., nonegotistical action and service in the world, leading to experiential knowledge of Reality and thus to salvation and liberation.

In our own time there has appeared a system that is intended specifically to enable men and women in the world, "good householders," to achieve spiritual change and to reach higher levels of consciousness. This teaching is called "the fourth way" (as distinguished from the ways of the fakir, the yogi, and the monk). The doctrine of the fourth way claims not to be new but to be an expression in contemporary terms of a universal spiritual "work" which always had existed. "The fourth way" and "the work" in the context indicated here are equivalent terms.

This system has evolved from the influence of two men and their followers and commentators. The first is G. I. Gurdjieff, an extraordinary and highly enigmatic person, who is regarded by some who knew him well as an authentic saint, by others as an eccentric if not a villain or a black magician, but by none as a neutral or uninteresting character. Gurdjieff brought to the West the knowledge of the principles which were developed in the teaching of the fourth way.

A Russian named P. D. Ouspensky studied and worked with Gurdjieff for a number of years beginning in 1915. Subsequently, in a series of lectures and personal teachings, he made possible the first widely published statements of the fourth-way system.

Ouspensky, trained as a mathematician, journalist, and philosopher, was a disciplined and audacious thinker. He was also a serious, a relentless, and in a certain cool way a heroic seeker for truth. Before his meeting with Gurdjieff he already had produced one of the most penetrating and revolutionary of modern essays in thought, a book entitled *Tertium Organum*. The lines of inquiry opened up in this work were followed further in a later book, *A New Model of the Universe*. Ouspensky's books which stem from his work with Gurdjieff and which are concerned specifically with the fourth way are *In Search of the Miraculous, The Psychology of Man's Possible Evolution,* and *The Fourth Way,* all published after his death in 1947. Ouspensky's collaborators and followers include Maurice Nicoll, who wrote *Psychological Commentaries on the Teaching of Gurdjieff and Ouspensky,* and Rodney Collin, who wrote *The Theory of Celestial Influence* and *The Theory of Eternal Life.*

The Rules

Spiritual awakening and growth in God are possible in ordinary life. But they come only to men and women who deeply long for the *truth,* who find and follow the *rules,* and who do the necessary *work.* These three — (1) the truth, (2) the rules, and (3) the work — are the ladder to success. We have already considered the place of truth in the quest for God. It is alpha and omega. Simple honesty, which any child can understand (but few children and fewer adults can practice), leads straight to the goal. By practicing honesty you win the grace of the Spirit of Truth. Then God himself, the Holy Ghost, becomes your inner teacher, the guide who takes you to your Lord and King. And he in turn enables you to understand the rules and do the work.

What about the rules? They are clearly stated in the great sources accessible to all: the Old Testament, the New Testament, the Bhagavad Gita, the Yoga Sutras, and the Buddhist scriptures. They can be epitomized so as to be readable in just a few minutes. It is assumed, however, that no one will take the brevity of the ensuing summary as grounds for underestimating the depth, sublimity, and binding necessity of the rules. Whoever takes the rules lightly or foolishly or fails to take them at all disqualifies himself not only for spiritual life but finally for any kind of life at the human level.

The following is a boil-down of the rules in contemporary terms:

A. *The Decalogue:*
1. First things first. Avoid idolatry: i.e., do not put lesser values above higher values or any love above the Supreme Love. This is a very hard rule to follow.
2. Do not kick sacred things around. Do not invoke God or use his name unless you are aware of what you are doing and unless you mean business.
3. Do not ignore basic cosmic rhythms and laws. There are, for example, cycles of activity and rest which have their roots in Divine Nature itself and cannot be violated with impunity by anyone, because no one can exist outside that Nature. Man's health and sanity depend on understanding and reverently accommodating his life to the profound implications of such traditions as the Sabbath.
4. The home, and particularly the relationship with father and mother, is a sacred institution. It reaches to the heights and depths of man's soul. It is the great analogue of man's relationship to his Creator. It is to be protected and honored.
5. Do not murder.
6. Do not commit adultery.
7. Do not steal.
8. Do not lie about your neighbor.
9 and 10. Do not covet your neighbor's wife or goods.

B. *The precepts of Christ (New Testament):*
1. (Quoted by Christ from the Law of Moses): Love God with your whole heart, soul, mind, and strength and your neighbor as yourself. Another hard rule to follow.
2. If you want to enter into eternal life, keep the commandments.
3. Repent, i.e., change your attitude, your outlook, your way of life, your mind; go beyond your present state, transcend yourself (Greek *metanoia: meta,* "change" or "beyond";

nous, "intellect," "mind," "understanding").

4. Wake up. Snap out of it. Pay attention. Watch (Greek *gregoreite*).

5. First things first: Leave all, sell all, and follow Christ (the Lord, the truth, the way). Deny yourself, observe and bear your unregenerate nature every day, and follow Christ.

6. Resist not evil; do not retaliate.

7. Do not be angry.

8. Do not touch a woman illegitimately, even in your mind.

9. Live one day at a time. Do not worry about tomorrow. Do not worry about food and clothes.

10. Pray always, and do not faint, do not collapse.

11. Heal the sick, cleanse the lepers, cast out devils, raise the dead.

12. Do not murder.

13. Do not commit adultery.

14. Do not steal.

15. Do not lie.

16. Honor your father and mother.

17. Be poor, and poor in spirit. (Let go of material *and* spiritual possessiveness.)

18. Mourn. (Let suffering and loss do their full work in you.)

19. Be meek (Greek *praos,* "disciplined," "trained," "nonresentful," "gentle," "tractable," "teachable").

20. Be hungry and thirsty after wisdom, justice, right knowledge, skill in the way.

21. Be merciful.

22. Be a peacemaker.

23. Be pure in heart.

24. Be perfect (Greek *teleios,* "complete," "undivided," "unlimited," "finished," "mature," "integral") as God is perfect.

25. Love your enemies; pray for anyone who abuses you.

26. Endure persecution and calumny cheerfully.

27. Believe and trust in God as your Father, hallow his name, seek his kingdom and his truth, ask him for what you need, knock at the door of God realization.

C. *The essence of the Bhagavad Gita:* Be devoted to God above all other interests. Work without craving for results or rewards.

D. *Pre-yogic moral disciplines* (Compiled from Gandhi, Vivekananda, Mees, Prabhavananda):

The five yamas (cardinal vows):
1. Harmlessness (non-violence, non-killing, non-resentment, meekness, *ahimsa*).
2. Truthfulness (non-falsehood in thought, speech, and actions, *satya*).
3. Non-stealing (not taking more than needed, not wasting).
4. Continence (refraining from illicit sexual experience, in thought, word, and deed, *brahmacharya*; further: restraint of all waste and leakage in the vital nature).
5. Non-possession (non-covetousness, giving up the sense of ownership, becoming "poor" and "poor in spirit").

The five *niyamas* (casual vows):
1. Purity (bodily cleanliness, outside *and* inside; mental cleanliness; regulation of diet, reading, and associations).
2. Contentment (non-worrying, non-fretting, non-striving, equanimity, even-mindedness).
3. Austerity (conserving energy and directing it toward the spiritual goal, *tapas*, training).
4. Study (reading and meditating on the scriptures and other works leading to God).
5. Devotion to and surrender to God.

E. *Buddhist guiding principles* (extracted and condensed from "Summary of Buddha's Dharma," Buddhist writings, Goddard, *A Buddhist Bible*):

The Four Noble Truths:
1. The universality of *suffering*.
2. The *cause* of suffering rooted in desire.
3. By ending desire, suffering comes to an *end*.
4. The *way* to end desire, and hence to end suffering, is to follow the Eightfold Noble Path.

The Eightfold Noble Path:

1. Right ideas.
2. Right resolution.
3. Right speech.
4. Right behavior.
5. Right vocation.
6. Right effort; following the ideals of
    a. unselfish charity,
    b. sincerity and fidelity in keeping the precepts,
    c. humility,
    d. zeal and perseverance,
    e. tranquillity and one-pointedness.
7. Right mindfulness.
8. Right *dhyana* (attention, meditation, concentration, rapture)

The Ten Bodhisattva Stages:

1. Gladness and joy.
2. Purity and peace.
3. Effortless patience.
4. Effortless energy.
5. Higher consciousness *(samadhi)* while retaining touch with this world.
6. Self-mastery and unshakable confidence.
7. The "turning about" from which one never again recedes.
8. Transcendental powers and utter acceptance.
9. Perfect wisdom and compassion, directed to the emancipation and enlightenment of the world.
10. Complete identification with the Great Truth Cloud; perfect integration with all lives.

F. *The seven things to avoid,* the capital sins (Christian tradition):

1. Pride.
2. Greed.
3. Lust.
4. Anger.
5. Gluttony.
6. Envy.
7. Sloth.

G. *The root trouble* against which all the rules are directed is *egotism* (exaggerated personal self-sense), giving rise to a condition variously termed craving, desire, lust, thirst, clinging, sticking, attachment, infatuation, delusion, beguilement — English: concupiscence; Greek: *epithumia*; Sanskrit: *moha*; Pali: *tanha*; Russian: *prelest*; modern American: "To hell with you, Jack. I've got mine."

The above survey of the rules is of course not complete, but it is carried far enough to indicate what the outstanding principles are, as stated in the main sources, and to show how they overlap, agree, supplement, and confirm each other. There is no substitute for consulting the sources themselves and really absorbing what they have to tell you.

For help in understanding the rules themselves, their truth and significance on the one hand and their utility and practice on the other hand, four work books are suggested (one Roman Catholic, one Anglican, one Hindu, and one Eastern Orthodox Christian): *The Spiritual Life* (a treatise on ascetical and mystical theology) by Adolphe Tanquerey; *The Warfare of the Soul* by Shirley C. Hughson; *How to Know God* (the yoga aphorisms of Patanjali), translated and with commentary by Prabhavananda and Isherwood (pp. 95-173); and *Unseen Warfare* (the *Spiritual Combat* of Lorenzo Scupoli, edited by Nicodemus of the Holy Mountain and Theophan the Recluse).

The *work* consists of the practical application of the rules in daily living. Spiritual work far exceeds any other kind of work in interest and meaning, in challenge and difficulty, and in real accomplishment and fulfillment; it is the subject of our next chapter.

CHAPTER TWO

The Practical Life
Means Practice

Practice in the spiritual life is the thing that separates the men from the boys. Lots of people today as always are ready to talk about it and hear about it; relatively few are ready actually to do it. But hearing without doing is impractical: i.e., it doesn't work. This is a hoary old truth, but some of us still manage to elude it.

> Whosoever heareth these sayings of mine, and doeth them, I will liken him unto a wise man, which built his house upon a rock. . . . And everyone that heareth these sayings of mine, and doeth them not, shall be likened unto a foolish man, which built his house upon the sand. . . .

> Matthew 7:24, 26

Questions as to whether seeking God is practical, i.e., whether it can be done at all by a mere mortal, are usually raised by men and women who have not yet really tried it, or who have tried it a little and found that it pinches pretty hard in the comfort or pleasure or self-esteem department.

Anyone who has begun to practice in full earnest will tell you that seeking God is practical enough in any circumstances, but that it is indeed very difficult. Of course it is also difficult to build sky scrapers, raise mink, or play a good game of golf, and there are plenty of people doing those things. The fact is that men, even more than ants and bees, stubbornly make their way over and under and through all kinds of difficulties on the way to objectives in which they *really believe* and which they *deeply desire.*

People balk at spiritual life not because of difficulties but because they are still asleep to the reality of it. They do not really believe in it (although they may be pious "believers"), and they do not really want it. The awakening to the reality is a gift of God; all we can do is pray for it. But when it comes, when a man gets a whiff of the joy of returning to God, it draws him far more strongly than money or sex or power. He then no longer talks of difficulties but quietly gets on with the work.

How do you work? *You start right where you are* and apply the rules in your own daily life. Whoever you are, wherever you find yourself, this is a big order. But fortunately there are several simple, proved, time-honored practices which help to clarify and channel the work as it proceeds and to make its accomplishment entirely possible for anyone who really means business.

The Practice of the Presence of God

Nicholas Herman of Lorraine was a big, clumsy man whose life was turned to God as a result of looking at a tree.

> He told me that God had done him a singular favor, in his conversion at the age of eighteen. That in the winter, seeing a tree stripped of its leaves, and considering that within a little time the leaves would be renewed, and after that the flowers and fruit appear, he received a high view of the providence and power of God, which has never since been effaced from his soul. That this view had perfectly set him loose from the world, and kindled in him such a love for God that he could not tell whether it had increased during the more than forty years he had lived since.
>
> *The Practice of the Presence of God*

Like certain men of Galilee in old times, Nicholas Herman was ignorant and uneducated. He was humble enough to enter a monastery, hoping "that he would be made to smart for his awkwardness." He was admitted as a lay brother among the barefooted Carmelites in Paris in 1666 and thereafter was known as Brother Lawrence. He was the monastery cook. From the uneventful life of this uncomplicated person there developed, almost by accident, one of the most influential and helpful of all books on the practical search for God.

The Practice of the Presence of God consists of conversations with Brother Lawrence recorded by M. Beaufort, Grand Vicar to the former Cardinal de Noailles, and letters written by Brother Lawrence himself, with no thought that they would ever be published. Emanating from a monastery, these spiritual counsels have been of greatest help to God-seeking men and women in the world.

The practice of the Presence of God can be done anywhere by anyone who is not dead, crazy, or asleep. It is direct; it is simple; it involves no theological or intellectual difficulties; it produces genuine spiritual power; it really works. (It does not work as well or as often as it could and should, but that is a curious question which we shall examine below.)

The appeal, the great practical value, and the wide popularity of Brother Lawrence's technique will be found to cut across denominational and interreligious lines. The practice of the Presence is praised and studied by Catholics and Protestants alike and has won considerable attention among devoted people outside the Christian tradition.

What is the practice? How do you do it? You can find out by reading the book. But do not be deceived by its simplicity. Do not read it and be charmed by it and put it aside as so many do. Read it slowly, a little bit at a time, daily for six months. And practice it daily. Only by doing it can you begin to know *what* the method is and *how* to do it.

You will notice that the practice of the Presence of God consists of three stages. The first is *recollection*. Brother Lawrence teaches us simply to remember — not as philosophy but as living realization in the midst of our ordinary occupations — what is the true state of affairs: God is everywhere. We are continually in his presence. We know this, and yet we do not know it. We alternate between very brief periods of faintly remembering it and very long periods of utterly forgetting it. The practice of the Presence begins with remembering more often and more vividly and forgetting for shorter periods and less completely.

. . . acquire a habit of conversing often with God, and forget Him the least you can. . . .

Let it be *your business* to keep your mind in *the Presence of the Lord.* If it sometimes wanders . . . the will must bring it back in tranquillity.

Let us thus think often that our only business in this life is to please God, and that all besides is perhaps but folly and vanity . . . let us begin in earnest; let us repair the lost time. . . .

One way to recall the mind easily in time of prayer . . . is *not to let it wander too far at other times* . . . being accustomed to think of Him often, you will find it easy to keep your mind calm. . . .

That useless thoughts spoil all; that the mischief began there, but that we ought to reject them as soon as we perceive their impertinence to the matter in hand or to our salvation, and return to our communion with God.

The second stage in Brother Lawrence's way to God is *conversation.* The first and second stages overlap; they are given in sequence here only for convenience. Recollection of the Presence and conversation with God are mutually supporting acts.

That we should establish in ourselves a sense of God's Presence by continually conversing with Him. That it was a shameful thing to quit His conversation to think of trifles and fooleries.

That in order to form a habit of conversing with God continually, and referring all we do to Him, we must at first apply to Him with some diligence. . . .

Conversation, like recollection, seems simplicity itself — when you are merely reading about it. When you actually practice it, you discover that the simplicity is real all right but that it is a surface beneath which lies a great depth and a great power.

Recollection of the Presence and *conversation* with God together represent a critical turning point in the inner life of man. Nearly anyone can remember God and converse with him, now and then. But when you are able to do it more often, and then still more often, a tremendous event is taking place in the soul. This is still a beginner's stage, but it is the *beginning of the true life in God.* Father Reginald Garrigou-Lagrange has written of this experience with wonderful clarity in his synthesis of the spiritual life, *The Three Ages of the Interior Life:*

> As soon as a man ceases to be outwardly occupied, to talk with his fellow men, as soon as he is alone, even in the noisy streets of a great city, he begins to carry on a conversation with himself. If he is young, he often thinks of his future; if he is old, he thinks of the past, and his happy or unhappy experience of life makes him usually judge persons and events very differently.
>
> If a man is fundamentally egotistical, his intimate conversation with himself is inspired by sensuality or pride. He converses with himself about the object of his cupidity, of his envy; finding therein sadness and death, he tries to flee from himself, to live outside of himself, to divert himself in order to forget the emptiness and the nothingness of his life. In this intimate conversation of the egoist with himself there is a certain very inferior self-knowledge and a no less inferior self-love.
>
> He is acquainted especially with the sensitive part of his soul, that part which is common to man and to the animal. Thus he has sensible joys, sensible sorrows, according as the weather is pleasant or unpleasant, as he wins money or loses it. He has desires and aversions of the same sensible order; and when he is opposed, he has moments of impatience and anger prompted by inordinate self-love.
>
> But the egoist knows little about the spiritual part of his soul, that which is common to the angel and to man. Even if he believes in the spirituality of the soul and of the higher faculties, intellect and will, he does not live in this spiritual order. He does not, so to speak, know experimentally this higher part of himself and he does not

love it sufficiently. If he knew it, he would find in it the image of God and he would begin to love himself, not in an egotistical manner for himself, but for God. His thoughts almost always fall back on what is inferior in him, and though he often shows intelligence and cleverness which may even become craftiness and cunning, his intellect, instead of rising, always inclines toward what is inferior to it. . . . The intimate conversation of the egoist with himself proceeds thus to death and is therefore not an interior life. . . . The interior life is precisely an elevation and a transformation of the intimate conversation that everyone has with himself as soon as it tends to become a conversation with God.

(1) Recollection of God and (2) conversation with God, as taught in the simple, uncomplicated, authoritative terms of Brother Lawrence, represent an outlook and a technique which lead to the third and culminating stage of the practice of the Presence, the condition of (3) sustained awareness.

When you reach this point, your own efforts become so blended with the grace of God that you who once had to swim so hard now find yourself drifting with the current of God's love and you who tried with such difficulty to walk toward God now find yourself upheld and carried, constantly, steadily, by an ever-present Power. Knowledge of God and communion with God in the stage of sustained awareness are spontaneous, effortless, and rarely interrupted. The Presence is known and communed with under all kinds of circumstances.

> That with him the *set* times of prayer were not different from other times; that he retired to pray, according to the directions of his Superior, but that he did not want such retirement, nor ask for it, because his greatest business did not divert him from God.
>
> He is now so accustomed to that *Divine Presence* that he receives from it continual succor upon all occasions. For above thirty years his soul has been filled with joys so continual, and sometimes so transcendent, that he is

forced to use means to moderate them, and to prevent their appearing outwardly.

That he had so often experienced the ready succor of Divine Grace upon all occasions, that from the same experience, when he had business to do, he did not think of it beforehand; but when it was time to do it, he found in God, as in a clear mirror, all that was fit for him to do.

There is a special power and appeal in Brother Lawrence's book. Many people are afraid of the spiritual life because it seems difficult and remote. Brother Lawrence presents it as easy and immediate.

> . . . Spend the remainder of your life only in worshipping God. He lays no great burden upon us; a little remembrance of Him from time to time; a little adoration; sometimes to pray for His Grace, sometimes to offer Him your sorrows, and sometimes to return Him thanks for the benefits He has given you, and still gives you, in the midst of your troubles. He asks you to console yourself with Him the oftenest you can. Lift up your heart to Him even at your meals and when you are in company; the least little remembrance will always be acceptable to Him. You need not cry very loud; He is nearer to us than we think.
>
> To be with God, there is no need to be continually in church. We may make an oratory of our heart wherein to retire from time to time to converse with Him in meekness, humility, and love. Everyone is capable of such familiar conversation with God, some more, some less. He knows what we can do. Let us begin, then. Perhaps He is just waiting for one generous resolution on our part.

Is it possible that Brother Lawrence was mistaken? Hardly. The power of the man and his work, the purity and authority of his words, are too great. But if the practice of the Presence of God is so easy and so effective, why is it that more people do not follow it through to the stage of sustained awareness as

Brother Lawrence himself did? *As a matter of actual fact, not many do. But why don't they?*

Getting down to contemporary cases, here is what we find: The practice of the Presence *is* easy to try. Let's say you are one of the many people who try it, and you find to your delight that in a few days you are making undoubted and exhilarating progress. And then . . . then . . . several months later you wake up and find that somehow, somewhere, you have dropped it completely and forgotten all about it. It is not consciously abandoned. No decision is made. The great adventure simply peters out, and you cannot tell for sure just where the stream disappeared in the desert.

But you are intrigued. You remember the joy of those few days when it was working so wonderfully and so easily. So you try it again. And again it works very well! You are thrilled. You resolve to be more alert and not to lose it again. Days go by, great days. And then . . . then . . . the strange drama is repeated. You come to, and you realize that you have not been practicing the Presence of God for weeks.

Some good comes from these sporadic and unsustained experiences in Brother Lawrence's technique. But the fact remains that they fall short of the thing Brother Lawrence is talking about, and they are distressingly in the majority.

Why?

First, probably because the ease and simplicity of the practice of the Presence are only a part of the picture. The practice is a long ladder. Its feet are comfortably planted at the easy levels where all may climb. But the upper rungs rise into clouds of glory. As the apostles did at the Transfiguration, you are apt to fall asleep in this rarefied atmosphere; and then you fall off the ladder.

The great quality, therefore, in practicing the Presence is the persistence to try again and again. Do not be discouraged when, time after time, you undergo the humiliating experience of falling asleep spiritually and simply forgetting that God is here and that we may converse with him always. This kind of sleep lies close to the root of the fall of man; it is embarrassing, but the difficulty is made bearable by the realization that you share it with the rest of the human race.

Anyone who wishes seriously to study and practice Brother Lawrence's way should read Gerald Heard's two essays on the subject, entitled "Notes on Brother Lawrence's Practice," in *Vedanta for the Western World*. With his combination of scholarship and spiritual insight, Heard shows that there is much more than meets the casual glance in *The Practice of the Presence of God*. Without wishing to detract from the appeal and comfort and usefulness of the book, he points out that it can be understood and successfully followed only after penetrating study of its content and meditation upon its real meaning.

> . . . That method [the practice of the Presence], though the description of it has been popular, has owed its popularity not to the fact that it is really simple or rudimentary but because we have felt sentimental about a pretty title and a charming old man. . . .
>
> The first thing that a careful study of these four conversations and fifteen letters discloses is that though the language is so simple, often even conventional, yet they contain far more specific information than the easy rapid reading suggests. . . . We find that this is not at all a beginner's book. . . . The system is simple because it is advanced. This is not a spiritual child speaking with unreflective simplicity. This is a man at the end of an intense, never-remitted struggle of a dedicated lifetime, having won to that consummate ease, that master's power to extemporize in any mode, which comes only to those who, at the top and climax of their form, having achieved all particular controls, now have such perfect command of expression and apprehension that every event becomes precisely that opportunity which allows fresh, inexhaustible creativeness to be exhibited.

Who is right — the people who see in Brother Lawrence and his way a direct, unconfused, and wonderfully easy method of living the practical life in God, or Gerald Heard, who sees in

Lawrence a man very far advanced in sanctity and in his practice an expert's, not a novice's, technique?

Both views may be true. So many ordinary people have been attracted to the practice of the Presence and greatly helped by it that we must agree with the enthusiasts who praise it as one of the great and basic spiritual practices. At the same time, so many give up serious attempts really to follow it after a few trials that we must also conclude that Gerald Heard is to be thanked for reminding us that the simplicity of this attractive, easy-to-try practice hides a master's way to the highest perfection.

For this very reason, however — just *because* it combines comfort and encouragement for the beginner with the scope and scale of deepest spirituality — it is a peculiar treasure of counsel in the quest for God. Let no one be put off by the paradoxical extremes of its range. Let the beginner be fed by its simplicity and clarity. And let the more mature seeker drink of its hidden springs. And let them respect and honor each other, so that the one will not be embarrassed by his novice's position or the other inflated by his own progress.

For the average person just starting out on the living of the life in God, Brother Lawrence's practice is a thoroughly sound guide, a perfectly possible and practical method to follow, containing a built-in challenge and test of his sincerity and his capacity to keep going when the practice would lead him into really deep awareness of the beloved Presence.

The Practice of Ego-reduction or Dying Daily

If God is so real and so near, why do we not see him and feel him? Why are we not constantly aware of him? What stands in the way?

That which stands in the way is an amazing thing, indicated by one of the shortest words in our language: "I."

I stand in my own way. The obstacle is nothing but what arises from the ordinary experiences of "I," "me," "mine." The terms most commonly used for this condition are "ego" and "egotism."

"Ego" is just a Latin word that means "I." In some modern systems of psychology it is used to designate the conscious individual. In spiritual teaching, however, the meaning is quite different: the "ego" there is universally recognized as *the root of self-ishness.* "Egotism," as a spiritual term, is not enlightened interest in oneself. It is a blind, narrow, and destructive obsession with the cravings and drives of the merely personal self. Egotism is a pampering of the lesser self at the expense of the true Self. It is "Saul" getting in the way of Christ. It is the individual arrogantly and foolishly pitting himself against the universal, the child against the parent, the human against the divine.

The ego is the self-centered brat in you. If you can't find him in yourself, it does not mean that he isn't there; it just means he has you hoodwinked.

Egotism leads to ignorance, sin, sickness, suffering, spiritual sleep, and spiritual death. The fall of man is a fall into egotism. The regeneration of man is a salvation from egotism. The eclipse of God — and the consequent loss of wisdom, health, and truth — comes from one thing only: egotism. The troubles of the world, *all of them,* come from one thing only: egotism. Your own troubles, whatever they may be, come from one thing only: egotism. No man can hope to deal with himself, let alone the world, let alone God, until he understands egotism. The job is to know (1) what it is, (2) how to reduce it, and (3) how to get rid of it.

You do not come to understand the ego, and most certainly you do not reduce it, by hearing words about it — even the wisest words. You begin to understand the ego by looking for it in yourself — by recognizing it and holding it under steady scrutiny in yourself, by struggling against it and separating from it in yourself, and finally by entering into the death grapple with it in yourself.

The final step — killing the ego — is beyond human strength (but not beyond human co-operation). The hand that strangles the snake at last is the hand of God, curiously and wonderfully united with your own hand. The first steps, however — watching for the enemy, recognizing him, and struggling against him — are well within the capacities of anyone who has seen the necessity of the encounter and is ready for work.

The first real glimpses of the ego in yourself are easy to recognize. They are accompanied by acute pain and a desire to run and hide somewhere. The recognition of your own egotism arouses embarrassment, shame, shrinking, and a sharp inclination to turn away from what is being perceived. But it is very important to persist, because this is *the* route to spiritual reality.

Ordinarily you cannot find God by a direct effort. The indirect effort of ego-reduction in most cases is the quickest and straightest way to the goal. For, as Meister Eckhart has said, when the false self is eliminated, God rushes into the soul as air into a vacuum. It is his nature to do so. As soon as you make room for him, there he is! And room is made by reducing and finally dissolving the ego.

> "Where is the dwelling of God?"
> This was the question with which the Rabbi of Kotzk surprised a number of learned men who happened to be visiting him.
> They laughed at him: "What a thing to ask! Is not the whole world full of His glory?"
> Then he answered his own question:
> "God dwells wherever man lets Him in."
>
> Martin Buber

Like all great movements in the truth-seeking life, ego-reduction is a paradox. It is very straightforward and simple, and very tricky and difficult, all at the same time. The best way to begin work on it is to begin. For example: you wake up this morning and something inside you says: "Let's turn the alarm off and catch a few more winks. We've got fifteen minutes before we absolutely *have* to get up." Another inner voice says: "Better get up now, take things easy, and get off to a good start for the day." You take the counsel of the first voice, oversleep forty-five minutes, bolt your breakfast, miss your first appointment, lie to the boss, and don't snap out of your snit till nearly noon.

This is a typical, ordinary egotistical mess. You must study this sort of thing in yourself and see where the ego enters in and how it keeps the stew cooking.

A man under grace sees that this state is not "normal" and

not "harmless," even if indeed it is "what everyone is doing." When egotism enters, precious energy is captured and curdled. The light of the intelligence is dimmed. The vitality is bled off into futile and destructive directions. The emotions are quickly poisoned. The life runs downhill. While it lasts the man is moving away from the kingdom of God and toward physical and mental illness, which may be more or less delayed in crystallizing out or may be checked by counterforces.

"Normal life" consists of spells of acute egotism relieved by periods of natural grace and good will, during which some healing and restoration take place. Spiritual life begins when you see the deadly nature of this situation, the precarious and dangerous balance involved, the constant liability to degeneration into the worst kinds of trouble, and the absence of any real security or hope for the future. At this point you see that *what the spiritual guides of humanity have always said is true:* the only way out is to face the ego in ourselves, submit to its reduction, and co-operate finally in its being rooted out. This procedure is at the base of every religion, and most certainly the Christian religion.

Ego-reduction requires intelligence and the grace of God right from the beginning. Courage and willingness to suffer are needed, but they are not enough. You have to learn how to work along with it as the job is being done. It is a skilled operation, and the skill can only be acquired slowly, by actual experience, by trial and error.

Certain phrases that are used to describe the practice must be taken in the right way. "Destroying the ego" and "killing the snake" must not lead to acts of self-persecution or self-violence, on the physical *or* mental level. The ego must not try to amputate itself. God is the surgeon. At the same time we must do our part, and do it sanely, without foolish excesses: ". . . Fasting and other forms of self-restraint . . . are needed for subduing the desire for sense objects, which however is rooted out only when one has a vision of the Supreme. The higher yearning conquers the lower yearnings" (*The Gita According to Gandhi*). Union of the lower with the Higher Self "is not for the man who overeats, or for him who fasts excessively. It is not for him who sleeps too much, or for the keeper of exaggerated vigils. Let a man be moderate in his eating and his recreation, moderately active, moderate in sleep and in wakefulness" (Prabhavananda and Isherwood, *Bhagavad-Gita*).

The following extracts bearing on this aspect of the process are from the notebook of a person who has been working on the ego problem for some time:

A particularly helpful and instructive dream: September 7, 1956. I am a member of a troupe of traveling actors. One of our troupe turns out to be a terrible liar and murderer. Several other members of the troupe and I decide that we must kill the murderer. We make many attempts to do so, and we have many fierce struggles with him, but he always escapes. He begins to impersonate the other members of the troupe so successfully that, in the attempts to kill him, we are in danger of killing each other. Once, trying to kill the liar, I almost kill my best friend.

This dream seemed to me to be of extraordinary significance for my life. I take it to mean that although the ego is a liar and a murderer, he cannot be eliminated by trying to use his own methods against him, i.e., by killing him or using violence against him. Not only does it not work, but it may do harm to the true individual (the dearest friend). The ego is really eliminated only when it is dissolved in truth. Neither arguments nor tricks nor hounding will do the job. It takes real spiritual experience and the opening of the whole being in the truth-atmosphere.

It is important to *paralyze or dissolve the ego.* If the ego is only injured or maimed, it is subject to all kinds of inflations, depressions, distortions and explosions; these set up repercussions at the personal level, and it is a very bad show all around.

The ego is an actual psychic structure; it is a sort of king-structure which holds a lot of other structures together. It may be literally paralyzed or dissolved; *or* it may be only hurt or crippled. *The distinction here is critical.*

A dissolved ego permits enlightenment and healing of body and mind. A crippled ego results in mental and/or physical illness. (Remember Ramakrishna's snake that had caught the frog and could neither cough it up nor swallow it? A very *exact* figure of the botched ego-killing job that results from clumsy spiritual disciplines or ignorant medical practices.)

Do not confuse the psychophysical aggregate, the body-and-bodymind, with the ego. It is *not* the ego, although it is the place where the ego arises, where the ego is entrenched, where the ego hides. The ego is only a stubborn and diseased self-notion which carries on a fugitive and precarious existence built upon an ignorant but powerful and persistent confusion of the psychophysical organism with the immortal individual. The ego is simply dissolved at the first full whiff of real truth. *But it may re-form.*

There are two kinds of real death which the ego can undergo: (1) small deaths, which are complete but temporary, and after which the ego re-forms, and (2) the Great Death, the final sacrifice and irrevocable dissolution which precedes and permits ultimate salvation and full entry into the Kingdom of God, of which Christ's death is the great example.

The psychosomatic organism is not an illusion. *But the ego, the normal self-notion,* quaintly and humorously *is* a complete illusion. The whole egotistical show is a tempest in a teapot. You can keep it boiling and bubbling exactly as long as you like. But for a man to live anything but the spiritual life is just silly. The ego-centered life is far beneath the real dignity of man and not at all commensurate with the real intention for man. Not everyone, of course, is meant to live a professed religious life, but, in whatever occupation, all are meant to live a spiritual life, a truth-centered life, a God-centered life.

One secret of successful ego-reduction is to realize as a fact that there are two selves in man, a greater and a lesser. When the lesser self presses its claims too far, we may speak of a true self and a false self, or even of a good self and an evil self.

These two selves are referred to in the New Testament as the first Adam and the second Adam, the old man and the new man, the earthly Jerusalem and the heavenly Jerusalem, the natural body and the spiritual body. "Plato, again, continually reminds us that there are two in us, and that of these two souls or selves the immortal is our 'Real Self'" (Coomaraswamy, *Hinduism and Buddhism*). In Eastern teaching the personal or lesser self is called the *jiva* and the Divine Self is called the *Atman*. The relationship is described in a famous statement in the Mundaka Upanishad:

> Two birds, companions who are always united, cling to the self-same tree. Of these two, the one eats the sweet fruit and the other looks on without eating. On the self-same tree, a person immersed (in the sorrows of the world) is deluded and grieves on account of his helplessness. When he sees the other, the Lord who is worshipped, and his greatness, he becomes freed from sorrow.

Paul's teaching is alive with the realization of the two selves. "I live, yet not I, but Christ liveth in me." And, speaking as the personal man diminishing as the Divine Man takes over the life, he says, "I die daily." This is perhaps the best short statement on record of what ego reduction actually feels like. The lesser self is not destroyed in this process. Only its arrogance, its ignorance, and its sense of separateness are destroyed. But these factors are so rooted in the vitality that their elimination is experienced literally as death itself.

The death of Jesus and his perfection in Christ is the great historical and traditional example of the redemption of the personal "I" in the Son of God, the salvation of the individual man in the Universal Man. Christ took our nature upon him, and our nature is egotistical to very near the core. The temptations in the wilderness all are appeals to egotism: "Enjoy wealth and power!" "Be a great world figure and leader!" "Amaze and conquer people's minds by spectacular demonstrations, and test God's patronage at the same time!" "Serve your own appetites by supernatural means!"

Christ's earthly life is a constant struggle against the more and more rarefied egotism in the humanity, culminating in the agony of prayer in the garden, "Let this cup pass from me," and the cry from the cross, "Why hast thou forsaken me?" The entire Christian demonstration is a complete triumph over egotism, the final and utter submission of the humanity to the Divinity, the death and resurrection of the lower nature in the Highest, the passion, transfiguration, and perfection of the flesh in the Logos.

The "I" in man — the sense of being and the power of identity is the principle which stands between the lower and the Highest. In a "normal" man this ego is pulled both ways. It is attracted to the Christ — the truly good, truly beautiful, and truly true Being — above. At the same time it is constantly tempted to a separate and ignorant service of the lower principles of intellect, emotion, and sensation.

The ego is capable on the one hand of rising to an experience of the One who named himself to Moses as "I AM" and who proclaimed to certain later Hebrews, "Before Abraham was, I AM." On the other hand the ego may fall to saying "I am" on its own part, separate and away from God. Thus it identifies with the psychophysical organism, binds itself to the transient and the perishable, gains perhaps the whole world but loses its own soul.

The lesser natures, intellectual, emotional, and sensual — find their true orientation only in a life surrendered to God. When these lower elements draw the ego into separate and selfish experience, they lose their proper power and dignity, debase the "I" (their natural lord), and lose contact with the Supreme Ruler. The "I" so debased is the "self" which must be denied, the "ego" which must die daily, in the Christ-centered life. Ego-reduction is nothing but the daily and hourly remembrance of the great central fact of spiritual life: "I . . . yet not I, but Christ. . . ."

The great Western treatise and "how-to" book on ego-reduction is the *Theologia Germanica.* This "spiritual noble little book,"

The ego stands between the Divine (expressed in the active triangle of beauty, goodness, and truth) above and the human (the instrumental triangle of intellect, emotion, and sensation) below. This is the prepared sacrifice, the cup, the cross.

When the man turns away from his Creator, the ego splits, hardens, and inflames the lower principles with a false light, false freedom, false movement. "Saul" persecutes Christ. This is "egotism," the sacrifice spilled, the cup defiled, the cross refused.

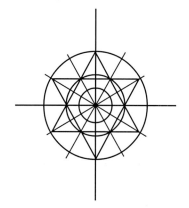

When the ego surrenders itself to God, the Divine nature penetrates the human, "Paul" receives Christ, and the man is made whole. This is salvation, the cross accepted, the sacrifice accomplished, the Holy Grail, the White Stone, the New Name.

as Luther called it, addresses itself directly, charmingly, and with great practical wisdom to the task of solving the ego problem.

What did the Devil do else? What was his going astray and his fall else, but that he presumed to be also somewhat, and would have it that somewhat was his, and somewhat was due to him? This presumption, and his I and Me and Mine, these were his going astray and his fall. And thus is he to this day.

What else did Adam do but the same thing? It is said: It was because Adam ate the apple that he was lost and fell. I say: It was because of his arrogating something to himself, because of his I, Mine, Me, and the like. Had he eaten seven apples, and yet never arrogated anything to himself, he would not have fallen; but as soon as he arrogated something to himself, he fell, and would have fallen if he had never bitten into an apple. . . .

Now when a man rightly knows these things in himself . . . he does not arrogate anything to himself, and the less he arrogates things to himself, the more perfect does his knowledge become.

The author of the *Theologia Germanica* is not known. He calls himself a "Frankfurter," a "Teutonic Knight," a "priest." Whoever he was, he probably wrote in the second half of the fourteenth century. Certainly he was greatly influenced by Meister Eckhart and John Tauler, and his book is strongly identified with the Rhineland mystics who called themselves "Friends of God."

The practice of the Presence of God as taught by Brother Lawrence and the practice of ego-reduction as taught by the *Theologia Germanica* are complementary and mutually interdependent experiences. If you practice the Presence you will find, as a corollary, that your ego is being reduced. If you work at dissolving the ego, you will find that the presence of God consequently becomes more real to you.

The practice of ego-reduction is facilitated not only by the practice of the Presence of God but also by a number of other disciplines. Several of these will be discussed in a later chapter: the practice of abandonment to the will of God, the practice of penetrating the cloud, the practice of continuous prayer. And there is

a most interesting and powerfully helpful procedure — the practice of *watching* — which is the subject of our next section.

The Practice of Watching

What, could ye not watch with me one hour?
Matthew 26:40

One of the best ways to sustain progress on the way to God
is to discover key words and find out what they really mean.
One key word is the term which in the New Testament is translated "watch." It occurs over and over again, in the Gospels, the
Acts, the Letters, and the Apocalypse.

It is easy to miss the tremendous meaning of this word
"watch." Christ Jesus commands us to "watch and pray," and we
say, "Sure, sure, I know, prayer is very important." And we do
spend some time trying to learn to pray, but we tend to slide
right over the command to watch, assuming that we know what
it means and that it is not essential anyhow. The fact is that we
cannot pray well until we have first learned to watch. Not by
accident does the command to watch come ahead of the command to pray. And not by chance is the double command,
"watch and pray," repeated so often and in such crucial settings.
A spiritual fact of the greatest importance is involved here, and it
is well worth while finding out what it is.

In order to understand what "watch" means, we must first
know that there are in the earth roughly four kinds of people: (1)
those who are spiritually *dead,* (2) those who are spiritually *asleep,*
(3) those who are spiritually *awake,* and (4) those who are spiritually *alive.* Notice that these terms describe *spiritual* conditions. A
man may be physically alive and spiritually dead ("let the dead
bury their dead") and physically awake and spiritually asleep.

It is a critical mistake for any of us to assume that we are
spiritually alive. The best of us, with very few exceptions, are not
even spiritually awake. We spend a large part of our time in
spiritual sleep, with only occasional flickers of awakening; and
rarely if ever do we experience moments of real life.

The *spiritually dead,* of course, are those who have unwittingly or deliberately severed all conscious contact with their Creator and are busy spending the capital they took with them when they left the Father's household. The end of this kind of "life" is death in the deepest sense, unless one has the good fortune to come to in the hogs and husks stage and start back home, where, in God's incredible softheartedness, a warm welcome is always waiting. I myself am a witness from the dead, having spent some years in that condition.

Spiritual sleep is the state of those who have not lost their faith, who are not sunk in deliberate and enjoyable evil, who perhaps practice their religion seriously and try hard to live right — but who at the same time have only a mental and theoretical knowledge of God, who are hopeful but dry, and who spend long periods in effective forgetfulness of what they really do know. This forgetting is the chief characteristic of spiritual sleep.

If you are *spiritually awake,* you see and know God directly just as directly as "normal" people know the air they breathe, the food they eat, and the solid earth under their feet. God is as obvious to an awakened man as sunshine is to the rest of us. The *how* of this can be understood only in the awakened state. It is possible for awakened men to pass some of their knowledge down to those in the sleeping state, but only under great limitations and in a severely modified form. The best favor which the awakened can do for the sleeping is to tell them, not what the awakened state is like, but how to awaken.

None of the tasks of human life can be understood, much less accomplished, in the state of spiritual death. A spiritually dead man, if he has a glimmer of insight left, can only hope and pray to come alive. (But when his prayer is answered he finds himself not yet in spiritual life but in spiritual sleep, with still a long way to go.)

A man's real problems can be dimly apprehended, and with hard effort painfully and partially resolved, in the condition of spiritual sleep. The objective of the sleeping man, however, must be not to dream better dreams but to wake up. For it is only in the awakened state that — with a crashing joy as of Beethoven's music — the problems are fully met and the great meanings and the triumphant solutions come pouring in.

What would it be like to be a man who is *spiritually alive?* We cannot say. There are examples, but we look at them as at direct sunlight and are dazzled or blinded. Jesus Christ was such a man. He represents a reality which profoundly shocks and upsets the ordinary personal consciousness. In order to teach us sleeping men Christ has to stoop to the level of spiritual awakening, and from there instruct us, because this is all that most of us can endure. As an awakened man who healed and helped people, he was popular. But when he stood up in his full stature and his quality of spiritual *life*, the rocks split, the elements sprang to obey him, and the Light of Glory streamed from his very garments. The three men who were chosen to witness his transfiguration were overcome by — sleep! People who heard him speak from his depths were not attracted but turned away: ". . . This is an hard saying; who can hear it?" The temporal and religious authorities of his own time could not and did not tolerate him. And after two thousand years our scholars, having failed to explain him, now spend much of their time trying to explain him away. Let's face it: we earth men are not pining for spiritual *life*; we are afraid of it. And properly so, because we are not yet awake.

What has all this to do with "watching"? We are coming to that.

From a practical, working standpoint, the critical relationship is that between spiritual sleep and spiritual awakening. Now put yourself in the position of a real spiritual teacher. He is in the awakened state, looking upon our present humanity, and what does he see? He sees even the best men and women wandering around in the state of spiritual sleep. *What would be his first command to such people?* Would it not be the command, "Wake up!"? And this is exactly what it is in the New Testament; this *is* the meaning of the word which is translated "watch."

"Watch" is not an inaccurate translation, but it is a seriously inadequate one. The Greek word is *gregoreite,* and it does indeed mean "be vigilant, pay attention, be watchful," but it also and more fundamentally and far more significantly means, "wake, wake up, keep awake." A perfectly good modern equivalent of the original meaning would be the command "Come to! Wake up! Snap out of it!" The word "watch" conveys the true meaning only if we read it as a sharp warning given to a sleepwalking man who is about to step off the edge of a building — *"Watch!"*

This one word is loaded, and it handsomely repays some digging. *Gregoreite* is the imperative form of *gregoreuo,* which comes from the root *egeiro,* a word rich in meanings, all of which relate directly to the great turning point in our life which would occur if we began to obey the directive: "Watch! Wake up!" These are the meanings: to awake, to take up, to lift up, to raise up, to rise again, to stand, to rouse from sleep, to rouse from sitting or lying, to rouse from disease, to rouse from death, to rouse from obscurity, to rouse from inactivity, to rouse from ruins, and to rouse from nonexistence.

There is real spiritual dynamite and an entire spiritual discipline packed into this one command, "Watch!" The discipline we shall examine in just a moment. The dynamite is in this, that *if we can hear it and obey it* this command will effectively change our lives and launch us — *really,* not just sentimentally or theoretically — on the way to God's living truth and to God himself.

What is the first sign that a spiritually sleeping man has heard the command "Wake up!"? It is that *he realizes he is sleeping.* He may not awaken right away, but he knows briefly that he is not awake. For just an instant he sees himself, not through a haze of ignorant imagination and self-deception, but in the aurora of truth. Such moments of realization are short and infrequent at first, but they are precious almost beyond estimate, because they signify not only that light has penetrated our darkness but that light *has been received;* it has pierced through into our awareness; it has revealed however fleetingly, our own true condition, our own state; it has shown us not yet where we are going but where we are and where we can start from. Thus in responding to the Christian command to watch, we simultaneously and inevitably also respond to the classical command, "Man, know thyself!"

Why does the command to watch precede the command to pray? Because otherwise we pray in our sleep! Any prayer is better than no prayer, but obviously awakened prayer is incomparably better than sleeping prayer.

Here is the explanation of whole lifetimes of "religious" and "spiritual" efforts which seem to achieve almost nothing. Some of us do not go anywhere because we are always getting ahead of ourselves. We press on to high school, whereas the knowledge we really need and could use, the power that could transform our lives, is still in kindergarten. We "pray" (and "read" and "worship" and "meditate") before we have learned to wake up. And so we pray and worship and meditate in spiritual sleep, and of course it is unsatisfactory, and finally it may become a tragic self-deception and frustration. We are perhaps better off than if we did not pray or worship or meditate at all, but at best we are spinning our wheels.

The cure for all this is clear. It is to embrace the terribly simple principle of first things first — swallow our spiritual pride, abandon our pretenses and our playacting, go back to low school, and pray God to teach us what it means to wake up, to come to, to snap out of it, to *watch!* (Hypocrites anonymous, rally round! Take notice! Let us be sure not to misunderstand: it is not somebody else who has to do all this. It is I, me, myself — just this smug little personality with my own dear name attached to it. That is who has to see himself and his own real status before the face of Christ.)

If we do succeed in having moments of first-degree awakening, what are we to watch? We are to keep an eye on *ourselves* — objectively, dispassionately, uncritically, and above all, honestly. Honest self-watching is the discipline that is included in this commandment of Christ, concurrent with the repeated shocks of self-awakening.

A wonderful thing follows immediately. We are able to pray! Now — truly, urgently — we can pray because we know and feel our need. Watching produces keen, *felt* experience of our own spiritual poverty. And this is the first beatitude, the basic blessing, upon which rests the foot of the ladder of bliss. When we actually (not theoretically or sentimentally or "piously") wake up and watch ourselves, we feel our great need for God's help as keenly as a starving man feels hunger, and we are able sincerely to ask for the food which will salvage our lives. Awakening and watching mean not just a change of mind but a change of state — *metanoia*. Nothing high yet, but clear and true.

I must speak here of my own experience with watching. I think it is perhaps impossible merely in books, in writing, to convey a real working knowledge of how to begin and pursue this basic practice. I think you need to come into personal, learning relationships with other people who know from experience what this great command means and how to do it. I am sure that when you pray to be brought into contact with such people you are always heard. My own instructors were a variety of people in many different stages of spiritual growth. They had the common denominator of admitting their own great need for God's help, of rigorous self-honesty, of willingness to watch themselves patiently and steadily and without blinking. And slowly, with reluctance and pain, I began to learn from them this lifesaving art.

A man who has been given the grace to begin the practice of watching sooner or later acquires the extended grace of beginning to see himself as an objective person. *He begins to see himself as he would see another man.* And in this way his self-watching becomes impartial, cool, penetrating, accurate. He is neither so easy on himself nor so hard on himself as he used to be. Regarding himself, he acquires a mother's heart and a surgeon's hand. He enters into himself and at the same time rises above himself. From this viewpoint, and only from this viewpoint, the work of co-operating in his own regeneration can be carried on.

Watching is a particular extension of the practice of the Presence: I observe Tom Powers in the light of the truth that whatever he feels, thinks, says, and does is felt, thought, said, and done in the presence of the living God. If you are able to do this — nothing more, just this — for any length of time, an amazing and powerful change takes place in your feeling, thinking, saying, and doing. You do not try to manipulate these functions. You don't change them. You simply observe them, and *they change* — wonderfully. Try it and see.

The practice of watching occupies a basic position in the universal spiritual teaching, and so it occurs in many traditions both within and without the Christian framework. It is known by different names, referring to the same essential practice. It is central, for example, in Buddhism. Recall that Christ's command means both "watch!" and "awake!" Then note that "the Bodhisattva is an 'awakening being,' or one of 'wakeful nature'; the Buddha is 'awake' or 'The Wake.'" In Zen Buddhism, the key word *satori* indicates a "sudden awakening." Original Buddhism itself is called "the Doctrine of Awakening." And one of the fundamental disciplines within the doctrine corresponds exactly to the Western discipline of "watching," in its aspect of viewing one's own person as an objective entity: ". . . one strives first of all for achievement of what is known as *ñana-dassana*, the vision which comes from knowledge, having as its object one's own person, in its totality. It is . . . a liberating . . . carried out by contemplation of oneself . . . as if one were another person or thing" (Evola, *The Doctrine of Awakening*).

In the Jewish spiritual tradition, watching is referred to within the scope of the key word *kavanah*. Abraham Heschel (in *God in Search of Man*) interprets it as follows:

> What is meant by the term kavanah? In its verbal form the original meaning seems to be: to straighten, to place in a straight line, to direct. From this it came to mean to direct the mind, to pay attention. . . . Kavanah, then, includes, first of all, what is commonly called *intention* . . . the state of being aware of what we are doing. . . . In this sense, kavanah is the same as attentiveness. . . . Kavanah is attentiveness to God . . . direction to God, and requires the redirection of the whole person. It is the act of bringing together the scattered forces of the self.

The practice of watching plays a prominent part in the psychology of Ouspensky and Gurdjieff, where it is broken down into two disciplines, "self-observation" and "self-remembering." The former is a way of watching oneself as an objective person; the latter is a technique of touching a higher level within oneself; both work together toward awakening from spiritual sleep. (See Nicoll's *Commentaries*.)

The Eastern Christian saint Nicephorus the Solitary speaks of watching as "guarding the mind," "attention of the mind," or just "attention," and describes it in these terms (italics supplied):

[Nicephorus first quotes St. Simeon]: Have you understood, brethren, that there exists a certain spiritual method swiftly leading whoever follows it to passionlessness and the vision of God? Are you convinced that the whole of active life is regarded by God as nothing but leaves on a tree which bears no fruit and that every soul which has no guarding of the mind will labour therein in vain?

[Then the followers of Nicephorus put this request to him]: We have learned . . . that there exists a certain doing which speedily frees the soul from passions and by love unites it to God. . . . But we beg you to teach us what is attention of the mind and how to become worthy to acquire it. For this work is quite unknown to us.

[And Nicephorus responds]: . . . I shall try as far as is in my power to show you what attention is and how, God willing, one can succeed in acquiring it. Some of the saints have called attention the safekeeping of the mind, others — the guarding of the heart, yet others — sobriety . . . and others again by other names. But all these names mean the same thing.

[And in the same tradition, St. John of the Ladder says]: Sitting on high, *observe, if only you know the art,* and you will see how and whence, how many and what kind of robbers are trying to enter to steal the grapes. When the sentinel gets tired, he gets up and prays, and then sits down once more and again resumes his work with new courage.

[Further, still in the Eastern Christian group, St. Isaac says]: . . . Every sentient being changes times without number and every man alters hourly. . . . His trials, day by day, have special power to make him wise in this, if he *watches over himself* with sobriety; so that, among other things, he may *observe himself* with his mind and learn what changes his soul undergoes every day, how it departs from meekness and its peaceful disposition and is suddenly thrown into confusion, and what unspeakable danger threatens him at such times.

The Philokalia

To awaken and pay attention is to stop living heedlessly, to stop drifting. When you have begun to watch, you are no longer wholly driven by pleasure, sucked under by habits, or carried away by dreams. You are now able to use the God-given and God-contacting faculty of *attention* as a power to edge your life toward its fulfillment. Attention is the key which lies ready at hand and yet is steadily ignored by most of us.

A man of the people one day asks the bonze Ikkyou: "Bonze, will you write for me some maxims of high wisdom?"

Ikkyou took up a brush and wrote a word, "Attention."

"Is that all?" said the man, "won't you add a few more words?"

Ikkyou then wrote twice: "Attention. Attention."

"All the same," said the disappointed man, "I don't see much depth or subtlety in what you have written there."

Ikkyou then wrote the same word three times.

Slightly irritated, the man said: "After all, what does this word 'Attention' mean?"

And Ikkyou replied: "Attention means attention."

Benoit, *The Supreme Doctrine*

Alas, the practice of watching, like the practice of the Presence of God, is easy to begin — and easy to drop.* A good exercise in establishing oneself in watching, in learning its meaning and feeling its importance, is to turn to those places in the New Testament where the practice is stressed and use them as a basis

---

* Watching, like the practice of the Presence, is superficially easy and fundamentally difficult; it seems to be a novice's technique but is really

for meditation. Notice that the command to watch is given in situations of urgency, of testing, of trial. But it must be carried out constantly in order that one may be ready for the trials. Observe that there is danger of crucial wrong turnings and grave loss if one does not watch. See how difficult, in spite of its simplicity, it is to watch. And see how watching is connected with the Lord's coming, with the actual experience of God, and with the capacity to sustain that experience. Note particularly Matthew 24:42-43; 25:13; 26:38, 40, 41; Mark 13:33-35, 37; 14:34, 37-38; Luke 12:37, 39; 21:36; Acts 20:31; I Corinthians 16:13; Colossians 4:2; I Thessalonians 5:6; Hebrews 13:17; I Peter 4:7; Revelation 3:2-3; 16:15.

Christ calls to us: *Gregoreite!* snap out of it! so that we will revive enough to reach out for our true life and the Power greater than ourselves who can lead us to it.

If by some rare grace we manage to glimpse what Christ is

---

a master's way. The novice *can* attempt it with real success, but he should not be deceived thereby into imagining that he has plumbed the possibilities of the practice. The beginner should not be dismayed at the immense ranges opened up by watching; neither should he be inflated by his early successes; rather should he be led on humbly over months and years of patient effort toward real mastery.

Some idea of the scope of self-knowledge into which the practice of watching leads can be gained from the works of Hubert Benoit who has made psychological studies specifically along these lines. Dr. Benoit is not easy to read, but if you have been attempting to watch for some time, you may find his views exceedingly helpful, because he discusses exact techniques for observing oneself at real depth. The following excerpt is from *The Supreme Doctrine:*

"In practice this work should entail inner gestures repeated, but short and light. It is not a question of laboriously dwelling upon it as though there were something to seize. There is nothing to seize. It is a question of voluntarily noting, as in the winking of an eye, instantaneous and perfectly simple, that I am conscious of myself . . . in that second . . . I succeed instantaneously or not at all; if I do not succeed at all I will try again later (this may be a few seconds later, but the gesture should be carried out at one go). It is to my interest to make this gesture as often as possible, but with suppleness and discretion, disturbing as little as possible the course of my dualistic inner life — I have to interrupt the consciousness that I habitually have of my dualistic life by a 'break' that is clean, frank, instantaneous, but without doing anything which modifies it directly. The normalizing modification will be carried out by the Absolute Principle through the instantaneous 'breaks' produced by this inner work."

revealing to us, if we begin to see that we are really and literally asleep, we may experience a brief moment of awakening and with it a shock. For the awakened man briefly sees the terrible problem: sleeping men, even if they know they are asleep, do not know how to awaken.

Clear instructions have been given to us on this critical point, but we find them exceedingly difficult to understand or to follow. Christ in the Gospels, the Buddha in the Sutras, Sri Krishna in the Gita, give plain directions which, if followed, would lead to full spiritual awakening — but not one man in a hundred thousand picks up on it.

All of the great religions contain these instructions, but they tend to get lost in the conventional way people take religion. Fresh, contemporary statements out of actual experience are urgently needed. One such is by G. I. Gurdjieff. The practice which Gurdjieff called self-observation is pure *gregoreite,* and Gurdjieff was able to present it in terms that are not easy but at least possible for a contemporary Western man to get hold of:

> To begin self-observation and self-study it is necessary to divide oneself. A man must realize that he indeed first of all consists of *two men.*
>
> So long as a man takes himself as one person *he will never move from where he is.* His work on himself starts from the moment he begins to feel at first *two men* in himself. One is passive and the most it can do is to register or observe what is happening to it. The other, which calls itself "I," is active, speaks of itself in the first person, and is in reality only an invented, unreal person. Let us call this invented person in a man *A.*
>
> When a man understands his helplessness in the face of *A,* his attitude towards himself and towards *A* in him ceases to be either indifferent or unconcerned. Self-Observation becomes observation of *A.* A man understands that he is not *A,* that *A* is nothing but the mask he wears, the part that he unconsciously plays and which unfortunately he cannot stop playing, a part which rules him and makes

him do and say a thousand stupid things, a thousand things which he would never do or say himself. If he is sincere with himself, he feels that he is in the power of *A* and at the same time he feels that he is not *A*. He begins to be afraid of *A*, he begins to feel that he is his enemy. No matter what he would like to do, everything is altered and intercepted by *A*. *A* is his enemy. *A's* desires, sympathies, thoughts, opinions, are either opposed to his own views, feelings and moods, or they have nothing in common with them. And at the same time, *A* is his master. He is the slave, he has no will of his own. He has no means of expressing his desires because whatever he would like to do or say would be done for him by *A*. On this level of self-observation a man must understand that his whole aim is to free himself from *A*. And since he cannot in fact free himself from *A* because he is himself, he must therefore master *A* and make him do, not what the *A* of the given moment wants, but what *he* himself wants to do. From being the master, *A* must become servant.

The first stage of work on oneself consists in separating oneself from A mentally, in being separated from him in actual fact, in keeping apart from him. But the fact must be born in mind that the whole attention must be concentrated upon *A*, for a man is unable to explain *what he himself really is.* But he can explain *A* to himself, and with this he must begin, remembering at the same time that he is not *A*.*

A modern man, intending to obey Christ's command *gregoreite,* would need to study these precise directions carefully and execute them faithfully. What is involved is something simple to do but easy to forget. Do not be led off into theorizing or arguing about it. Just do it.

If you will go ahead and do it, and keep doing it, you will find that it works. Self-observation really does produce moments

---

* This and the next quotations are from *Psychological Commentaries on the Teaching of G. I. Gurdjieff and P. D. Ouspensky* by Maurice Nicoll (London, 1964: Vincent Stuart).

of awakening and periods of freedom from the bad dreams of resentment, self-pity, despondency, anxiety, boredom, and the lot.

One caution needs to be kept in mind constantly. A big danger is that we will fall into *imagining* that we are self-observing when we are not. Maurice Nicoll, one of Gurdjieff's commentators, writes:

> Many of you think that Self-Observation consists merely in noticing that you feel moody, that you feel unwell, that you feel negative or bored or gloomy or depressed and so on. Let me assure you that this is *not* Self-Observation. Self-Observation begins with the establishing of Observing "I" in your own inner world. Observing "I" *is not identified* with what it observes. When you say: "*I* am feeling negative," you are not observing yourself. You *are* your state. You are identified with your state. There is nothing distinct in you that is standing outside your state, something that does not feel your state, something that is independent of it, and is looking at it, something that has a quite different feeling from your state. If you say: "*I* wish *I* were not negative," this is quite useless. It is "I" speaking the whole time. You are taking yourself as one mass. You are not dividing yourself into two, which is the beginning of Work on yourself. You are not saying: "Why is *it* negative?" but "Why am *I* negative?" You are taking *it* and *you* as the same. Try to understand what it means to divide yourself into two — an observed side and an observing side — and try to feel the sense of "I" *in the observing side* and not in the observed side.

There is amazing power in the practice of watching. You cannot appreciate it, and indeed you can hardly believe it, until you experience it. When the personal self is watched, it reacts as a small child with both hands in the forbidden cookie jar who suddenly realizes that someone is observing him; the child simply and sheepishly withdraws. Likewise, when the eye of truth is open, without any great tension or struggle much stubborn mischief just ceases. This is not brought about by picking on oneself; it is done by a simple, clear, uncritical but unsparing glance within.

The mere act of watching, of patiently and calmly and honestly observing oneself, brings peace and inner healing which no amount of guilt or chagrin or self-castigation can begin to accomplish. Watching is not faultfinding or internal henpecking. It is simply — watching. When it is done right, it produces results. If there are no results, you just have not learned how to do it yet. You must be at least slightly awake to do it at all. And you have to try it yourself over a considerable time before you begin to realize how great the results can be.

The man who watches also dies daily, because the ego can thrive only in the dark; when observed, it begins to shrivel like a spider in a flame. The watcher finds himself, furthermore, practicing the Presence of God, because he sees his true relationship to God, keenly feels his need for God, and prays for the supplying of that need. He prays inevitably, by reflex, as a drowning man says "help" and a bee-stung man says "ouch" — and with the same elementary sincerity.

And finally the watching man finds himself behaving with wisdom and love in personal, family, business, social, and political situations. Not by overdependence on theories but rather by the direct power of truth, he begins to know what to do and *to be able to do it.*

PART THREE

God's Will:
How to Know It
and Do It

CHAPTER ONE

God's Will Is the Door;
Prayer Is the Key

Do you want to succeed in life? Do you want to be really happy? Do you want to find the highest adventure, the greatest wealth, the utmost growth, and the most wonderful fulfillment possible for you?

It is very simple to attain these goals: just *know* the will of God and *do* it. If God exists at all, he sees what our greatest good is, beyond our fondest hopes and dreams; furthermore he is able to bring us to that good. So it is only a matter of discovering his will and carrying it out. The will of God is the door to our heart's desire.

Alas! as an answer this is too simple. It is a true answer. It is what we all have to do. But how do you know God's will, and how do you do it? If we stay in the realm of mere philosophy we can chirp along making rather bright noises about this great question. Talk is cheap and pleasant. If we buckle down, however, and begin to do some experimental work, several tough but reliable and interesting facts emerge:

Fact number one is that in our normal state we do not know the will of God and *cannot* know it. Self-deception on this point, even the most "well-intentioned" self-deception, is among the surest ways to abort the second birth.* To know and to do the will of God quite simply is to live in paradise. And that is where, in our usual condition, we do not live. We are fallen from there, not in some "old biblical" and remote sense, but strictly, techni-

---

* Loose imagination miscalled vision, pigheadedness miscalled faith, and undisciplined notions about the will of God combine to produce what is known as "illuminism," the watchword of which runs something like this: "I've got the inside track, boys. God has spoken to me. Clear the way. Here I come!"

cally, immediately, and effectively. Jacob Boehme, a man who knew these things from direct experience, puts it this way: *"What, and where is Paradise, with its Inhabitants?* We have hinted . . . that it is in this world, yet as it were swallowed up in the Mystery; but it is not altered in itself, it is only withdrawn from our sight and our source [property, or sense]; *for if our eyes were opened, we should see it* [italics supplied]. Nay, God in his Ternary is with us; how then should Paradise be lost? We have lost its source [property, or working] and fruit in the outward life, as the devil lost God, when he wilfully exalted himself as a haughty spirit, and would be lord; so it is with us" (*The Forty Questions*, p. 297).

Now don't get excited and don't go away. If you have not been schooled and drilled in honesty, you will never face this condition, you will just go on forming pretty good notions of what the divine intention for you may be and pretending and "believing" that these notions are the will of God. In other words, a kind of self-deceit on the subject will be translated (with the monkey's help, of course) into a kind of "faith."

But let's back up a bit. A sincere person cannot help making the *best possible estimate* of what God wills for him. It is right and highly necessary to do so, if one is merely to live sanely, let alone grow toward truth. So far so good. But it usually goes farther, and here is where the trouble starts. The estimate of God's will — which is the closest we can come to the truth — is taken for certainty. If there are any doubts, they are smothered by "faith." The enlightened guess — which is the best we can do — is taken for knowledge. You can practice this kind of deceit on yourself without really noticing what you are doing, or you can half-notice and actually congratulate yourself on your "power of belief." A lot of this monkey business goes on today; there are even teachers of the art. But it is the devil's own gambit, and God help you if you don't find a way out of it.

Here is the place where a man who really means business in the quest of truth must rigorously stop kidding himself. He must sternly rid himself of such moonshine. Concerning God's will for you, make the best estimates and the most enlightened guesses you possibly can. Your physical, mental, and spiritual health depend on your doing so. But do not tell yourself that this is *know-ing*. Test and find the truth for yourself in your own life: except for rare moments of inspiration or exaltation, an ordinary man does not know and cannot know the will of God.

A further and more difficult point: Even if we knew it for sure, we are normally incapable of doing the will of God. We may and must approximate doing it. But actually and fully do it? No. In the problem of doing as in the problem of knowing, it is equally easy and equally dangerous to pretend.

Pause. Consider. If you were able for just one hour to do the will of God you would begin abruptly to behave very much like Jesus Christ. You would give sight to the blind, heal the sick at a glance or touch, raise the dead, and do other things just as great. People for miles around would be thunderstruck. No, no. We ordinary men do not do the will of God. We do not often come close to doing it. Let us never imagine that we do. Let us at least refrain from any such dreadful flattery of ourselves. Good Lord! millions of us can't even stop lying or masturbating or backbiting or overeating for a few days or weeks on end; other millions, sunk in such miseries, don't even hope or try to break out. And yet we have quick and easy courses for knowing and doing the divine will!

Can you face this? *Can you feel it?* It bears repeating: our greatest need is to know and to do the will of God. At the same time the most striking fact of our present life is that we do not know it and we cannot do it. Realization of this state is a salutary shock. It is a sharp taste of the first beatitude: spiritual poverty. It is the way, and the only way, to real prayer. "Thy kingdom come" ceases to be a bored and mumbling little recitation and becomes a cleansing agony of spirit. "Thy will be done" is lifted up from a dumb and fearful acceptance of a bleak unknown to a passionate hunger and search for the one thing needful.

Furthermore, once you move out of the region of sentimentality and dream religion, once you come to grips with this terrible situation of man's position and God's will, the more interesting it becomes. For example, how very odd it is that we do *not* know the divine intention, for it is the sober truth that God is not far from us and he is not silent to us. . . .

God Speaks Continuously . . .

Look, really look, at a seascape, a field of corn or a city lot full of rubbish. Look and (even in the disorder) see the law, the beauty, and the indelible significance. See the meaning within meaning, even in the foam and the soil and the trash.

The attempt to explain away the universe as an idiot's delight has been made and has failed. You may take an idiot's-eye view if you choose, but that does not change the cosmos. And a chastened, truly modern science will no longer support you. It is now obvious that this present world and this present power are at once the expression and veil and crucifix of a Higher Power.

In the most ordinary things, God confronts us. All children (except very sick children and perhaps even they) know this. You do not need to know the word "God" to know the truth of it; little children are alive with it, and to it. The bulk of the human race in nearly all eras has known it. We are living in one of those fortunately rare times when very many adults have forgotten it. Perhaps that is why, in a teaching addressed particularly to this age by One who entered deeply into its pain, we are commanded to turn and become as little children.

You do not need books and laboratories for this (although indeed they may help). But just go and look at the trees. How could they *be*, by accident? Take up a handful of summer soil and see the tiny lives moving in it. Sit before a clump of marigolds and watch the bees industriously, ecstatically, wisely, and efficiently working them over. And then notice the birds . . . ah, God, the birds! — no wonder that in the language of heaven to speak of a bird is to speak of a spirit

There is no harm in analyzing the trees and the bugs and the birds if we would only *see* them first. Our young children see them, but we do not. We see shadows, and we exhaust our lives classifying and arguing and actually fighting about shadows. And the shadows grow harder and colder and deader, and they assume meaningless and chaotic forms, and finally it is a hideous dream which confronts us, which we blasphemously call reality.

All nature is enacting God's will and singing God's song, and not only every beautiful creature but every lump of garbage is pregnant and bursting with holy significance, but we do not hear it and we do not see it. God help us. Can we not find the grace at least to admit our so painful and so obvious blindness? Do please help us. Merely to admit our helplessness is the beginning of redemption. In mercy, carry us that far if we cannot or will not walk to it!

God confronts us everywhere. "That which is before you is it in all its entirety and with nothing whatsoever lacking."* This is not "mysticism" or "Pantheism" or any other special cuss word which some academic toe dancer may wish to bang onto it. It is the truth. And therefore it is a fit subject for religion and science and common experience. ". . . The One is totally, infinitely present in all particulars."† This is not an abstraction but a statement of tremendous, empirical fact. "Wherever there are two, they are not without God, and wherever there is one alone I say I am with him. Raise the stone and there thou shalt find me; cleave the wood and there am I."‡ This is not something you can swallow up in classifications and name-callings. It is the staggering but simple truth, which the humblest man can prove to his own utter satisfaction, if he will. His ego will be shattered in the process, *but he will know the truth.*

God confronts us everywhere. If we even faintly know it, life is full of meaning, satisfaction, and joy. If we do not know it and will not probe it, life is full of frustration, misery, and idiocy. I did not learn this from books (although certain books clearly tell of it). I learned it from living it, both ways. I have been a self-appointed, frustrated, miserable idiot in this very life. I wouldn't mind so much having reached that state if it weren't so unnecessary. But God's mercy is inexhaustible: when the idiocy gets bad enough, it becomes the seed of its own cure. One is reminded of

---

* Huxley, *Heaven and Hell,* p. 37.
† Hsi Yun, *The Huang Po Doctrine,* p. 23.
‡ "Sayings of Jesus," Dunkerly, *Beyond the Gospels,* pp. 133 ff.

the toast attributed to Gurdjieff and spoken presumably in his imperfect English: "Here's to hopeless idiot. When he knows he is hopeless idiot, he is no longer hopeless idiot."

God confronts us everywhere. The whole universe as it changes from moment to moment is a perfect expression of the will of the Unchanging. It is a complete and lucid statement of the will of God, faultlessly adapted to the understanding of every creature from the man to the star to the atom to the squirrel on the fencepost. Everything that happens to you, good or bad, is a messenger of God's will for you. Your whole life is a consummately articulated script of God's will for you.

Since it is so obvious, since we are surrounded at all times and immersed in a great, coherent, beautiful, and unfailing expression of God's will for us, since God speaks without ceasing to the human heart, telling it what he wishes and intends, why do so few understand it, even a little bit, and why do even fewer do it, even a little bit? Here is a mystery.

God confronts us everywhere, and he is not silent to us. He speaks. God's voice — the thundering, crashing, sparkling, warning, encouraging, and pleading symphony of God's Word — is sounding down all the aisles of creation, from high heaven to the remotest sinks of outer darkness, without interruption. It is sounding right where you are and right where I am at this very moment. God speaks continuously. . . .

But Who Can Hear Him?

On this earth, very few men can hear him. It is a wonder that God speaks, and it is an almost equal wonder that we are deaf to him. It is not "hope" or "faith" but cruel and deadly foolishness to deceive ourselves on this point. Thank God the heart of humanity is stirring in its sleep. Many today are yearning, seeking, praying, watching, and listening. But how many truly *hear* that Voice and how many truly *do* his will? Few, very few. Let us be ready to give our lives that their number may increase!

Far from hearing God's voice, far from knowing what God's will is, not one man in a thousand has even an adequate rational idea of what the will of God *may* be and how it *may* operate in human affairs. To clear one's mental sights is a minimum move if the subject is to be touched at all. One of the very best ways I know to begin to do this is to study Leslie Weatherhead's brief but powerful book called *The Will of God.*

If you have never thought it out, the question of God's will can be painfully confusing, and in a personal emergency or tragedy it can arise suddenly as a fierce and insistent challenge. We all know, vaguely, that nothing can happen outside the scope of God's will.

Does he, then, will that bombs fall on helpless and harmless little babies? That men die in slow and futile agony of battle wounds, cancer, and alcoholism? Does he will that people burn to death while trapped in wrecked automobiles and airplanes or drown wretchedly in sunken railway coaches? Does he intend that our insane asylums be filled to overflowing?

"Not my will but thine be done," said Jesus, and we know the sequel. Was it really the deliberate and coolly calculated will of the omnipotent God that this good and blameless man be shamefully and brutally tortured to death? That is what the story seems to be telling us. Is there some mistake? Is God himself after all some kind of bloodthirsty monster? The question, if it presents itself seriously, is a horror too great to be borne. It threatens one's sanity quite directly. From it, men turn to atheism with profound relief.

Clear, unevasive, and unsentimental answers to such questions are desperately needed. The answers must be rooted not only in scholarship but in experience. Dr. Weatherhead's remarkable book *The Will of God* takes us into the area of such answers. God's will, he says, bears upon human beings in three different aspects: (1) God's *intentional will*, that is, his original plan, including his intention to create man as a free being; (2) God's *circumstantial will*, that is, his revised intention in the face of evil circumstances with which free men are free to confront him; and (3) God's *ultimate will*, that is, the triumphant outcome of his over-all plan, in spite of, and often by means of, the very evil that opposed it.

Here is a view that smells to me of the truth, a welcome

odor in a field of inquiry where, particularly in our time, the savor of truth often has been lost in the unfaced terror of a terrible question. If Leslie Weatherhead's thesis is sound, we really need not play ostrich with the obvious facts of evil. We need not embrace the evil of lying to ourselves about evil, of pretending against the voice of our whole soul that evil does not exist. Neither need we accept the outrageous alternative that the good God actually approves of men's torturing themselves and other men. Gods full will, his three wills taken and understood as one, includes all the facts of life in a love that is absolute: absolutely good and absolutely true. "All," as our Lord said to the Lady Julian, "*is* well." The ultimate and utterly satisfying understanding of the sublimity of God's holy will must await the meeting of our souls with the Uncreated Light. But such explanations as Leslie Weatherhead's help us to keep clear heads while our hearts are being opened.

Meanwhile, for working purposes, let us take our places where the vast majority of us belong: among those who do not yet *know* but who are only able to yearn, seek, pray, watch, and listen. Let us humbly and frankly face our exile, our inability to hear our Father's Word, and our impotence, if we did hear it, to obey it. We need solid foundation for our hope, our encouragement, and our final triumph in God. Let us seek such undergirding in a present effort to understand our present failure, our amazing refusal to receive the King of the Universe into the councils of our hearts.

This is the fall of man we are talking about. It is not a gag, and it is not an "old tribal belief." It is the bones and bowels of the human problem. And it is not solved by brash excursions into certain kinds of self-hypnotism mislabeled "faith." It is also not solved by crossless Christianity, by biblical emasculation masquerading as biblical scholarship, by logical positivism and materialism masquerading as science, or other kinds of modish whistling in the dark.

But we mustn't quarrel about these things, either. Even the best-intentioned religious and scientific disputes in our time can be nothing more than folly. We do not (perhaps fortunately) have time to argue with each other. The only real hope for a solution must lie in opening ourselves — spirit, soul, and body — to what the Eternal is now telling us and eternally has been telling us. The way out for mankind, and for every individual, is not in more bright ideas but in listening to God. If we won't do that, of course there will be consequences. Our freedom is real, and so is our responsibility.

The glorious and terrible fact is that God's will is in exquisite reciprocal relationship with the will of man. Evidently he wants it that way and will not have it otherwise. He has arranged it so that our redemption depends not alone on him but on our co-operation with him. A right relationship with God can arise only out of this root. There is no use trying to ignore him; on the other hand it is no good trying to play him for a patsy; furthermore we cannot blame him for withholding blessings or permitting disasters. All of our cute little tricks with him are beginning to appear about as bright and attractive as a stubborn case of paranoia. We know better than this; he has given us the power of knowing better; we cannot even claim his pity.

Obviously, even so, he does pity us. But his mercy is inexorable. What happens to the human race and to particular men is up to him all right, but he puts it right back up to us. It still depends on what we do and what we do not do — as a species, as nations, as families, and as little frightened individuals under the covers at night.

Maybe we had better start watching, praying, and listening real hard. It is getting late.

In the end, as C. S. Lewis has pointed out, there are only two kinds of men: those who say to God, "Thy will be done," and those to whom God says, "*Thy* will be done." A child of God may well pray for many things, for his everyday needs — "give us this day our daily bread," for example. But prayer that remained in this area alone would be dangerous, because if we actually have advanced to the point where our requests are beginning to be granted, and if at the same time we are not wise enough to know what is really good for us, we are in for trouble. We must include in our asking, as the great prayer does, things even nearer to the deepest human necessity — the power, for instance, to cancel moral indebtedness and to have our own debts canceled.

But the ultimate and only wholly safe refuge is found in the greatest request and the greatest gift of all: *the power to receive God's intentions and to be ruled by them.* This is the answer to everything. "Thy kingdom come, thy will be done." Or, as the salvaged alcoholics say — they who have known in their very blood the hell of separation from his holy order and the incredible joy of return — "[We] sought through prayer and meditation to improve our conscious contact with God, as we understood Him, *praying only for knowledge of His will for us and the power to carry that out.*"

Our situation, then, with regard to God's will (the door to all happiness) and prayer (the key to the door) is simple but difficult. The facts we need to keep in mind are few but inescapable:

Our failure to know and do God's will arises not because he does not give knowledge and strength but because we have lost the capacity to receive. Two revolutionary steps lead from the life of the spiritually dead to the life of the living: (1) *realization that we have lost the capacity* to know and do the will of God and that life is fruitless without it and (2) *asking* with humility and courage and a sufficient awareness of desperate need *that the capacity be restored* to us.

This kind of asking constitutes the very metal and mold of the key: the life of prayer. And that is our next consideration.

CHAPTER TWO

How to Use the Key

What is prayer? It is the simplest and most wonderful thing in the world. It is an infant cuddling with his Mother. It is a child talking with his Father.

In some systems this talking is called "low prayer." "Middle prayer" occurs when the child speaks to his Father of the needs of other children. And in "high prayer" the child is rapt beyond personal concerns and immersed in pure worship and adoration of the living flame of Love which is his Source and Goal.

But let us not go beyond low prayer too soon, or indeed ever. Our Lord, the night before he died, used low prayer. It is well not to lose the capacity to be just a child talking to his Father. For all our high flights, there are moments in life, perhaps the greatest moments, when we are returned to being just a child talking to his Father. Please, Father, don't let thy gifts of glory ever make us forget our eternal childhood in thee.

Prayer is the most wonderful and beautiful thing in the world. But like everything else which is entrusted to men, its beauty shines through a cloud of confusion and distortion.

"Prayer" is like "love," a great word that is burdened almost to death by loads of free and easy talk on the subject. Many a man who goes in for seeking God soon finds himself talking, often with exhilarating glibness, about high states of "prayer" and about the great power of "love." (I personally have been in this bag up to my ears, so I am level with the other offenders and not looking down my nose at anyone.) In the midst of certain kinds of cocksure talk about "love" and "prayer," however, I feel a deep uneasiness. For the fact is that prayer and love are profound and sacred mysteries about which most of us know very little and can do even less. The little we can do is immensely important, but it is still little. "Optimistic" and "positive" feigning to the contrary is not really healthful but, since wholeness depends on truth, eventually is sickening.

The confrontation of this situation is unpopular; the writer, therefore, had better stay in the first person, which is the only sound place to be in difficult discussions, stop talking about the "other offenders," and describe his own experience. I do notice that many persons are involved in eager, well-meaning, and largely unconscious pretense in the key areas of prayer and love. But a far more disturbing observation is that I myself am not able to stay out of this charming and mutually seldom criticized daisy chain. Like a lot of other eager beavers I have learned what I *ought* to be doing in prayer and love, and what the great saints and God-lovers *have* done in prayer and love, and the temptation to talk as if I were at least in ninth or tenth grade in these subjects is almost irresistible. Indeed, sometimes it *is* irresistible.

But occasionally the Self-Existent visits me in his marvelous and little-appreciated quality of *geburah*: rigor, severity. And then it is brought home to my reluctant attention where Tom Powers really stands in these matters. And I see, quite apart from any monkey-play of pious inferiority or phony humility but very simply as the truth, that in the practice of prayer and love I am in subkindergarten. (I will not speak for anyone else, but I will say that I do not feel lonely here. I have company.)

I am a beggar and a clodhopper when it comes to prayer and love. In my normal state, that is. There *are* periods when the grace of God moves through me and I become for the time a vessel of love. Again, the Holy Spirit acts and I become a channel of prayer. But this is not my love or my prayer. I am entirely conscious, indeed unusually conscious, while all this is going on. But afterward it is very hard to bear true witness to what happened, because ego elements intrude in spite of good intentions. Perhaps the truest thing that can be said is that *only God prays* and *only God loves*. In my worst times I am miserably divorced from prayer and love. In my middle times I hopefully grope toward loving and praying.

And in my best moments I am caught up in real love and real prayer — not mine, but his.

I do not wish to confuse things which are beautifully simple, to make easy acts difficult, or to make vinegar out of the wine of God's truth. I recognize that love and prayer are as natural and spontaneous as breathing — for the pure in heart. But for myself, and for many another yet-unpurified seeker, there is a need to crouch low going through these great doors, just because the spirit of hypocrisy insinuates himself in such subtle ways where prayer and love are concerned. *Mephistophel,* the corrupter-liar, is very active right here. Wouldn't you be, with his assignment?

In approaching a discussion of prayer I must come at it from this conservative angle — because prayer, in its lowest form, is as high as God. Either it reaches to God or it isn't prayer. And so it breaks out beyond heaven and sinks lower than hell. It is more intimate than sex and more necessary than eating. I can't help this. I didn't invent prayer. It is just the way it is. Every fool who prays knows this.

I cannot avoid flying high in speaking of prayer, and so I want to be well anchored at the start at least. I do hope constantly to remember who provides the air and the wings and the heart for such flights and to remember that without grace I am quite incapable of prayer. Finally, I hope that my limitations as a commentator on prayer may be divested of any mock "humble" aspects and appear clearly as just what they are — facts, which may be useful to other men, similarly limited.

All right, so prayer is the key. Before talking about how to use it, may we examine the key itself just briefly:

It is an ancient key, as old as mankind and possibly very much older, and being a gift of God it is purest gold. But before we can use it we have to clean it off and brush it up a bit, for it is smeared with the adversary's rancor and smudged with human perversity and weakness. Prayer and purity are necessarily related.

And so we need to say a word about *morals:*

This, of course, is another twentieth-first-century hot potato.

The puritans love it excessively, and the libertines hate it excessively, and between the two an ordinary mortal is inclined merely to skip it.

But no skipping is possible here, if we are to consider prayer at all. The science of right and wrong (morals) must accompany the science of divine access (prayer). Observe why: genuine prayer, even the most rudimentary kind of prayer, is an approach to the divine Life, and therefore to sacred power (*mana*, *Kraft*, virtue). If the approach is right, prayer is the greatest of all human activities. If the approach is wrong, prayer is literally and very seriously dangerous. For the divine Life is real, and sacred power is power; and such things are not given to nitwits, unless the nitwits insist, and then they may wish they hadn't. Holy virtue immemorially has been surrounded by specific safeguards, to ignore which is folly. If you touch but the hem of the garment of Truth, you touch and draw into yourself his living sap, his sacred Life-stream. This is not a pious fiction. It is more real than electricity.

Any prayer at all is better than no prayer, and generous fools sometimes may succeed where the stingily prudent fail, but let us not be deceived for all of that: there are right and wrong ways to approach God, and we are sternly cautioned to learn what they are and to observe them in our practice. "Friend, how comest thou in hither not having a wedding garment? . . . Bind him hand and foot, and take him away." (Matt. 22:12-13.)

In an emergency you can and should forget the hygiene and pray just as you are, even if you are right in the trough with the pigs. But otherwise certain preparations for prayer should be made. The most obvious of these is that you should clean yourself up morally before you pray. Nothing complicated or obscure is suggested. Just clean up in the simplest possible sense. Specifically: so far as you are able, stop lying, stop cheating, stop deceiving, stop guzzling, stop gorging, stop loafing, and stop fornicating. Stop envying, judging, and condemning. Stop wallowing in self-pity, self-hatred, and self-concern. Stop hating or fearing your fellow men. Unless you are delirious or deranged, you know what you are doing and which of these little pastimes are on your list. It is not a philosophical matter at all. These things, spiritually considered, are dirt. Prayer is a movement toward holiness (wholeness, oneness, integrity, health). And dirt and holiness do not mix. It is not the holiness which suffers in an improper contact, it is the dirt. If you touch the holy in an unduly dirty condition, you are liable to be burned. I know. I've been there.

But now here is something for all of us to remember always: if a man waited to approach God until he had perfectly cleaned himself up, he would never pray at all. Because it is not in our power to accomplish our own purification. Again, the situation is very simple. We are required to clean up *as much as possible* before turning to God. As always, something remains to our responsibility, and on that the whole wheel of grace turns; we must do our part. *Then* we go to him, and we are warmed in his fire, certainly never burned beyond our capacity to endure, if we have done an honest cleanup job in preparation.

Out of prayer, and out of the warmth and the benign burning, comes the capacity for further cleansing; this permits deeper prayer; and thus God and man cooperate in the basic redemptive phase of purgation, which nobody — note: *nobody* — escapes. God is Author and Lord of love, and he is by no means above loving whores. But they end up washing his feet in their tears.

Prayer is the key to the will of God. Prayer is easy and simple; it is also deep and difficult. This is a typical paradox of the way to God; and like all such mysteries it is also a very practical fact. The first motions of prayer are humbling to the rational mind, because we would not have to pray at all if the rational mind were as competent as it sometimes thinks it is. Nobody really understands prayer, so that he could analyze it and explain it. And yet everyone, for his own direction, has to understand as well as possible.

There is no end to the ways in which one may speak of prayer. It may be said, for example, that prayer is a holy instinct, a holy art, and holy breath.

Prayer obviously is an instinct, the deepest of all. The act of praying, of calling for help, for life, for sustenance, for love and understanding and guidance, is built into us far below the level of language and conceptual thought. It is in our very cells. It is in our vegetable, animal, and infantile natures, which we never lose no matter how old and sophisticated our minds become. A sudden upset is apt to throw us back to these levels at any time. And this is gain, not loss, if it enables us to recover the primitive capacity of the creature to seek help from its mother the universe and its Father the Spirit of the universe.

The whole creation up to the human level is one vast orchestration of need and fulfillment, hunger and food, seeking and finding. This is not yet the language of religion but of existence. If man has lost the feeling of his participation in the universal prayer life at that level, it is because egotism has cut him off from nature as well as from God. But he *can* recover, because prayer is in his very bones, and it is apt to find its voice whenever the person's outer shell is scratched. If the shell is actually *cracked,* the voice sounds loud and clear. Sometimes a light tap will break the personal shell, and the instinctual prayer is heard easily and sweetly. Sometimes, particularly nowadays, a real whack is required. For emphasis, I give an extreme example:

I know a man who went off his rocker in early middle life and was given shock treatment. (He is a nice man who since has fully snapped back and today is as healthy in the head as anybody and maybe more so than many; so I guess his report, strange as it is, may be trusted.) As I said, he broke down and was given shock. This was in the pioneering days of shock treatment; he was getting it (without premedication) with Metrazol, and it was rough.

One day they had not quite matched the dosage to his increasing physical tolerance for the drug, and he began to go into shock in full consciousness. Several times he passed out but then returned to the body consciously, still in the shock. Once, on the edge of returning to consciousness, he heard someone screaming. "God!" the cry went. "God! . . . Help! . . . God help me! . . . God! . . . God! . . . God! . . . ." For a while the man wondered calmly and objectively who was doing the screaming. Then his focus changed, and suddenly he knew that it was *he himself* who was screaming.

Afterward, when he had a chance to think it over, the man was surprised, because he was a cast-iron atheist and had been for many years. He realized then for the first time, and upon further observation and reflection very much more so, that there are levels of being at which no man is an atheist. He saw that atheism is a phenomenon strictly confined to people who do not know their own depths.

The above is an example of low-low prayer, and it really is built into every one of us, deep, deep down. Prayer in the most literal sense is an instinct.

Prayer also is an art. When we have recovered our animal-vegetable instinct for prayer (which is apt to restore our health and to give us a considerable measure of release from neurotic self-concern), we are ready to advance to the specifically human levels of prayer, to the *art* of prayer, properly so-called. Nothing fancy is indicated here. It is just the threshold where, consciously and with full human rationality and freedom, we reach out to contact and offer ourselves to the Higher Power who broods above us and within us, to be "a reasonable, holy, and living sacrifice" unto him.

There are no rules of prayer in the sense of stiff regulations or sharp do's and don'ts. But over the centuries a lot of major and minor artists in prayer have left us a rich legacy of records of their experiments, their trials and errors and achievements, their discoveries and surprises, their techniques and their soarings above technique. This literature constitutes a gold mine of wisdom for our encouragement and instruction in learning the art of arts.

Beyond instinct and art, prayer is breath. Beyond intentional training, as its flower and fruit, there is the life of spontaneous aspiration, receiving and reciprocating continuously the love of God and mediating it to the creation, rising above personal self-consciousness as a sort of higher instinctual octave in which the rationality and self-direction of the human nature are transformed in a greater Intelligence and greater Guidance. Prayer now is as steady as the heartbeat and the breath, but with full and joyous conscious participation. It is indeed the synchronization of the human breath and the Holy Breath. Prayer at this level is not learned from books or from people, but from the Holy Spirit of God himself.

Prayer is the key both to the human heart and to the Heart of God. In the use of this precious key there are three great traditional practices, and every child of God who is groping his way back toward his Father's house should know them.

The Practice of Abandonment

How can you clear the way to true prayer? At any moment shock or emergency may clear it spontaneously and abruptly (but temporarily). But otherwise two steps are indicated: (1) a moral cleanup, which we have already considered, and (2) a surrender to God, a giving up of the self-direction of your life and affairs and abandoning them to the divine will and the divine providence. For convenience, we can call this act just "surrender" or "abandonment."

Surrender seems to be a firm and indispensable prerequisite to any real spiritual progress. Many balked or bogged-down attempts to realize God can be traced back to failure or refusal to surrender.

Abandonment or surrender is a definite, technical, critical phase of the truth-seeking life. If you want to work with it, you must first understand what it is and then realize that it is not only important but inescapable as a condition which permits real, living, breathing, knowing contact with the Higher Consciousness. In brief, if you want to get to God, you've got to surrender.

So what is surrender? It is a giving up of the egotistical, self-centered notion that I, just as I am, can direct and run my own life effectively and well. Surrender or abandonment is preceded by a keen appreciation that without conscious co-operation with the Higher Power I do not properly know how to eat, to sleep, to work — and most certainly I do not know how to love or pray or rejoice in life.

This realization is not cheap, and, particularly for people with good animal health and a medium to large bank roll, it is exceedingly difficult to grasp at the working level, that is, at the point where it becomes a moving force and not just a pious notion. It is true that nobody can live his life well for a single day without intentional contact with God. But people who are "doing all right" in this world find it hard to believe, to know, and to *feel* this truth.

What can be done about it? First of all, you must be alert to a certain kind of event which varies greatly from person to person but which no life is without: crises, disasters, tragedies, injuries, and illnesses. These are great aids in the process we have been considering. A major aspect of their significance in the human moral and spiritual economy no doubt lies in just this peculiar power to help in abandonment to God.

When these things come, you are wasting your life if you do not seize them as means to bring you to surrender at the feet of the Lord. The harder it is to take, the more powerful is the potion. It is necessary to refuse the false anodynes of whining and self-pity, to reject the gall of cursing and complaint, and to gaze steadily through the darkness toward the ever-present Light. But *then* when the scalding cup of pain or loss is drunk right down, it takes you into the Presence as nothing else can.

Of course disasters and illness are not to be self-induced or self-sought. In many a soul there is a monkey-governed twist, usually buried but still often effective, which draws the person toward sickness and accident for wretched and weirdly egotistical reasons of its own. Do not say too quickly that you could not be guilty of this; you may be; it is a very common condition. The probe of truth must be thrust right into this stinking boil. Any tendency in yourself toward fraudulent illness or tricked-up tragedy should be faced, watched, and strictly denied influence in the heart or mind or body. You will never know the redemptive power of real pain unless you have rejected phony pain. The true cross is the straight road to the Highest, but false crosses are about the meanest and most injurious kind of pretending, conscious or "Unconscious," to which a human being can stoop. If you must play-act, do not do it at this level. It is not just bad theater; it is a travesty of the deepest revelation of truth that this earth has yet received. Do not dare to provoke or improvise the most terrible of all mysteries. Leave the cross alone until it is given to you. *Do not fake suffering.* It is the gateway to God. The Father on his sapphire throne expects his own anointed Son — not some miserable ham.

Suppose you are not in any difficulty. Suppose you *are* "doing all right" in this life. Suppose you are not caught in false suffering and the aid of genuine suffering is denied to you for the present. Suppose at the same time you do see the necessity for surrender to God and abandonment to his will and providence. Suppose you are willing to surrender, so far as you can be willing in spiritual sleep (which is where most of us are, remember?). Where do you go from there?

Well, if your experience is like a lot of other people's, you lock yourself in the bedroom or bathroom or wherever you have decided to experiment with conversation with That which is above you, and you say something like this: "Hello. Are you there? I'm feeling well, thank you, and actually doing rather well, it seems (correct me if I'm wrong). But I've been hearing about a thing called surrender. It makes sense to me, and I want to try it. I see that it probably would be good for me, and that it may be necessary in any event. Please make me understand it and give me the grace to do it, or begin doing it."

Then when you emerge from prayer, during the rest of that day you try to *get out of the driver's seat.* Try to let God run your life and you go along for the ride. The secret is just to remember to do it. The actual attitude and act are not so hard, but we are heavily prone to forget. Patiently and with good humor in spite of failures, make the effort to remember. Make little quick prayers for the grace to remember. It is simple but tricky. Just remember — to remember. You cannot realize how much hangs on remembering until you try it. But first you've got to remember to try it.

The monkey really hates this business and will inevitably counterattack on two fronts, first with a tweezers and later on with a wrench. His first tweezer touches, in the phase in which you are trying to remember to surrender, are so light and so deft that you have to be an old campaigner to notice what is actually going on. All a neophyte can observe is that, somehow, in spite of good intentions, he is forgetting to surrender. Automatically, with no conscious knowledge of how it happened, again and again he winds up in the driver's seat and running his own life like a fire engine. So he tries again to surrender, and again, but less often as time goes on.

After a while, when he does remember his original intention, he may feel a faint discouragement and distaste for the effort involved. Somewhat later it may occur to him that the whole idea is probably unsound. "After all, why wind up throwing your life to the winds and acting eventually perhaps like a spineless dope. . . . A man does need to have at least some of the control of his own affairs in his own hands. . . . It's only natural. . . . Responsibility is something we all have to remember" etc., etc., etc. By this time, of course, the end of the enterprise is in sight. The monkey wrench never appears at all and soon Jocko will feel safe to sheathe the tweezers until the next nasty little threat to the kingdom of ego arises, if it ever does.

Maybe you think this is a jolly overportrayal. On the contrary, it is taken right from life, my own and others'. And, again, it is much more likely to happen to you than you can possibly realize until you yourself really try to surrender.

What is the proper strategy in such a case? I say it is not just to go on making harder efforts and kicking yourself for a chump when you fail. The ground needs to be reconnoitered on an empirical basis. And what do we find? Those whom the adversary succeeds in tricking right out of the game are the *loners*. So the secret lies not only in more determined efforts but in more determined efforts *plus* constant association with other people who are making the same effort. Here you really need the group, the *ecclesia*, to lift you up and carry you on. You need pretty regularly to swap experience with other laborers on this particular section of road. You need, also, occasional contact with journeymen who are further along, who are in veritable contact with the

Master, and who can reflect his know-how back into this rocky stretch in which the ego is first learning to let go and let God.

Maybe you are remembering that wrench and wondering when the monkey uses it. He brings it to bear if and when the tweezers fail. If you succeed over any considerable period of time in remembering to surrender, if you really do begin to get out of the driver's seat, if the attitude of abandonment begins to become habitual and to involve the heart — then the infernal little chum begins to clobber you with the wrench. That is to say, he drops the subtlety, steps out in the open, and confronts you directly with his own special version of an old production called "Frank and Fearful Possibilities." The lines go something like this: "What! Are we to have *no* part in the government of our very own life — *none at all*? Does God wish to destroy our *integrity*? Having given us the innate and sacred thirst for freedom, does he now propose to make a *puppet* of us? Is he after all a God of *slaves*? Are we finally to have no privacy, no choice, no adventure, no noble individual and personal striving? Is all to be swallowed up in this ghastly 'Surrender'? It's a swindle and a shame. To hell with it. We won't have it, that's all. We will just forget all about it and get back to normal, back to sanity, back to real life. . . ."

This kind of concern — whatever the language in which it may appear — is a heavy-handed attack against our progress toward full abandonment, and it is likely to strike home not only in the mind but in the deep emotional nature. Something very profoundly rooted in the primordial part of every human being fiercely and passionately does not wish to surrender to anybody or anything. Particularly it does not wish to be subordinate to a "God" in which it does not believe and which it regards as a piece of pious idiocy (if it is under the sway of Ahriman, the devil of obscuration and materialism) or a God whom it knows to be real but whom at the same time it loathes and execrates as a cosmic and eternal enemy (if it is under the rule of Lucifer, the devil of pride and false light). The monkey aspect finally is seen to be an amiable and misleading disguise. The real face of the enemy is a death's-head, and it is mortally opposed to the surrender of this life into the hands of its Creator.

In order to press firmly on toward effective and sustained abandonment, you must remember first of all to practice the art, and then you must be prepared to persist in the face of a determined and prolonged enmity, entrenched deeply within yourself. The opposition is so heavy just because the lines here are clearly drawn and the stakes are high. And the adversary knows it.

Fortunately in this crucial area there is available today a written work (published as two books) which mediates to the life of him who reads, understands, and receives its message the most authentic and workable wisdom of God.

I wish I could tell you that these two little books *(Self-Abandonment to Divine Providence* and *Spiritual Letters* by J. P. de Caussade) are easy to read and to follow, but at first I did not find them so. Some beginners do, and some do not. The books were recommended to me by a friend whose insight I greatly respect, and therefore I tried earnestly to study them and to practice what they teach. But I got almost nowhere; perhaps it would be correct to say really nowhere at all. And after some months I gave up and put this particular source into my suspense account, intending to return to it later. A considerable period of time ensued, during which my search for truth ran along other lines.

Then suddenly I found myself in the midst of one of the worst difficulties of my life. It involved my family and my marriage, and both my physical and emotional natures were so influenced that my mind was clouded and literally numb — at a time when, perhaps as never before in this lifetime, I needed to think clearly; a great deal depended on it. For some time I was quite unable to read, although at the same time I felt a keen need for the help certain kinds of reading can bring. And then one day I found myself reading *Self-Abandonment,* and not only reading it but drinking into my soul the precious light it has to give.

I could read no other book during the time my trouble lasted (and it continued over some months), but I could and I did regularly read *Self-Abandonment.* Never, never before had I even half-realized the power of a holy man of God to reach out over the centuries and across the oceans and to give to a modern man, so far separated from him in the flesh, his blessing of living knowledge, living courage, living love.

The full name of the man into whose debt I have so deeply entered in this way is Father Jean Pierre de Caussade. He was a Jesuit, living in France from 1675 to 1751. The writings* in which his greatest work is embodied are two collections of letters, incomplete and incorrectly copied, of counsel and encouragement addressed to a few Visitation nuns.

Before you decide that you could not receive help from so unlikely a person, do yourself the favor of sampling him. He is one of the men who have made me practically, unsentimentally, and utterly sure of the communion of saints.

Please don't be put off by the fact that Caussade writes in the style of another century or (if you are a Protestant) that he is a member of the Roman Church. Don't mind that he is not a clever or amusing writer. As a matter of fact he writes very well, but he is overwhelmingly an influence, not at all an entertainer. He is a rare genius in understanding and communicating the art of surrender. Be patient in opening yourself to him. If you can receive him, he is a tremendous teacher. I wish there were more like him, but it seems to me that, in this great specialty of abandonment to God, in the West and East he stands alone. All men of God know and teach abandonment, but I have encountered none who teaches it so single-mindedly, with such passion and flame, and yet with such clear common sense and practical concern. Maybe I am partial to this man. Read him yourself and be my judge.

Father de Caussade is quoted twice already in this present book. I will not quote him further. I would not rob you of the joy, the profit, and perhaps the blessed and strengthening difficulty of reading his great words in his great books themselves. I

---

* Of the translations available, those by Algar Thorold seem to me greatly superior, so much so that I would caution anyone reading Caussade for the first time to seek out Thorold's work in preference to any others.

will only say in summation: if you wish to surrender your life to God, read Caussade. Do what he tells you to do. Find and work with your friends in God who also are entering the deep, sweet, swift current of abandonment. Keep it up. Do not be discouraged. Of all ways, this way leads most directly to true prayer, and to the Goal of prayer.

The heart of Caussade's teaching is in what he calls "the sacrament of the present moment." It is not necessary, he says, to know the will of God in advance but *to accept it,** to abandon yourself to it as it unfolds in your life *from moment to moment*. Ordinarily we get all mixed up about the will of God because we are straining to know it either in advance or in retrospect. We want to know what it is going to be two weeks from now or tomorrow or five minutes from now. Or we brood and scratch over what it might have been yesterday or five years ago or in 486 B.C. We jump and bounce around like fleas in a windstorm, while the thing we are seeking and forever missing lies in the calm eye of God's *present* intention for us. The human mind continually and obsessively and indeed pathologically runs behind or ahead of the point where the will of God actually may be contacted and accepted, if not "known." We crave forecasts and enjoy rehearsals. We want elaborate descriptions and blueprints of God's will, whereas he steadily and faithfully gives us his whole will in the living moment.

This makes complete sense if you will take the trouble to think it through. To state it properly is easy. But to grasp and hold it is exceedingly difficult, because it is encapsulated in a stubborn illusion and a stubborn habit of thought to the contrary. Hard-won flashes of the truth of the magic of *now* are likely to disappear as mysteriously as they appear.

---

* How can you accept something you don't know and don't understand? It's easy. You do it all the time. You breathe and you eat, but do you really *know* air? and do you *understand* food? Of course not. If acceptance did not naturally and continually precede full knowing, none of us could live the day out. What Caussade recommends is as simple and sensible as eating a steak. You don't require a laboratory analysis in advance. You just have a good look at it, take a good sniff of it, and then you sink your teeth into it.

Caussade's method is a combination of "watching," i.e., continual awareness of your own life, moment by moment, and the practice of the Presence of God, i.e., unwavering attention to God's grace and his will as they bear upon you from moment to moment — plus a patiently and diligently repeated act of abandonment to the divine providence, in the exact circumstances of your daily life, from moment to moment.

The secret — and it is a great one — is in focusing upon the present moment. Caussade's gift lies in himself realizing, and then in transmitting to us, a single tremendous insight: the truth that once you are centered in the present moment, the sacrament of surrender becomes simple, easy, joyful. It is not a burden and not a drudgery; it is a leap, a shout, a kiss, a dance. It is not "ideally" so but actually and literally so. And it is so not for healthy and rich folks only but also — and perhaps especially — for the inadequate and the undistinguished.

If you are looking for an easy way to God, this is it. The ease lies not in the absence of pain or trouble but in the fact that pain and trouble and everything else are caught up into the deluge of God's love and mercy from moment to moment. You don't have to be a spiritual giant to do this; all you have to do is remember, from moment to moment. You may not do it very often to begin with, but do it as often as you can; that is absolutely all that is required.*

Believe me, a miracle takes place every time you succeed in entering the present moment and surrendering. The "doing" of it is quite possible for anyone. To sustain it, however, is frankly not easy. We forget. Or we lose the blessed simplicity necessary to

---

* We must beware of misunderstandings at the extremes of such practices as self-abandonment. Because it is so easy at the beginning extreme, let us never forget that at the other and final extreme abandonment is the greatest of all difficulties. Not just the practice of surrender as a discipline but the utterly effective, final, and irrevocable self-abandonment of the spirit into the hands of the Father — the act which Christ Jesus accomplished upon the cross — this is beyond our view at this time. All prayer, all spiritual life, leads toward it, but it is beyond the scope of the present discussion. (See Jean-Nicolas Grou, *Manual For Interior Souls*, Chapter LXIII, "On Entire Abandonment.")

enter into a simple grace, and begin again automatically and thoughtlessly to seek complicated "solutions" that are going to help us, when? . . . tomorrow!

But abandonment must be practiced, and can only be practiced, *now*. We must ask God what he wants of us *now*. We must ask him for what we need *now*. We must open our eyes and our ears and our hearts to what he is telling us *now*.

Experiment with this in your life, now, today, beginning with this moment. Do not juggle words about it or get into inner arguments about it. That is just exactly the monkey's dish. He has a great assortment of "reasons" why so simple and effective a practice as abandonment to God from moment to moment "won't work." It "excludes foresight," of course, and it "cuts out memory," and it "leaves no place for planning." (Ah, planning! *That's* what we need more of, isn't it?) Let this kind of talk run on inside yourself if you want to, but try to see how much captious gibberish is mixed up in it. And inner debates, even without the gibberish, never yet brought anybody to God.

If you will postpone the grand analysis and get on with the *practice,* you will find that, as the moments of self-abandonment to God's will flow into hours, and as the hours flow into days, foresight and memory are not lost or weakened. They are clarified, rather, and they find their proper places as servants, not tyrants. They are not forever getting in the way now. They do not bug you so much any more.

Abandonment to God is prayer, and it is also the great preparation for other kinds of prayer: "the practice of penetrating the cloud," for example.

The Practice of Penetrating the Cloud

Nearly all men live in a cloud of ignorance of God. "Penetrating the cloud" is a term which describes a certain kind of prayer: broadly speaking, it is prayer done in *time specifically set aside* for the purpose.

There are ways of praying throughout the day in the midst of other activities, and there are even ways of praying continuously. But the particular kind of prayer which is practiced in specially reserved time every day occupies a position of central importance in the way to God, and very few can get along without it.

You must learn how to practice penetrating the cloud, but even before that you must *find the time* for it.

Further, you must continue without interruption to find the time for it. A few days or weeks of this practice will do you no harm, but they probably won't do you much good, either. The practice of penetrating the cloud must become like eating your meals, sleeping, or going to the bathroom. When the time is at hand every day, you just do it, period. Unless you can put it on that basis (and everybody can who really wants to), you are merely stirring around in the cloud, not practicing the penetration of it.

Time must be set aside at least five days a week and preferably six. (You may want to take a seventh-day rest, even from this blessed kind of work.) Morning is best for most people, although evenings will do, and any time of day is all right in a pinch. It should be done at the same time every day; a few lapses on this point are permissible, but not many.

How much time every day? At least ten minutes to begin with. That is my own estimate of the need; opinions vary widely; one of the most experienced men I know says you cannot do much in less than half an hour. Ten minutes obviously is less than a good working minimum, but it is a *possible* time for anyone, and it will serve to get things going and keep them going. For a starter, it is not presumptuous and not a strain, and nobody can lie his way out of the daily appointment on the plea that it is too much for him. It seems to me that in many cases these advantages outweigh the admittedly grave disadvantages of so short a time.

An old man who was teaching me started me out at this level. He instructed me in what he called the "wedge system." Said he: "Ten-minute periods faithfully and regularly held every day are far better than half-hour sessions held occasionally or in spurts. When the ten-minute wedge is firmly inserted in your daily routine (and this might take six months or a year), then you can drive it in a little further, maybe expanding the time to fifteen minutes — later to twenty — later to thirty — and so on, up to what your real capacity for daily practice of this kind turns out to be. It is wrong to lag, but it is no good trying to be a saint overnight, either."

When I first began to listen to this man, he questioned me about my habits of prayer. "How long do you go?" he asked. "About two hours at a stretch," I said, trying with a great effort to appear modest. (It was true. I was less than twelve months out of a moral and physical collapse in which I had been floundering for years. But I had been reading books, and I am inclined to excess, and I *was* practicing, at that time, two hours at a clip.)

My old spiritual father looked at me narrowly.

"You do this every day?" he said.

"Well, no," I said.

"You do it for a few days and then skip a few days?" he said.

"Yes," I said.

"And sometimes you skip a few weeks, perhaps?" he said.

"That's the way it goes," I said.

"Ten minutes a day for you," he said. "No less *and no more.*"

Thank God I found my way into the old man's hands. In another few months I probably would have blown some fuses or soured myself on prayer forevermore, the way I was going. The point is, to begin with a time period which is not beyond your ability to sustain, however humble and indeed however humiliating that period may be. If you want to be a star performer, fine; but take it easy, at least at first. There are real heroes in this game, and it is a good thing to emulate them, but it is also possible to get something like a spiritual hernia. If the ten-minute beginner's time really is too easy for you, by all means increase it, but not too much and not too fast. On the other hand, after a while if you are not succeeding in keeping the ten minutes clear at least five days a week without fail, drop back to five minutes. Find out what time you *can* keep, and *keep it.* Then you are on the way, not otherwise.

Now a word about the place in which you practice. So far as

possible it should be the same place every day. It would not serve our purpose here to go into the reasons why, but it does make a difference. (If you are traveling, you just do the best you can on the road, using whatever places are available, and try to stay to a regular place at home.) A bedroom is fine. A bathroom will do. The room should have a door with a lock or bolt, if possible. Again, this is not the occasion to develop the rationale, but it makes a difference to work in a room secured against accidental intrusion. A certain animal level of the mind remains distractingly alert unless it knows it won't be watched or butted into from the outside. Why waste time trying to argue with it or reassure it, when you can so easily just lock the door?

How do you use the time? That depends. There are many sources of instruction in the art of penetrating the cloud. Using them as little or as much as makes sense, you've got to find your own way, or rather, the application of the one Way in your particular case. Some common knowledge along these lines, arising out of my own experience and the experience of those who have shared their lives with me, may be of interest here. The following discussion, of course, is directed to the problem of the householder, the man or woman in the world. The science of penetrating the cloud is very highly developed in certain religious communities and particularly in enclosed orders. On the other hand, as William Temple has pointed out, God is by no means exclusively or even preferentially interested in the formally religious affairs of the world. The monk in his oratory may *or he may not* have clearer access to the ear of God than the father of a family locked in his bedroom for a few minutes before rushing off to his day's work.

The attitude, the mental and emotional set, with which you approach and enter your daily period of prayer is important. You have put aside a time for a meeting with God. Either it is that, or it is nonsense. If the President of the United States agreed to meet with you and to give special consideration to your personal, family, and vocational needs, you would come up to the meeting with your face washed, your attention well focused, and your heartbeat stepped up. In prayer, either you are meeting with the

Executive and Sovereign Monarch of the Universe, or you are kidding yourself. Make up your mind which it is. And try to let the truth sink home, even as you approach prayer. Try to get out of the area of lukewarm half-knowledge and half-belief; it is almost worse than no knowledge and unbelief. Either you are a silly fool muttering to himself, or you are entering into an interview with the omnipotent God. This hasn't anything to do with your spiritual status or capacity. It is just a cold-turkey question with a cold-turkey answer. Either you are talking to Papa or you aren't. If you are, go in on your toes.

The first consideration, when your time has come around and you have entered your room and locked the door, is what to do with the body.

There are a number of possibilities. You may want to walk around for a while at first, just to get loosened up. This is a good time to stretch and yawn a bit, to break up tensions. And sometimes it is good to pray standing. Prayer while standing upright has a long traditional background, and in certain conditions nothing is the equal of it.

Kneeling, of course, has a profound effect upon both body and soul. For me, kneeling was a crisis in my return to communion with God. Over many years I had lost my faith completely, and for a while even after I began trying again it was exceedingly difficult for me to pray at all. Then I got to the point where I could pray, but I could not bring myself to kneel. At last I slid out of bed where I had been trying to pray one cold February night, and I actually *did* kneel — and it made a great difference. It broke something down inside me. After so long a struggle to rule in my own place, it was an act of profound significance to put myself finally in this position before God — the attitude of a servant before his liege Lord. It spoke more powerfully in my soul than any words I could have uttered. It took me at once below and above my proud mind. It not only moved me, it moved the Lord himself toward me. I don't have to guess about this. I know.

So the physical position you take in prayer is not a matter of indifference; it is something worth reverently experimenting with.

Standing up, kneeling, and lying down are positions of great utility in certain states of mind and heart. But each of them has its disadvantages, too. Standing or kneeling over any considerable period of time usually induces a degree of fatigue and discomfort which is distracting. Praying while lying down is peculiarly useful if you are ill or injured. Some of the very greatest prayers, the prayers of the dying, are uttered in this position. Ordinarily, however, lying-down prayer is apt to go very well for a while but then to merge ever so gently into sleep. This is not a bad way to end the day, but it is not suited to the regular attempt consciously to enter and to remain in the presence of the living God.

The physical disposition which seems best suited to sustained work in practicing the penetration of the cloud is sitting. Just plain old comfortable sitting down. With certain qualifications, however. Sitting must not be confused with its cousin, lounging. That is one position which is definitely contra-indicated. You would not lounge in an important business interview; do not lounge in the presence of the Creator. Sit as comfortably as possible, but do not slump, sag, twist, lean, crouch, coil up, or collapse. We get into these contortions so often that they actually come to seem comfortable; but if you try to stay in one position for more than a minute or two, as you must in prayer, you will find that any of the varieties of lounging certainly are not comfortable; indeed, they are very soon unendurable.

You may sit in a chair or cross-legged on a folded blanket on the floor. Sit bolt upright, with the spine straight and the head floating lightly on top like a pumpkin balanced on a pole. Then, while remaining bolt upright, deliberately relax. *It can be done.* Relaxation need not involve wilting. Straight does not mean stiff. There is a golden mean between the ramrod and the dishrag. Quite easily, by a simple and direct effort, you can achieve real relaxation while simultaneously sitting up as straight as a string. Just try it, and see.

The upright, relaxed, sitting position — with the hands resting on the thighs or folded in the lap, and (if you are in a chair) with the feet about three to six inches apart and flat on the floor

— is wonderfully comfortable. It takes some learning and some getting used to, of course. You must learn particularly how to relax the muscles of the face, back, and neck. But the position is amazingly easy and invigorating when achieved, and you can remain in it for considerable periods of time with little attention, little effort, little fatigue, and therefore with little distraction. At the same time the very physical attitude tends to keep the mind awake and alert. For these reasons it is ideally adapted to the practice in which, by deliberate effort, you intend to present yourself — body, soul, and spirit — at the court of the Great King.

Now something needs to be said about breathing. When you are sitting right and the mind is released somewhat from over-concern with the physical frame, the attention is likely to be drawn to the breathing. Ordinarily we pay little or no attention to breathing, unless we have to run for a bus or something and the laboring and aching lungs then force us to notice. But in prayer, when the body is quiet and the mind is alert, the breath is apt to become prominent in the field of awareness.

Do not try to ignore it. Without considerable training, it is impossible to do so, and it is not necessarily desirable to do so. At the same time, do not deal with the breath foolishly or recklessly. Right at this point certain things may be done which are powerfully effective, i.e., which will produce quick and striking and real results, but which for that very reason are exceedingly dangerous unless they are done under the direct guidance of an experienced and competent instructor. There is a delicate and intimate connection between the instinctive rhythm of the breath and the total instinctive balance of the body. Whoever deliberately assumes control of the breath had better know what he is doing.

Specifically: *do not do any "breathing exercises," do not manipulate, direct, "control," or play any tricks at all with the breath,* unless you are in immediate, personal, and responsible touch with someone *who really knows what needs to be known* about the relationship of the human breath to the entire human body-and-mind.

You can do the following with complete safety. When the breath calls attention to itself, give it what it asks: attention. Give it all the time it wants, too; do not be in a hurry to move on to something else. Observe the breathing. Let the mind dwell upon it, and *in it*. This in itself has a soothing and balancing effect upon the whole organism. Quietly, calmly, noncritically, and nonmanipulatively, notice the breath. Observe it in the nose, in the throat, in the lungs, in the head. Observe how it penetrates to parts of yourself you never suspected it would; indeed, on a subtle level it fills the entire body. All you are doing is noticing the breathing. You are merely paying attention (for once). Without directing it, *allow* it to become quiet — peaceful — steady — unhurried — quiet — peaceful — steady — unhurried — quiet — peaceful — steady — unhurried. . . .

You may combine your first prayers with your breathing. You may say "Thy kingdom come" on the in breath and "Thy will be done" on the out breath, for example. Or you may repeat the name of God calmly a number of times on the in breath and say "Bless me . . . bless me . . ." on the out breath. If this is a possible thing for you, the Spirit of Truth quite clearly will teach you your own best ways of doing it.

Even this elementary degree and amount of inner working may open the way to marked changes in you. Already there may occur, at a certain point, a definite change of consciousness. It may be something rather like the opposite of going to sleep, a gentle but pronounced kind of awakening. It may be accompanied by joy. It may induce tears. There are a number of ways in which it may come; to describe them in too much detail would not help and might hinder by suggesting something which, if it is to come at all, should come of its own motion and the motion of grace. If this does happen, and if you are unprepared for it, you may find yourself retreating hastily. But there is no cause for alarm. You have done nothing wrong or bad in this attempt at communion, nothing unauthorized by the laws of God, man, or common sense. There is nothing to be upset about. You have just succeeded a little bit, that is all. It is quite safe to go on praying. God surely will guide and protect you.

At the same time it is well to take the changes which may occur in prayer very seriously. Either prayer goes nowhere (I wonder if it ever does go just nowhere?), or it goes toward the great deeps, the ocean of psychic and spiritual life upon which every personal life floats. One need never be uneasy in sincerely approaching God, but it is a good thing for the mind to be somewhat prepared for what may happen. This is a razor's edge. If there is too much mental preparation, it leads to guessing games, pseudo experiences, and a shameful kind of egotism. If there is too little preparation, you may be unduly and unnecessarily frightened when things really do begin to happen in prayer.

There are ways of briefly covering the ground in advance, and they may help in this connection. After having made your preparations and before actually beginning to attempt any movement toward the deep contact, you may address yourself to the Holy Spirit in some such terms as these:

"I am about to begin to pray again, but as usual I really do not know what I am doing. I have read books and talked to men, but I am still ignorant and a fool, now possibly more than ever. And at the same time, although I can talk glibly about my attraction toward you, when the Light begins to appear I am a coward. When the Door begins to open I am afraid. I have withdrawn, you know how many times.

"Now take pity on me again. In my deepest heart I do seek you, and I want you regardless of consequences. Let me die if necessary in the act of seeking which is about to take place. On the other hand, let me not ignorantly injure these instruments, this body and mind, which you have put under my care and control.

"Guard me against my timidity and lack of courage on the one side and my rashness and blind irresponsibility on the other. Be my guide and my strength against these enemies within. And by thy grace, let me confidently and easily and with childish trust now enter into prayer."

If no changes in your mental, physical, or conscious state occur, that is fine and perfectly normal, too. Progress in prayer does not depend on their happening or on their not happening. If they do not happen, be of good cheer and proceed without them. Some masters of prayer regard this as the more auspicious way.

If changes do occur, proceed with caution but without worry or fear. You cannot choose which of these ways you will go. Temperament and many other factors enter in. Go the way God leads you. Do not be discouraged by lack of "results," and do not be afraid when results appear.

Spiritual awakening, in or out of prayer, is one thing; psychic phenomenalism, in or out of prayer, is something else again — the two may be related, and they may be quite unrelated or even opposed. There are no hard and fast formulas for distinguishing them; you need to rely heavily and directly on the inner Spirit of Truth.

In certain natures there may be physical or mental phenomena: visions or monitions for example, even quite early in the practice. Your attitude in the face of such happenings must be quietly but firmly neutral. You must turn immediately to the Supreme Guide with some such words as these: "I wish neither to accept nor to reject these things for their sake or for my own sake. I want only the truth. If what is occurring here is of the truth, let me receive it, and please help me in receiving it. If it is any other kind of intrusion, let it be removed at your pleasure, and show me how to bear myself toward it while it remains, or if it recurs." Such a prayer never falls on empty air. The Lord will direct you in terms that are right and effective for you. You can count on it.

Visions and such things *may* be messages or messengers from God; or they may be a kind of trash — or worse. They may bring true enlightenment and encouragement; and they may lead off into the bogs and sloughs of the lower psychic realms — *where egotism flourishes as nowhere else in all the worlds,* where truth and falsehood are jammed together in one vast suet pudding, where the psychic and the spiritual are hopelessly confused, and where the life of prayer quickly may be sucked down to death, drowned in silly and ghoulish parodies.

Complete protection against these dangers, however, is always at hand. If you cling sincerely to honesty and humility, and if you turn quietly and constantly to the ever-present Light of Light for help, then visionary and phenomenal experiences need not trouble you, by their presence or by their absence. You may be helped by reading St. John of the Cross in this regard (*The Complete Works,* Vol. I, pp. 143-58).

Now may we return to the actual details of practice. To begin the period of prayer, sometimes a few minutes of reading, in the Bible or other basic work, are helpful. The saying of a favorite prayer or two is a good way to get started, the Lord's Prayer, for example, or the Twenty-third Psalm, or the Collect for Purity ("Almighty God, unto whom all hearts are open, all desires known, and from whom no secrets are hid, cleanse the thoughts of our hearts by the inspiration of thy Holy Spirit, that we may perfectly love thee and worthily magnify thy Holy Name. . . ."), or the Serenity Prayer ("God grant me the serenity to accept the things I cannot change, courage to change the things I can, and wisdom to know the difference").

When the body is composed, when the breathing is easy and steady, and when the mind and breath are in harmony, you can say such prayers in a way not ordinarily possible: slowly, a phrase at a time, with long, calm pauses in between, during which new and wonderful light is apt to break out from the old familiar words.

We have stayed close to the common, ordinary, strictly kindergarten aspects of the kind of prayer which may be called the practice of penetrating the cloud. But do not for that reason underestimate the power and the possibilities in such an approach. If you do your part in it, your life is highly apt to be revolutionized. If — say, for a couple of years — you will do no more, but also no less, than the simple everyday practice outlined in this chapter, if you will faithfully do the elementary work, take the elementary precautions, and observe the elementary rules, expanding your daily time as you are able, then your guidance into deeper and higher regions of communion with God will be very sure and *very* competent, because it will come unmistakably from God himself.

A book like this present one can do little more than to give you hints on getting started and to suggest other and more detailed sources for your immediate and future consideration. Actual progress will be very much a matter between you and God.

One final word of caution: You sometimes hear talk of "making the mind a blank" in prayer. This is impossible. The true mind already is a blank, a void, a virgin. But the blank is normally filled with objects, with phenomena, with images — in medieval terminology, with "creatures." Those who speak of making the mind a blank actually are talking, often quite ignorantly and nearly always prematurely, about the advanced, technical, and difficult stage of spiritual training known in both the West and the East as "detachment from sense objects" and in the Rhineland school and in other schools of Christian teaching as "leaving imagery" or "leaving the creatures." It does not mean that you make your mind a blank, and it does not mean that you leave your wife or your dog or your automobile and go away somewhere. It means something quite else. When the time comes to do it, by grace you will know how to do it.

You must leave the creatures, sure enough, but you *can do it too soon* and you can get yourself terrifically worked up and continentally confused in the attempt, unless the Spirit is leading you directly, or unless you are in touch with experienced compeers and teachers. Read what the *Theologia Germanica* says on the subject (Chapter XIII, entitled "How a man often casts aside imagery too soon"):

> Tauler says: There be some men at the present time who take leave of imagery too soon, before truth and knowledge have shown them the way thence; hence they are scarcely or perhaps never after able to understand the Truth aright. For such men will follow no one, hold fast to their own understandings, and desire to fly before they are fledged. They would fain mount up to heaven in one flight. . . .

When it is time to go to high school, unmistakable signs will appear. Meanwhile just plug along with the kids in grade school.

It is safer and surer and better all around. Remember that you cannot normally make your mind a blank, in prayer, sleep, meditation, or any other condition. Indescribable states most certainly may be reached, but not blanks. Even deep sleep, trance, anesthesia, and coma are not blank areas in the life, as often popularly assumed. They are states of which the ordinary man retains no memory. There are men who know how to enter and leave such states with intact memory, and they report something *very much other* than a blank.

The "void" *(sunyata)* of Buddhism, the "Unqualified Absolute" *(Nirguna Brahman)* of Advaita Vedanta, and the "divine darkness" of the deepest and most orthodox of Christian mysticism* — these are simply terms which cannot possibly be understood, and can hardly fail to be actively misunderstood, by an unprepared and inexperienced person. There is nothing snobbish about this. It is just a plain fact. It is very much the part of wisdom to leave such considerations humbly and reverently aside until some years of training and actual practice in prayer have been lived through. Nothing is accomplished by mental groping and flights of speculation on the margins of such abysses of Reality, and much harm is done if the heart is filled with hopes and horrors that have no basis in the Truth.

Do what you can do with your mind, especially in prayer. You can learn to entertain such "creatures" — i.e., such impressions, thoughts and ideas — as by God's will are appropriate and ordained for your present condition. You can learn to see, honestly and steadily, what phenomena do as a matter of fact habitually occur in your particular mind. You can learn to distinguish your true friends from your actual enemies and to extend hospitality to the one and to deny your consent and your vitality to the others. *This* is the inner work for a long time. This is not yet knowledge of God, but it is knowledge of the road to God.

And some day, when the road is clear and the time has come to enter the naked ignorance, stripped of its phenomenal rags, you will be strong and humble and ready for the task. *Then* you

---

* See St. Dionysius (Dionysius the Areopagite), *Mystical Theology.*

may probe out beyond the mind, stabbing with the heart's primordial fire of love into that "cloud of unknowing" which lies between the fallen human being and the face of Almighty God.

I shall not speak of that task here. Certain documents, and certain people, are available, and exceedingly well able, to help you when your time comes. For all I know, of course, you may be ready now. In that case it needs only to say that the books which can help you are well known. There are many, but you may note particularly the works of Poulain, Augustine Baker, Teresa of Jesus, John of the Cross, Walter Hilton, and John of Ruysbroeck.

There is one book which addresses itself (indeed, by its very title) so directly and with such skill and power to the deeper phases of the kind of prayer we are considering that it is worth special attention and study. It is also worth quickly putting aside if you find that it does not suit you at present. Put it aside so that you may come to it again by grace at the time when it *will* be useful for you.

I would hate to steer anyone off who could possibly profit from reading *The Cloud of Unknowing*. But at the same time I take the unknown author's warning, which is set down at length in the Prologue, very seriously. He repeatedly "charges" and "beseeches" the reader — "in the name of the Father and of the Son and of the Holy Ghost" and "by the authority of charity" — to leave the book alone unless you are going to take the time to read it "all over," as he says.

In other words, we are warned that this is not a book for spiritual posy-sniffers or pious dabblers, and that such may be harmed by it. And I agree and entirely believe that *indeed they may be harmed by it.* I would echo the old author in saying earnestly to anyone: "Leave this book alone unless you understand what area of life it is dealing with, and unless you utterly mean business in that area."

The writer of *The Cloud* has a specific list of the kind of characters who should lay off: "Fleshly janglers, open praisers and blamers of themselves or of any other, tellers of trifles, ronners [gossips] and tattlers of tales, and all manner of pinchers [nig-

gardly or greedy types], cared I never that they saw this book."
Now maybe you don't fit in any of those quaint old categories,
but try this one on for size: ". . . neither they," he says, "nor any
of these curious, lettered, or unlearned men."

Here the word "curious" is the key. If it is curiosity —
"spiritual," psychological, literary, academic, artistic, vulgar, or
any other kind of mere curiosity — that has brought you to *The
Cloud of Unknowing* and not a deep heart's hunger for the invis-
ible and inscrutable God, then you have come to the wrong book.
So says the man who wrote it, and again I entirely agree.

The Practice of Continuous Prayer

There *is* a way of praying continuously. Not absolutely continuously at first — for not only the in-working of the Holy
Spirit but a lot of practice on our own part is required — but
continuously for considerable lengths of time, even in the beginning. As you gain proficiency, it is possible in this way to pray
for a whole day at a time, without interfering with your duties,
but on the contrary with a great gain in light and strength for
duties. And finally, I am reliably told and I believe, this practice
leads to a point where prayer is absolutely continuous, uninter-
rupted even by the most demanding occupation or by sleep.

> It would be a misunderstanding of the whole matter if
> we supposed that the occupations of life are a hindrance
> to this sort of prayer. On the contrary they are, or at least
> often may be, our way of practising it and there is a kind
> of prayer which is rightly named the prayer of action. . . .
> If an animal action such as eating or drinking does not in-
> terrupt the continuity of prayer, it is still less likely to be
> interrupted by the labors of body or mind or of any kind
> of domestic affairs or by the duties of our occupations.
> There is nothing in any of these concerns in themselves to
> distract the heart from its union with God, nothing to ar-
> rest the actions — of the Holy Spirit or the soul's inward
> conformity with it. That is an understatement; indeed all
> these things tend to unite us more closely to God and to

maintain the hidden communion of the Holy Spirit and the soul.

Grou, How to Pray, p. 82

So here is something that starts conveniently low and rises very high indeed. Imagine the revolution that would be accomplished in a life in which prayer had become absolutely continuous! This development is frankly way ahead of most of us, but the practice that leads there starts from where we are, wherever that may be. Furthermore, this is something which no Christian can afford to ignore, because it is commanded to him — not recommended but commanded by clear precept — by the Lord, Christ Jesus himself. Père Grou, a real authority, leaves no doubt at all on that score:

> This section on continual prayer requires, both for its own sake and for the consequences which flow from it, to be treated with great care and read with attention.
>
> *Men ought always to pray*, says the Gospel, *and not to faint* (Luke 18:1).
>
> Let us weigh these words. *We ought:* it is a precept and not a counsel; it concerns a matter of obligation and not a counsel of perfection. If we fail in this we are sinning more or less seriously. *We ought:* it is a general duty which concerns all Christians. It is said not only for ministers of the Church, not only for those who are consecrated by religious vows, but for all those who profess to believe in the Gospel and to follow it as their rule of conduct, whether they live in the world or are withdrawn from it. *Men ought always to pray:* not only to have a fixed time for prayer and not allow a day to pass without prayer, but to make prayer our continual practice, never suspended or interrupted.
>
> That these words: *to pray always*, must be thus understood is shown by what follows: *and never faint*. The Gospel commands us first to pray unceasingly and then forbids us to cease doing so, thus uniting these two ways of express-

ing one precept. You will not find in all Scriptures a precept which is laid down in stronger or more definite terms.

But this precept, if we understand it as applying to vocal prayer, or even to that form of mental prayer which we call meditation, is plainly impossible. So those who do not recognize any other kind of prayer, have thought themselves justified in restricting the obligation to certain fixed times. No doubt they would be right were there no other way of praying to God, except by the lips or by the application and concentration of the mind.

But the words of the Gospel take us further and might have opened their eyes to the necessity of allowing another kind of prayer, of such a nature that every Christian can practice it unceasingly.

What kind of prayer is this? It is the essence of prayer, the only kind that attracts God's attention and which gives value to all the other kinds, in a word the prayer of the heart. This prayer can continue without interruption, as no other can.

Ibid., pp. 79-80

What the French Roman Catholic master of prayer here calls "prayer of the heart" is designated also by that identical term in a great Christian tradition of which Père Grou hardly can have had any direct knowledge: the Hesychast tradition of the Eastern Orthodox Christian Church.* We shall hear more of that, and of how the Hesychast "prayer of the heart" has been brought down to modern times, in a moment.

Meanwhile, at the outset, I would like to describe in the simplest possible terms one of the most powerful of the methods of inducing and co-operating with continuous prayer of the heart, namely, *japam* or repetition. The very simplicity of this way is for many people the chief obstacle to its serious practice. The sophisticated modern mind often cannot bring itself to admit that any-

---

* Indeed, Père Grou seems to be entirely unfamiliar with the Hesychast *method* of attaining continuous prayer of the heart, repetition of "the Prayer of Jesus," and I think we may assume complete nonacquaintance on his part with the Eastern Christian *practice* in this kind of prayer.

thing as simple as repeating the name of God could be effective
in life, let alone life-transforming.

Repetition of a name of God, or of a short phrase incorporating
a name of God, is basically all you do in this practice. How you do
it makes an immense difference, but still that is all you do.

Any beginner can use this method with real effect, real results, real benefits. And yet the same method is useful to the pro-
ficient approaching the radiant mountaintop of consciously be-
holding God's very face. I never heard of a method of prayer
which covers such a range — which can be practiced in such a
potpourri of life conditions by such a variety of persons — with
such power and authority on all levels.

We observed earlier the desirability in some natures of a
weekly one-day rest from the practice of penetrating the cloud.
Nothing like a vacation from prayer itself was indicated, but only
a rest from a specific kind of work in prayer. But no such rest is
necessary or desirable in the practice of prayer of the heart. By
grace and without forcing it, the nearer it comes to absolutely
continuous prayer the better.

Inevitably and immediately, the mind raises questions and objections to *japam* or repetition of God's name. May I say right away
that few of the objections are valid, and all of the questions can be
fully and satisfactorily answered. We shall see, as we go along.

There is one book which describes — simply and basically and
workably — this universal practice of prayer in its deeply traditional Christian form. That book is *The Way of a Pilgrim* (and *The Pilgrim Continues His Way*). Let me first bear witness briefly to my own
experience of this great book and this great way of prayer and to
the experience of my friends in God who know this blessing, too.
Then I shall let the Pilgrim speak for himself, and shall refer you
further to the other sources which are qualified to describe this
prayer and to instruct you if you are willing to learn it.

I first read *The Pilgrim* twenty-five years ago, and since then
I have read it again and again and have practiced the method of
prayer it teaches. It has been a great power for good in my life.
No book, not even the Bible itself, has been of more practical
help to me. Nowhere have I found such clear insight on how to

"pray without ceasing." Many friends of mine have had similar experiences with it.

The Abbot of St. Michael's Monastery at Kazan discovered the manuscript of *The Way of a Pilgrim* in possession of one of the monks at Mount Athos. He made a copy of it, and this was printed at Kazan in 1884, the year of the Abbot's death. The name of the author of *The Pilgrim* is not known; all we know is that he was a Russian pilgrim, and in his narrative he tells of his experiences as he wandered about from one holy place to another in Russia and Siberia, evidently in the period after the Crimean War of 1853 and prior to the Liberation of the Serfs, which occurred in 1861. He tells how an old monk, his *starets* or spiritual teacher, taught him the method of prayer which he calls "the Prayer of Jesus." He describes the prayer as follows:

> The continuous interior Prayer of Jesus is a constant, uninterrupted calling upon the divine Name of Jesus with the lips, in spirit, in the heart, while forming a mental picture of his constant presence, and imploring his grace, during every occupation, at all times, in all places, even during sleep. The appeal is couched in these terms: "Lord Jesus Christ, have mercy on me." One who accustoms himself to this appeal experiences so deep a consolation and so great a need to offer the prayer always, that he can no longer live without it, and it will continue to voice itself within him of its own accord.

Specific instructions are given as to how to develop this prayer within oneself, and the objections which inevitably arise in the skeptical mind are met and answered:

> Many so-called enlightened people regard this frequent offering of one and the same prayer as useless and even trifling, calling it mechanical and a thoughtless occupation of simple people. But unfortunately they do not know the secret which is revealed as a result of this mechanical exercise; they do not know how this frequent service of the lips imperceptibly becomes a genuine appeal of the heart, sinks

down into the inward life, becomes a delight, becomes as it were, natural to the soul, bringing it light and nourishment and leading it on to union with God.

This type of prayer, of course, is not confined to Christianity. In Hinduism it is called *japam* (recitation of the divine Name) or *Ramanama* (repetition of the Lord Rama's Name). *Ramanama* was the mainstay of the spiritual life of Mohandas Gandhi. To a question by a missionary friend whether he followed any spiritual practices, Gandhi said:

> I am a stranger to yogic practices. The practice I follow I learnt in my childhood from my nurse. I was afraid of ghosts. She used to say to me: "There are no ghosts, but if you are afraid, repeat Ramanama." What I learnt in my childhood has become a huge thing in my mental firmament. It is a sun that has brightened my darkest hour. A Christian may find the same solace from the repetition of the name of Jesus, and a Muslim from the name of Allah.* All these things have the same implications and they produce identical results under identical circumstances. Only the repetition must not be a lip expression, but a part of your very being. . . . One should pour one's soul into it. . . . The Mantra becomes one's staff of life and carries one through every ordeal . . . it is my constant support in my struggles.†
>
> Gandhi, *Ramanama*, pp. 5, 6, 11

---

* The repetition of the Name is a basic discipline in Islam, as in most of the great religions of humanity. Carl Vett reports the ensuing bit of conversation, following his introduction to a Muslim teacher by a friend called "the Bey": "'Very successful!' said the Bey as we left. 'It almost seems that you have roused the old man's interest. . . . What kind of impression would it have made on you, if the master had had you do nothing but repeat the name of Allah out loud five thousand times a day? And that is one of the commonest exercises for a beginner'" (Vett, *Dervish Diary*, p. 55).

† A description of the power of repeating God's name occurs in the work which Gandhi regarded as "the greatest book in all devotional literature," the *Ramayana of Tulasidas*:

"Install the luminous gem in the shape of the divine Name . . . on the threshold of the tongue at the doorway of your mouth, if you will

The Prayer of Jesus as given in *The Pilgrim* actually is the principal means to union with God in the Hesychast tradition of Eastern Orthodox spirituality. Frithjof Schuon (in *The Transcendent Unity of Religions*) says:

"This method [Hesychasm] has been handed down, through the Desert Fathers, in a direct line of descent from primitive Christianity . . . all the forms of Hesychasm are derived with strict traditional fidelity from something that existed in Christianity at the beginning . . . it is the Hesychast Tradition, from the Desert Fathers to the 'Russian Pilgrim,' which undoubtedly represents in its most unaltered form the inheritance of primitive Christian spirituality — that which properly can be called 'Christ-given.'" If there is any possibility that this tremendous statement is true, it deserves the electrified attention of every Christian.

The great book containing the treasured writings of the centuries of this tradition is *The Philokalia*, mentioned again and again by the Pilgrim. *The Philokalia* writings specifically indicated in *The*

---

have light both inside and outside, O Tulasidasa.

"Yogis (mystics) who are full of dispassion and are wholly detached from God's creation keep awake (in the daylight of wisdom) muttering the Name with their tongue, and enjoy the felicity of Brahma (the Absolute), which is incomparable, unspeakable, unmixed with sorrow and devoid of name and form. Even those (seekers of Truth) who aspire to know the mysterious ways of Providence are able to comprehend them by muttering the Name. Strivers (hankering after worldly achievements) repeat the Name, absorbed in contemplation, acquiring superhuman powers. . . . If devotees in distress mutter the Name, their worst calamities of the gravest type disappear and they become happy. . . . Theory of the Name is supreme in all four Yugas [ages] and all the four Vedas, particularly in the Kali age [the dark or iron age, the present age] in which there is no other means of salvation.

"Even those who are free from all desires and absorbed in the joy of devotion to Sri Rama have thrown their heart as fish into the nectarine lake of supreme affection for the Name. . . .

"(Not only in this Kali age but) in all the four ages, at all times (past, present, and future) and in all the three spheres (viz., heaven, earth, and the sub-terranean region) creatures have been rid of grief by repeating the Name. . . . In this terrible age the Name alone is the wish-yielding tree, the very thought of which puts an end to all the illusions of the world. . . . In Kaliyuga neither Karma (action) nor Bhakti (devotion) nor again Jnana (knowledge) avails; the Name . . . is the only resort.

"The Name repeated either with good or evil inclinations, in an angry mood or even while yawning, diffuses joy in all the ten directions" (*Sri Ramacharitamanasa*, Tulasidas, pp. 40, 41, 45, 46).

Pilgrim are found in a volume entitled *Writings from the Philokalia on Prayer of the Heart*. See also *Early Fathers from the Philokalia*. See further *On the Prayer of Jesus* by Bishop Ignatius Brianchaninov.

The practice of continuous prayer of the heart (achieved by means of repetition of the Prayer of Jesus, or of the name of Allah or by the name of a Bodhisattva, or by *Ramanama)* is taught or recommended by many of the major spiritual teachers of the world,* including, in or near our time, Sri Ramakrishna and Sri Ramana Maharshi. *The Gospel of Sri Ramakrishna* contains many references to the power of repeating the divine Name. Brahmananda, a direct and beloved disciple of Ramakrishna and a tremendous teacher in his own right, strongly urged *japam,* repetition of the Name, upon the young aspirants in his charge:

> The mind rules the senses. Therefore it must be controlled. . . . Always be on your guard until you have transcended the mind. . . . Plunge yourself deeply into the practice of japam and meditation. The mind is gross and feeds on gross objects. But as japam and meditation are practiced, the mind becomes subtle and learns to grasp subtle truths. Practice. Practice. See for yourself if there is really a God.
>
> Brahmananda, *The Eternal Companion,* pp. 142-43

Prabhavananda, who knew Brahmananda directly, and who edited *The Eternal Companion,* comments upon Brahmananda's teachings of *japam* as follows:

> In his teachings, Maharaj [Brahmananda] lays great stress on the value of japam.
>
> Japam may appear monotonous and mechanical when not accompanied by meditation. Nevertheless, it

---

* For an example of the Buddha's teaching of the power of uttering the name of the Bodhisattva Avalokitesvara, see *Samantamukha Parivarta,* "the Lotus of the good Law," the twenty-fifth chapter, known as "The Kwannon Sutra" (Suzuki, *Manual of Zen Buddhism,* pp. 30-32). In Mahayana Buddhism *Nembutsu* is "a ceaseless invocation to Amida Buddha" and is markedly stressed in the Jodo sect.

has a good effect. If one persists, the monotony will break, and the presence of God will be felt. Through japam, an inner joy and sweetness will arise which will help the aspirant to devote himself more and more to the practice of the Presence of God.

Ibid., p. 223

And further, in his commentary on the sutras of Patanjali, Prabhavananda gives one of the clearest and most cogent expositions of the power of repeating the Name:

People who have never tried the practice of repeating the name of God are apt to scoff at it: it seems to them so empty, so mechanical. "Just repeating the same word over and over!" they exclaim scornfully. "What possible good can that do?"

The truth is that we are all inclined to flatter ourselves — despite our daily experience to the contrary — that we spend our time thinking logical, consecutive thoughts. In fact, most of us do no such thing. Consecutive thought about any one problem occupies a very small proportion of our waking hours. More usually, we are in a state of reverie — a mental fog of disconnected sense-impressions, irrelevant memories, nonsensical scraps of sentences from books and newspapers, little darting fears and resentments, physical sensations of discomfort, excitement or ease. If, at any given moment, we could take twenty human minds and inspect their workings, we should probably find one, or at most two, which were functioning rationally. The remaining eighteen or nineteen minds would look more like this: "Ink — bottle. That time I saw Roosevelt. In love with the night mysterious. Reds veto Pact. Jimmy's lying to get my job. Mary says I'm fat. Big toe hurts. Soup good . . ., etc., etc." Because we do nothing to control this reverie, it is largely conditioned by external circumstances. The weather is cloudy, so our mood is sad. The sun comes out; our mood brightens. Insects begin to buzz around us, and we turn irritable and nervous. Often, it is as simple as that.

But now, if we introduce into this reverie the repetition of the name of God, we shall find that we can control our moods, despite the interference of the outside world. We are always, anyhow, repeating words in our minds — the name of a friend or an enemy, the name of an anxiety, the name of a desired object — and each of these words is surrounded by its own mental climate. Try saying "war," or "cancer," or "money" ten thousand times, and you will find that your whole mood has been changed and colored by the associations connected with that word. Similarly, the name of God will change the climate of your mind. It cannot do otherwise. . . .

Mere repetition of God's name is, of course, insufficient — as Patanjali points out. We must also meditate upon its meaning. But the one process follows naturally upon the other. If we persevere in our repetition, it will lead us inevitably into meditation. Gradually, our confused reverie will give way to concentrated thought. We cannot long continue to repeat any word without beginning to think about the reality which it represents. Unless we are far advanced in spiritual practice, this concentration will not be maintained for more than a few moments; the mind will slip back into reverie again. But it will be higher kind of reverie — a reverie dominated by sattwa rather than by rajas or tamas. And the Name, perpetually uttered within it, will be like a gentle plucking at our sleeve, demanding and finally recapturing our attention.

Patanjali, How to Know God, pp. 58-61

At what is perhaps a considerable risk of confusing the subject, I have included references to continuous prayer of the heart (as aided by repetition of the name of God) from many different places and times. It seems to me that the risk is justified in order to bring out the important fact that in historical times it is one of the most widespread, most practical and helpful, and most seriously practiced of all forms of prayer. From the Desert Fathers in the West and the devotees of Rama and Avalokitesvara in the East, the practice of the repetition of the Name has come down recently through *The Pilgrim* to becoming in our day a prominent subject in two stories by J. D. Salinger in *The New Yorker* magazine. God works in mysterious ways indeed.

May I conclude these references by sharing briefly with you a few experiences of my own with this kind of prayer of the heart.

Until I read *The Pilgrim* I had no idea that any such prayer existed, much less that it would be a possibility for me. I had encountered references to *"japam,"* "chanting God's name," "repeating the *mantram,"* etc., etc., in Eastern teachings, but they were just words and phrases as far as I was concerned. They all seemed to me to refer to practices that were local, special, and frankly a little bizarre — you know, fine for those Hindus but not for me. I didn't tumble at all to what they were talking about, and certainly I never guessed what a mine of grace I was skipping over so lightly.

But then I came upon *The Pilgrim,* and although at first I did not suspect the full power and depth of the Prayer of Jesus, nor did I then realize the place it occupies historically and traditionally in Christianity, still I did recognize right away that there were real possibilities in this kind of prayer, and I set out to explore them. (Only much later did I begin to see the connection between the Jesus Prayer and similar practices throughout the spiritual life of humanity as a whole.)

I began experimenting with "Lord Jesus Christ, have mercy on me" (or "Lord Jesus Christ, have mercy on us," if I had someone else in mind), said silently and inwardly, on a train commuting to New York City five days a week. There was about a twenty-minute run between my home town of Chappaqua and the change engines stop of North White Plains, less than halfway to the big city, and in that period I began to work the prayer every commuting day.

At first it was odd and difficult and clumsy, and I soon saw that I was trying too much at a time, so I cut it down to the stretch between Chappaqua and Hawthorne, about ten minutes.

Then it went rather well for a while. Of course I encountered the early kind of difficulties that everybody else does. I worried quite keenly, for example, that the other commuters would notice what was happening and that they would be powerfully confirmed in an impression that a real live nut got on the train every morning along with the solid citizens at Chappaqua. But I carefully said the prayer inwardly and with no motion of the face or lips; so the only thing unusual was that I was sitting up straight and otherwise unoccupied. As a matter of fact lots of people doze or gaze absently about on a train. Nobody of course paid the slightest attention to me. By holding an open book or newspaper on my lap I felt my disguise to be complete, and I proceeded without further concern on that score.

The next development, as the prayer was going on, was that one of my crew of inner voices began to point out that our Lord has cautioned us against *vain repetition* (this voice was one of the pious, scripture-quoting members of my crew). I had the grace, however, to see the wisdom of another inner voice (one of the work gang), who called attention to the fact, which was quite obvious as soon as observed, that whether the repetition was vain or not turned upon an interesting point: it depended upon whether I was able to keep my attention even faintly on the words and to realize even a very little bit what they mean.

At times, in spite of all efforts, the repeating of the phrase would sink out of the circle of fully conscious attention and thus into the realm of vain repetition. *But not quite.* It was not entirely vain. Because as long as it kept going, as long as I did not forget it entirely and drop it, even the mechanical repetition served finally to pull the attention back, and the prayer immediately arose for a time above the vain level. It was indeed, as Prabhavananda says, "like a gentle plucking at the sleeve." And therefore I realized early in the game the really quite remarkable value of the practice even at its humblest, least esteemed, and most criticized level.

Then there were times, rare at first and brief, when the prayer rose, of its own momentum or of a hidden momentum, to a kind of peak, where it seemed right on the point of breaking out into some kind of light, right on the edge of another kind of knowing and feeling. This happened in every case spontaneously, never when I was pushing or struggling with the practice in any way, or when I was strenuously hoping for a rise or a break in it. Whenever I tried to direct the prayer toward such a peak, the exact opposite or nothing at all occurred. It just kept on at the ordinary level or sank to an even duller plane than usual. I soon saw that the peaks cannot be promoted or manipulated in any way. They come, I am now very certain, as a result of grace, and so do other and deeper involvements of the prayer. The quantity, as Bishop Brianchaninov points out, is somewhat within our choice and control. The quality is not.

Of course there were many ups and downs and hiatuses, but the ten minutes in the morning finally were going so well that I added a similar bit on the train coming out in the evening. The run from Grand Central to 125th Street is a hair short of ten minutes, and so it suited the need very nicely.

Then, when it felt as if I had solid bases in the two periods, morning and evening, I experimented with extending the time. It was much easier to do so successfully in the morning than in the evening (I think that this was simply a matter of available energy and the fatigue threshold). At the end of a year I was able occasionally to maintain the prayer with good attention all the way from Chappaqua to New York. The first time I did so, I got off the train in Grand Central in such a state of inner joy that I had to stop the repetition and pray: "God, please help me to get my feet down on the ground; I've got a day's work to do."

There is nothing much worse than getting into athletic feats in prayer or endurance contests with yourself or anyone else. But in this particular kind of prayer it *is* helpful, with no thought of setting any records, to extend the periods of practice gradually up to what you are fully capable of, and then to accustom yourself to being in this continuous prayer as you go about your daily affairs. Abbot Chapman's observation is profoundly true: "The more you pray, the better it goes." I think that my early attempts with the Prayer of Jesus represent about an average beginning experience, which any serious experimenter would find himself able to duplicate or exceed quite easily.

It seems hardly possible when you have just heard about it and are trying to figure it out, but when you actually get to doing it you find that you are able to keep the prayer going in the midst of all kinds of activities, including sometimes even hard mental work.

Repetition of the prayer while walking is excellent. I found also that it went very well while mowing the lawn. It works fine, too, while driving a car, particularly on longish trips. (Note to the National Safety Council: I testify that this practice positively does not interfere with proper attention to the serious business of driving; on the contrary: the back of the mind of everyone who drives a car is filled with random thoughts, more or less chaotic, more or less angry or fearful or otherwise sour-emotional, and more or less distracting; but the back of the mind of one who repeats the Jesus Prayer is occupied with a calming, steadying influence which clarifies rather than obstructs the outer attention and assists rather than hinders one in any such occupation as driving a car.)

There are many occasions during the day that are particularly suited to establishing prayer of the heart: times when you are waiting for an appointment, when you are walking from one building or place to another, when you are doing routine chores of any kind, such as brushing your teeth or washing the dishes. I found that the quiet hours spent on a trout stream were a perfectly wonderful time for it. Mealtimes of course are ideal, because they present opportunities to combine the prayer with the essentially sacramental and holy acts of eating and drinking.

Times of illness and difficulty are specially suited to repetition of the Name. The place of this practice in healing is a very important one. It is indeed one of the greatest aspects of the prayer, but it is a large subject in itself and I cannot develop it here (see Gandhi, *Ramanama*).

You might think that mixing prayer with the daily life in this way would tend to induce woolly or abstracted or slightly dissociated states, but the exact opposite is true: The practice of continuous prayer of the heart makes one much more alert and awake in all his faculties and much better able to do work of any kind. I realize that it is hard and perhaps impossible to visualize in advance how this could be so, but I assure you, from my own experience and that of many others, that it is so.

In order even to begin to experience the validity and authority of the Prayer of Jesus, it is necessary to say it "in the heart." You should take the trouble to understand what is meant by the "heart" in this context. It involves the physical heart, but something very much beyond that, too. *The Pilgrim* gives clear instructions for bringing the prayer into the heart. I would say that this phase in the development should be undergone at first in quiet and undistracting circumstances, because when the prayer actually does enter the heart there are repercussions throughout the whole being. One of the best simple modern expositions of what the "heart" is in universal spiritual teaching, and what its powers and functions are, is given in Austin Pardue's *Create and Make New* (particularly pp. 17-39).

Continuous prayer of the heart, *in* the heart, is like the practice of the Presence of God, the practice of watching, and the practice of abandonment, in that it is easy to start and difficult to maintain. But that difficulty seems to be a characteristic of all of the really basic movements of the truth-seeking life. I guess it is just the part that is left to our own volition; and for most of us volition toward God is a frail element which needs tender nursing and plenty of patient, unhurried, undiscouraged exercise.

I am going to close with something I've been avoiding all along: a scale or map of the territory covered by prayer.

I am uneasy about systems and maps of prayer (although some of the greatest men of prayer have used them), because they sometimes tend to intimidate beginners and to inflate premature proficients. Further, they tend to give a mechanical and academic dress to something which should be fresh and natural and uncalculated. "Systems" of prayer sometimes provide not a ladder but a series of artificial hurdles between the praying man and the

A MAP OF PRAYER

I.
The PRAYER of
ATTENTION

. . . within
our control
and initiative.

A. VOCAL prayer: Talking with God. Petitions: "low prayer." Intercessions: "middle prayer." Thanksgivings. Spoken group prayer. Sung prayer. Liturgical and congregational prayer. Spoken repetition of the Name.

B. MENTAL prayer: Meditation. Quiet prayer. Attention of the mind to God. Unspoken repetition of the Name.

II.
The PRAYER
of GRACE

. . . *not* within
our control
and initiative.

C. CORDIAL prayer: Preternatural clarity and truth. Warmth. Joy. Rapture. Bliss. Unction. Tears. Fire. Ecstasy. *Bhakti*. The Love of God. Compassion (leading to) service (leading to) sacrifice. Prayer of the heart: repetition of the Name in the heart.

D. TRANSCENDENTAL prayer: Direct realization of God. Living Light. literally beyond all description.

Reality to whom he prays.

On the other hand, a good map does enable you to see the ground in which you are working and to confirm and guide your own experience within a rational, empirical, and traditional framework. One of the simplest and most useful maps I know is compiled from all traditions but follows, in its structure and terms, the view of prayer held in Russian and Greek (Eastern Orthodox) Christianity.

You will observe that the practice of continuous prayer by means of repetition of the Name takes one from the vocal, through the mental, to the cordial level, and from the Prayer of Attention right up into the Prayer of Grace, that is, from the place in which you are your own man to the place in which you are God's man. This is a tremendous transition. Note the critical distinction between the Prayer of Attention and the Prayer of Grace. In the one, *quantity* is involved, and that is up to you. In the other, *quality* is involved, and that is up to God.

And so, as my last word in this book, I would like to make some observations as to how one may bear oneself in this transitional area, this crucial flash point between one's own action and the action of the Grace of God:

The Prayer of Attention, in all its varieties and ranges, is *within our voluntary control* (unless we are willingly in the grip of vice, in deliberate hatred, or in some other deadly sin or God-eclipsing condition). If we set ourselves to it we can pray a great deal — even four or five hours a day — just by deciding to do so and sticking to it. God has put this area of prayer within the range of our effective choice and implementation to a very considerable extent. Few of us exercise the amount of effort and do the amount of work we could do in the Prayer of Attention. The chief problem is to find the time and, even when there is the time, to remember to do it. Mainly it is a problem of remembrance, because, as we have seen, there are ways of praying even in the midst of business. A very busy man, *if he remembers,* will find himself doing a remarkable amount of the Prayer of Attention in the interstices of his daily affairs, even if they are extremely crowded. The point is that the Prayer of Attention is up to us, except in states of deadly separation.

The Prayer of Grace on the other hand is *not* within our voluntary control. *It cannot be attained by us.* The Prayer of Attention clears the way and prepares the ground for the Prayer of Grace, but *it is not at all the cause* of the Prayer of Grace. To bear this in mind is of the greatest importance. Unless we do a lot of the Prayer of Attention we shall probably have very little or none of the Prayer of Grace. And yet, no amount of the Prayer of Attention will *result* in the Prayer of Grace. There must be an erasure of any and all thoughts of cause and effect that arise here. *The Prayer of Grace is always the gift of God.* You may strive and struggle in the Prayer of Attention. You must not strive or struggle in or for the Prayer of Grace. Ask for it, yes. But do not grasp for it. Ask and wait.

Don't get tired asking and don't get tired waiting. And when it does come, it is to be welcomed in the deepest possible gratitude. We never know how we are going to behave when the Prayer of Grace comes to us. I have often withdrawn in fear. I felt that God was giving me something I was afraid to receive and requiring something of me that I was afraid to give. Such reactions are normal enough, and with time and continued grace they are outgrown. The ideal attitude is to relax in perfect trust and let God have his way with you. But at first this may not be possible. Just do the best you can. He understands.

In addition to strengthening and cleansing joy, the Prayer of Grace always brings with it a subtle and wonderful guidance. If we are alert to this and if we will give ourselves up to it, then we are beautifully led and taught how to receive the comfort and bliss. When this type of prayer is well developed (which usually takes some time), then God himself becomes the man's teacher, and he needs to rely less and less on exterior counsel, while remaining humbly open to it at all times.

In the meantime, as always, there are dangers to be guarded against. Every advance in spiritual life, in addition to its advantages, brings difficulties and perils that must be surmounted. This is outstandingly true of the advance into the Prayer of Grace.

One danger, which we have already looked at briefly, is that the man, hearing about the Prayer of Grace or actually having tasted it, will try by various methods to induce it. This is futile, because, as we have seen, the prayer by its very nature is a gift. And the striving leads to psychic indigestion or worse. The ego, which is by no means amputated yet, at this point may become subtly but seriously inflamed by these clear tokens of God's encouragement and approval, and the *persona* may begin to strut and preen itself in hidden and tricky ways in the light which God has introduced into the soul. No man may say, "Oh, that could never happen to me." It could happen to anyone and has happened to many. On the one hand we must be alert and humble; on the other hand we must not fall into scruples. (1) A *childlike trust* in God and (2) a *cheerful willingness* to see secret faults in ourselves and to be corrected by the Truth in the areas of our deepest experience — these two attitudes are our refuge and protection against all danger when the Prayer of Grace is starting.

You cannot force God. But by surrendering, by seeking to penetrate the cloud of your own ignorance, and by trying to pray continuously, you can break your heart for him — and he does not remain unmoved at that. With all your work and sweat you cannot cause anything to happen — but a great deal does happen. Nobody is ever going to figure it out, but that is the way it is.

For books helpful in the practice of prayer, see Special Book Listings, page 215.

Bibliography

Books indicated throughout the text are listed here in alphabetical order. The approximate "weight" of each book is indicated by notations ★, ★★, or ★★★ immediately following the listing: ★ means light reading; ★★ means medium reading; ★★★ means heavy reading.

Please use caution in interpreting these marks. They are intended as a rough index of ease of reading, but they must be applied with discrimination. It would be a misuse of this device, for example, if you were simply attracted to the easy books and repelled by the difficult ones. Some of the not-so-easy works may be among the most useful and enjoyable of all books for you. The Bible, for instance, is marked ★★★ because, like all sacred writing, it is difficult to understand thoroughly. But at the same time it is of the greatest practical value even to people who are not used to hard reading.

On the other hand a single ★ does not mean that the work so checked is frivolous or shallow; it just indicates a book that treats its subject in an elementary way or in terms that are quite easy to comprehend. For instance, Brother Lawrence's *Practice of the Presence of God is* marked ★ because it is easy reading; nevertheless it is a profound spiritual treatise, as you may discover for yourself by reading it over four or five times a year and experimenting with the practice it suggests. So take these ★s, ★★s, and ★★★s with a grain of salt and an eye to your own particular situation. Used that way, they should serve you without misleading you.

For a listing of books grouped according to special purposes, see Special Book Listings beginning on page 207.

Albert the Great, St. *Of Cleaving to God.* London, 1954: Mowbray. ★★.

Alcoholics Anonymous. Anonymous. New York, 1955: Alcoholics Anonymous World Services. ★.

Alcoholics Anonymous Comes of Age. Anonymous. New York, 1957: Alcoholics Anonymous World Services. ★.

Aquinas, St. Thomas. *Basic Writings.* Edited by Anton C. Pegis. New York, 1945: Random House. ★★★.

————. *Summa Contra Gentiles.* Translated by Anton C. Pegis. 4 vols. Notre Dame, Inc., 1975: University of Notre Dame Press. ★★★.

————. *Summa Theologiae.* 60 vols. New York, 1976: McGraw-Hill. ★★★.

Aristotle. *The Basic Works of Aristotle.* New York, 1941: Random House. ★★★.

The Art of Prayer: An Orthodox Anthology. Compiled by Igumen Chariton Valamo. Translated by Kadloubovsky and Palmer. London, 1966: Faber. ★★★.

Ashton, Joan. *Mother of All Nations: The Visitations of the Blessed Virgin Mary and Her Message for Today.* San Francisco, 1989: Harper. ★.

Attar, Farid al-Din. *Muslim Saints and Mystics.* Translated by A. J. Arberry. Boston, 1973: Routledge and Kegan Paul. ★★.

Augustine, St. *The City of God.* Edited by Vernon J. Bourke. New York, 1950: Doubleday. ★★.

————. *Confessions of St. Augustine.* Translated by Rex Warner. New York, 1963: New American Library. ★★.

Aurobindo, Sri. *The Life Divine.* New York, 1949: The Sri Aurobindo Library, Inc. ★★★.

Austin, Lou. *You Are Greater Than You Know.* Winchester, Va., 1955: The Partnership Foundation. ★.

Baker, Ven. Father F. Augustine. *Holy Wisdom.* Wheathampstead, Herts, England, 1964: Anthony Clarke Books. ★★★.

The Baltimore Book of Prayers. Roman Catholic Books. ★★.

Baly, Denis. *The Geography of the Bible.* New York, 1974: Harper and Row. ★.

Bar Hebraeus. *Book of the Dove.* Translated by A. J. Wensinck.

Leyden, Holland, 1919: E. J. Brill. ★★★.

Beevers, John. *Storm of Glory: The Story of Thérèse of Lisieux.* New York, 1977: Doubleday. ★.

Benoit, Hubert. *The Supreme Doctrine.* New York, 1968: Penguin. ★★★.

Bernard, Theos. *Hatha Yoga.* New York, 1950: Weiser. ★★.

Bernard of Clairvaux, St. *On the Song of Songs.* Translated by Kilian Walsh. Kalamazoo, Mich., 1976: Cistercian Pubs. ★★★.

Bhagavad Gita. Of special value, because of Gandhi's great personal demonstration of the Gita's teaching, is *The Gita According to Gandhi.* Ahmedabad, India, 1946: Navajivan Publishing House. ★★★. Gandhi himself considered Arnold's the best English translation:

————. *The Song Celestial.* Translated by Sir Edwin Arnold. London, 1948: Routledge and Kegan Paul. ★★★.

Other translations:

————. *Bhagavad-Gita, The Song of God.* Translated by Prabhavananda and Isherwood. Hollywood, Calif. 1973: Vedanta Press. ★★★.

————. *The Bhagavadgita.* Translated and with commentary by S. Radhakrishnan. New York, 1948: Harper. ★★★.

For interpretation and study:

————. *Essays on the Gita.* By Sri Aurobindo. New York, Sri Aurobindo Library. ★★★.

————. *Talks on the Gita.* By Vinoba Bhave. London, 1960: George Allen and Unwin. ★★★.

————. *The Yoga of the Bhagavat Gita.* By Sri Krishna Prem. London, 1938: Watkins. ★★★.

Bible. The word "bible" means simply "book." The Bible is "the Book" (although really it is a collection of books). The Christian faith is based upon the Old and New Testaments of the Bible. The New Testament is a group of writing about Jesus of Nazareth, the Christ, and his disciples. It consists of the Gospels, which tell of the life and teachings of Jesus and describe his death by crucifixion, his resurrection, and his ascension; the Acts of the Apostles, an account of the activities of the first followers of Christ Jesus; the Epistles, letters of counsel and doctrine written by Paul, James, Jude, Peter, and

John; and a concluding prophetic book, the Revelation of John.

The Old Testament contains books that are held sacred in both Christianity and Judaism. These books deal with the Creation, the Prophets, Psalms and Proverbs, stories like Ruth and Esther, and great psychological and spiritual treatises like Job and Ecclesiastes.

The effect of the Bible upon mankind is quite incalculable. It has inspired Christianity and Judaism directly, and Islam indirectly, and the influence of the peoples of these faiths upon the rest of the world has been enormous.

The Catholic Bibles.

————. *The Holy Bible.* Douay-Rheims Version. Rockford, Ill.: TAN. (This is the traditional English-language Catholic Bible, first published in 1582.) ★★★.

————. *The Holy Bible.* Ignatius Press. (This is the Catholic edition of the Revised Standard Version of the Bible [see below, The Protestant Bibles], said by some modern commentators to be the best modern Catholic Bible for general use.) ★★★.

————. *The Navarre Bible.* Four Courts Press. ★★★.

The Protestant Bibles. In England, between 1525 and 1611, no less than eight Protestant translations appeared: the Tyndale (1525), the Coverdale (1535), Matthew's (1537), the Great (1539), the Geneva (1560), the Bishops' (1568) — and finally in 1611, the King James Version, which became, and to this day remains, the most popular English Bible.

It is almost impossible to exaggerate the influence of the King James Bible. So highly esteemed was it by all denominations as an inspired and masterful rendering of the Word of God that no major subsequent translation appeared for 273 years, until the Revised Version in 1884.

In the present century — and especially since 1950 — a host of new English translations have appeared, incorporating advances in biblical scholarship and seeking to improve upon the unfamiliarity of the language of the King James Version. Two of these modern translations deserve special mention: The Revised Standard Version (1952) is highly regarded for its scholarly accuracy and for its readability, and now exists in both Protestant and Catholic editions. The Amplified Bible (1965) provides full and precise translations of key words in the ancient texts; and, by bracketing explanatory words and phrases directly in the text, it eliminates the need for footnotes or other "helps."

———. *The Amplified Bible.* Zondervan. ★★★.

———. *Holy Bible with Apocrypha and Book of Common Prayer.* King James Version. Preservation Press. ★★★.

———. *The New Oxford Annotated Bible with Apocrypha.* Revised Standard Version. New York: Oxford University Press. ★★★.

———. *New Testament Apocrypha.* Westminster/John Knox Press. ★★★.

———. *The Scofield Study Bible.* King James Version. Edited by C.I. Scofield. New York: Oxford University Press. ★★★.

The Bible of Judaism. One thousand years ago the rabbinical scholar Saadia Gaon observed: "Israel is a people only by virtue of the torah." This is no exaggeration. Without the bible it is impossible to imagine that the Jews could have survived as a distinctive people or as a religious fellowship through so many centuries and through so many vicissitudes. Actually the bible is not just one book. It is a "library" or collection of sacred Jewish writings. Regarded throughout the English-speaking Jewish community as the standard English translation of the Holy Scriptures, the *Tanakh* has been acclaimed by scholars, rabbis, and lay leaders — Jews and Christians as well.

Here in a single volume are the Torah (the five Books of Moses), the Prophets (including the early prophets, Isaiah, Ezekiel, and Jeremiah, and the twelve minor prophets), and the Writings (including the Books of Psalms, Proverbs, Job, Song of Songs, Ruth, Lamentations, Ecclesiastes, Esther, Daniel, Ezra, Nehemiah, and the Chronicles I and II.)

———. *Tanakh.* Philadelphia, 1983: The Jewish Publication Society. ★★★.

Boehme, Jacob. *The Aurora.* Greenwood, S.C., 1960: The Attic Press. ★★★.

———. *The Forty Questions.* Translated by John Sparrow. London,

1911: John M. Watkins. ★★★.

———. *Mysterium Magnum*. Translated by John Sparrow. 2 vols. London, 1924: Watkins. ★★★.

———. *The Signature of All Things*. Greenwood, S.C., 1960: The Attic Press. ★★★.

———. *The Way to Christ*. London, 1964: Watkins. ★★.

———. See also Franz Hartmann.

Boisen, Anton T. *Religion in Crisis and Custom*. New York, 1955: Harper. ★★.

Bossuet. *Letters of Spiritual Direction*. London, 1958: Mowbray. ★★.

Brahmananda, Swami. *The Eternal Companion*. Compiled by Swami Prabhavananda. Hollywood, Calif. 1944: Vedanta Press. ★★.

Brianchaninov, Bishop Ignatius. *On the Prayer of Jesus*. London, 1953: Watkins. ★★★.

Brother Lawrence. *The God-Illuminated Cook: The Practice of the Presence of God*. Hankins, N.Y., 1975: East Ridge Press. ★.

Buber, Martin. *Eclipse of God*. New York, 1957: Harper. ★★.

———. *For the Sake of Heaven*. New York, 1969: Atheneum. ★★.

———. *Hasidism and Modern Man*. New York, 1958: Harper. ★★.

———. *I and Thou*. New York, 1970: Scribner. ★★★.

———. *The Legends of the Baal-Shem*. New York, 1969: Schocken. ★★.

———. *Tales of the Hasidim*. 2 vols. New York, 1973: Schocken. ★★.

Bucke, Richard M. *Cosmic Consciousness*. Secaucus, N.J., 1970: Citadel. ★★.

A Buddhist Bible. Edited by Dwight Goddard. Boston, 1970: Beacon. ★★★.

Bulwer-Lytton, Sir Edward. *Zanoni*. Blauvelt, N.Y., 1971: Rudolf Steiner Publications. ★★.

Bunyan, John. *Pilgrim's Progress*. New York, 1970: Dutton. ★★.

Butler, Alban. *Butler's Lives of the Saints*. Christian Classics. ★★.

Carrel, Alexis. *Prayer*. London, 1947: Hodder & Stoughton. ★.

———. *The Voyage to Lourdes*. New York, 1950: Harper. ★.

Catherine of Genoa, St. *The Treatise on Purgatory*. Westminster, Md., 1946: Christian Classics. ★★.

A Catholic Dictionary. Edited by Donald Attwater. New York,

1961: Macmillan. ★★.

Catton, Bruce. *This Hallowed Ground.* New York, 1955: Doubleday. ★.

Chapman, Dom John. *Spiritual Letters.* Edited by Dom Roger Huddleston. New York, 1935: Sheed & Ward. ★★.

Chesterton, G. K. *Collected Works.* Volume 3. Ignatius Press. ★.

————. *The Everlasting Man.* New York, 1953: Dodd, Mead. ★.

————. *Orthodoxy.* Wheaton, Ill.: Harold Shaw Publishers. ★.

————. *St. Francis of Assisi.* New York, 1957: Doubleday. ★.

————. *St. Thomas Aquinas: The Dumb Ox.* New York, 1956: Doubleday. ★.

The Choice Is Always Ours. Edited by Dorothy Berkley Philips, Elizabeth Boyden Howes, Lucille M. Nixon. Wheaton, Ill., 1975: Theosophical Publishing House.

Cleckley, Hervey. *The Mask of Sanity.* St. Louis, 1964: Mosby. ★★.

The Cloud of Unknowing. Anonymous. Edited by Evelyn Underhill. London, 1946: Watkins. ★★.

————. Edited by Abbot Justin McCann. London, 1952: Burns Oates. ★★.

————. Translated by Clifton Wolters. New York, 1968: Penguin. ★★.

————. Translated into modern English by Ira Progoff. New York, 1957: Julian Press. ★★.

————. Shortened version in modern English. New York, 1948: Harper. ★★.

Collin, Rodney. *The Theory of Celestial Influence.* New York, 1954: Weiser. ★★★.

————. *The Theory of Eternal Life.* New York, 1974: Weiser. ★★★.

Collins and Lapierre. *Freedom at Midnight.* New York, 1980: Ballantine. ★.

Colson, Charles. *Born Again.* Baker Book House. ★.

————. *Life Sentence.* Baker Book House. ★.

Common Prayer, The Book of. (Episcopal.) New York, 1928: Oxford University Press. ★★.

Confucius. *Analects.* Translated by Arthur Waley. New York, 1966: Random House. ★★★.

————. *The Wisdom of Confucius.* Translated and edited by Lin Yutang. New York, 1948: Modern Library. ★★★.

Coomaraswamy, Ananda K. *Am I My Brother's Keeper?* Plainview, N.Y., 1947: Books for Libraries. ★★.

————. *Buddha and the Gospel of Buddhism.* New York, 1964: Harper. ★★★.

————. *Hinduism and Buddhism.* Westport, Conn., 1971: Greenwood Press. ★★★.

Cranston, Ruth. *The Miracle of Lourdes.* New York, 1955: McGraw-Hill. ★.

Cruz, Joan Carroll. *The Incorruptibles.* Rockford, Ill.: TAN. ★★.

Daily, Starr. *Release.* New York, 1942: Harper. ★.

Dante. *The Divine Comedy of Dante Alighieri.* Translated by Dorothy L. Sayers. 3 vols. New York, 1974: Penguin. ★★★.

Daumal, Réné. *Mount Analogue.* Translated by Roger Shattuck. San Francisco, 1952: City Lights. ★★.

Davenport, Russell W. *The Dignity of Man.* Westport, Conn., 1973: Greenwood Press. ★★.

The Dead Sea Scriptures. Translated and edited by Theodore M. Gaster. New York, 1956: Doubleday. ★.

De Caussade, Jean Pierre. *On Prayer.* Translated by Algar Thorold. London, 1949: Burns Oates. ★★★.

————. *Self-Abandonment to Divine Providence.* Translated by Algar Thorold. Rockford, Ill., 1985: TAN. ★★★.

————. *Spiritual Letters.* Translated by Algar Thorold. London, 1948: Burns Oates. ★★★.

Dechanet, J. M. *Christian Yoga.* Westminster, Md., 1972: Christian Classics. ★★.

De Laredo, Bernardino. *The Ascent of Mount Sion.* New York, 1952: Harper. ★★★.

De Molinos, Michael. *The Spiritual Guide.* London, 1907: Methuen. ★★★.

De Monval, Maurice Boutet. *Joan of Arc.* New York, 1980: Viking. ★.

De Sales, St. Francis. *Introduction to the Devout Life.* Edited and with introduction by Thomas S. Kepler. Cleveland, 1952: World. ★★.

De Voragine, Jacobus. *The Golden Legend.* Princeton University Press. ★★.

The Desert Fathers. Translated by Helen Waddell. Ann Arbor,

Mich., 1957: University of Michigan Press. ★★.

The Dhammapada. Translated by S. Radhakrishnan. New York, 1974: Oxford. ★★★.

Dionysius the Areopagite. *The Mystical Theology and the Celestial Hierarchies.* Nr. Godalming, Surrey, 1961: The Shrine of Wisdom. ★★★.

————. *Theologia Mystica.* Translated by Alan W. Watts. West Park, N.Y., 1944: Holy Cross Press. ★★★.

————. *On the Divine Names and the Mystical Theology.* Translated by C. E. Bolt. New York, 1940: Macmillan. ★★★.

Dunkerly, Roderic. *Beyond the Gospels.* New York, 1957: Penguin. ★★.

De Nouy, Lecomte. *Human Destiny.* New York, 1947: New American Library. ★★.

Dostoyevsky, Fyodor. *The Brothers Karamazov.* New York, 1957: New American Library. ★★.

————. *The Idiot.* New York, 1935: Random House (Modern Library). ★★.

Durant, Will and Ariel. *Caesar and Christ.* New York: Simon & Schuster. ★★.

————. *Age of Napolean.* New York, 1939: Simon & Schuster. ★★.

————. *The Life of Greece.* New York, 1939: Simon & Schuster. ★★.

————. *Our Oriental Heritage.* New York: Simon & Schuster. ★★.

Eckhart, Meister. *Meister Eckhart: A Modern Translation.* By R. B. Blakney. New York, 1941: Harper. ★★★.

————. *Meister Eckhart.* Translated by C. de B. Evans. 2 vols. London, 1947 and 1952: Watkins. ★★★.

————. *Breakthrough: Meister Eckhart's Creation Spirituality in New Translation.* Translated and with commentaries by Matthew Fox. New York, 1980: Doubleday. ★★★.

————. *Meister Eckhart and the Rhineland Mystics.* By Jeanne Ancelet-Hustach. New York, 1957: Harper. ★★★.

Ehrenfeld, David. *The Arrogance of Humanism.* New York, 1978: Oxford. ★★.

Ellul, Jacques. *Apocalypse: The Book of Revelation.* New York, 1977: Seabury. ★★.

————. *The Betrayal of the West.* New York, 1975: Seabury. ★★.

————. *The Judgment of Jonah.* Grand Rapids, Mich., 1971: Eerdmans. ★★.

————. *The Meaning of the City.* Grand Rapids, Mich., 1970: Eerdmans. ★★.

————. *The Subversion of Christianity.* Grand Rapids, Mich., 1986: Eerdmans. ★★.

————. *The Technological Society.* New York, 1964: Knopf. ★★.

————. *Violence.* New York, 1969: Seabury. ★★.

Emmerich, Anne Catherine. *The Dolorous Passion of Our Lord Jesus Christ.* Hawthorne, Calif. 1968: Christian Book Club. ★★.

————. *The Life of the Blessed Virgin Mary.* Compiled by Clemens Brentano. Rockford, Ill., 1970: TAN. ★★.

————. *The Life of Jesus Christ.* Edited by The Very Rev. Karl E. Schmoger. 4 vols. Rockford, Ill.: TAN. ★★.

————. See also Schmoger, The Very Rev. K. E.

The Essential Gandhi. Edited by Louis Fischer. New York, 1962: Random House. ★.

Evans, Sebastian. *The High History of the Holy Graal.* Greenwood, S.C., 1969: Attic Press. ★★.

Evans-Wentz, W.Y. *The Tibetan Book of the Great Liberation.* With commentary by C. G. Jung. New York, 1954: Oxford. ★★★.

————. *Tibet's Great Yogi: Milarepa.* New York, 1951: Oxford. ★★.

Evola, J. *The Doctrine of Awakening.* Translated by H. E. Musson. London, 1951: Luzac. ★★★.

Faber, Frederick. *Self-Deceit.* Wallingford, Pa.: Pendle Hill. ★.

Fedotov, G. P. *A Treasury of Russian Spirituality.* New York, 1948: Sheed & Ward. ★★.

Fenelon, Francois. *Christian Perfection.* Minneapolis, 1975: Bethany Fellowship. ★★.

Ferm, Vergilius. *Religion in the Twentieth Century.* Westport, Conn., 1948: Greenwood. ★★.

Fischer, Louis. *The Life of Mahatma Gandhi.* New York, 1962: Macmillan. ★.

Fosdick, Harry Emerson. *The Meaning of Faith.* New York, 1950: Association Press. ★.

————. *The Meaning of Prayer.* New York, 1962: Association Press. ★.

Fox, George. *Journal.* New York, 1924: Dutton (Everyman's Library). ★★.

Francis of Assisi, St. *St. Francis of Assisi: The Legends and the Lauds.* Edited by Otto Karrer. New York, 1948: Sheed & Ward. ★.

————. See also G. K. Chesterton; *The Little Flowers of St. Francis.*

Friedlander, Ira. *The Whirling Dervishes.* New York, 1970: Macmillan. ★.

Gandhi, M. K. *An Autobiography: The Story of My Experiments with Truth.* Boston, 1972: Beacon. ★.

————. *Ramanama.* Ahmedabad-14, India, 1949: Navajivan. ★.

————. *Self-Restraint vs. Self-Indulgence.* Ahmedabad-14, India, 1928: Navajivan. ★.

————. See also Bhagavad Gita; Collins and Lapierre; Louis Fischer; Vincent Sheean.

Garrigou-Lagrange, Rev. R. *God: His Existence and His Nature.* 2 vols. St. Louis, 1934: Herder. ★★★.

————. *The Three Ages of the Interior Life.* 2 vols. St. Louis, 1947: Herder. ★★.

Gaucher, Guy. *The Story of a Life: St. Thérèse of Lisieux.* San Francisco, 1987: Harper. ★.

Geoffrey of Monmouth. *History of the Kings of Britain.* Translated by Sebastian Evans. New York, 1958: Dutton. ★★.

Gilson, Etienne. *The Christian Philosophy of St. Augustine.* New York, 1960: Random House. ★★★.

————. *The Christian Philosophy of St. Thomas Aquinas.* New York, 1960: Random House. ★★★.

————. *History of Christian Philosophy in the Middle Ages.* New York, 1955: Random House. ★★★.

Ginzberg, Louis. *The Legends of the Bible.* Philadelphia: The Jewish Publication Society. ★★.

————. *The Legends of the Jews.* 7 vols. Philadelphia, 1909: The Jewish Publication Society. ★★.

Gobbi, Fr. Stefano. *To The Prists: Our Lady's Beloved Sons.* St. Francis, Maine: The Marian Movement of Priests. ★★.

Goethe, Johann Wolfgang Von. *Faust.* Part I. Translated by Alice Raphael. New York, 1930: Jonathan Cape and Harrison

Smith. ★★.

————. *Goethe's Faust.* Parts I and II. Translated by Albert G. Latham. New York, 1910: Dutton (Everyman's Library). ★★.

Gollancz, Victor. *From Darkness to Light.* New York, 1956: Harper. ★★

————. *A Year of Grace.* New York, 1955: Penguin. ★★.

Govinda, L. A. *Psychological Attitude of Early Buddhist Philosophy.* New York, 1970: Weiser. ★★★.

Grimm, George. *The Doctrine of the Buddha.* Mystic, Conn., 1973: Verry. ★★★.

Grou, Jean-Nicholas. *How to Pray.* Greenwood, S.C., 1964: Attic Press. ★★★.

————. *Manual for Interior Souls.* London, 1952: Burns Oates & Washbourne. ★★.

————. *Spiritual Maxims.* Springfield, Ill., 1961: Templegate. ★★.

Guardino, Romano. *The End of the Modern World.* New York, 1956: Sheed & Ward. ★.

Guénon, Réné. *Man and His Becoming According to the Vedanta.* London, 1945: Luzac. ★★★.

————. *The Reign of Quantity.* London, 1953: Luzac. ★★★.

Hall, Francis J. *Theological Outlines.* New York, 1961: Morehouse-Barlow. ★★★.

Hartmann, Franz. *The Life and Doctrines of Jacob Boehme.* Blauvelt, N.Y., 1977: Rudolf Steiner Publications. ★★★.

————. *Paracelsus: Life and Prophecies.* Blauvelt, N.Y., 1973: Rudolf Steiner Publications. ★★★.

Heard, Gerald. *Is God Evident?* New York, 1948: Harper. ★★★.

————. *Is God in History?* Hollywood, Calif. 1950: Vedanta Press. ★★★.

————. *Training for the Life of the Spirit.* Hankins, N.Y., 1975: East Ridge Press. ★★.

Heller, John H. *Report on the Shroud of Turin.* Boston, 1983: Houghton Mifflin. ★.

Hermes Trismegistus. *Hermetica.* Translated and edited by Walter Scott. 4 vols. Boston, 1975: Shambhala. ★★★.

————. *The Fathers of the Church: The Apostolic Fathers.* Edited by

Ludwig Schopp. New York, 1947: Christian Heritage. ★★★.

Heschel, Abraham. *God in Search of Man*. New York, 1966: Harper. ★★.

Hildegard of Bingen, St. *The Book of Divine Works*. Edited by Matthew Fox. Bear & Co. ★★★.

———. *Mystical Visions*. Translated by Bruce Hozrski. Bear & Co. ★★★.

———. See also Dr. Wighard Strehlow

High Holyday Prayer Book. 2 volumes. Translated by Philip Birnbaum. Hebrew Publishing Co. ★★.

Hilton, Walter. *The Stairway of Perfection*. New York, 1973: Doubleday. ★★★.

Hordern, William. *A Layman's Guide to Protestant Theology*. New York, 1957: Macmillan. ★★.

Hsi Yun. *The Huang Po Doctrine of Universal Mind*. Translated by Chu Ch'an. London, 1947: The Buddhist Society. ★★★.

Huang Po. *The Zen Teaching of Huang Po*. Translated by John Blofeld. New York, 1959: Grove Press. ★★★.

Hughson, S. C. *Contemplative Prayer*. West Park, N.Y., 1935: Holy Cross Press. ★★.

———. *The Warfare of the Soul*. West Park, N.Y., 1942: Holy Cross Press. ★★.

Huxley, Aldous. *Heaven and Hell*. New York, 1971: Harper. ★★★.

———. *The Perennial Philosophy*. New York, 1970: Harper. ★★★.

The Hymnal of the Protestant Episcopal Church in the United States of America, 1940. New York, 1940: Church Pension Fund. ★.

Ignatius of Loyola, St. *St. Ignatius' Own Story*. As told to Luis Gonzales de Camara. Translated by William J. Young. Chicago, 1956: Regnery. ★.

The Imitation of Christ. Variously attributed to Thomas â Kempis, Tauler, and others. Whitford translation. Edited by Edward J. Klein. New York, 1941: Harper. ★★.

Inge, William R. *Christian Mysticism*. New York, 1956: Living Age (Meridian). ★★.

———. *Mysticism in Religion*. Chicago, 1948: University of Chicago Press. ★★.

————. *The Philosophy of Plotinus*. Westport, Conn., 1968: Greenwood Press. ★★.

————. *The Platonic Tradition in English Religious Thought*. Folcroft, Pa., 1977: Folcroft Library Editions. ★★.

Iyengar, B. K. *Light on Yoga*. New York, 1973: Schocken. ★★.

James, William. *The Varieties of Religious Experience*. New York, 1958: New American Library. ★★.

John of Ruysbroeck. *The Spiritual Espousals*. Translated by Eric Colledge. New York, 1953: Harper. ★★★.

————. *The Adornment of the Spiritual Marriage, The Sparkling Stone, The Book of Supreme Truth*. Translated by Dom C. S. Wynschenk. London, 1951: Watkins. ★★★.

————. *The Seven Steps of the Ladder of Spiritual Love*. Translated by F. Sherwood Taylor. London, 1944: Dacre Press. ★★★.

John of the Cross, St. *The Complete Works*. Edited by E. Allison Peers. Translated by P. Silverio de Santa Teresa. 3 vols. Westminster, Md., 1945: Newman. ★★★.

John Paul II, Pope. *Catechism of the Catholic Church*. Ignatius Press. ★★★.

————. *Celebrate 2000!*. Servant Publications. ★★.

Johnson, Raynor C. *The Imprisoned Splendour*. New York, 1953: Harper. ★★.

Julian of Norwich. *Revelations of Divine Love*. Translated by Clifton Wolters. London, 1973: Penguin. ★★★.

Jung, Carl G. *Answer to Job*. Princeton, N.J., 1972: Princeton University Press. ★★★.

————. *Psychology and Religion: West and East*. New Haven, 1938: Yale University Press. ★★★.

Keller, Helen. *My Religion*. New York, 1973: Swedenborg Foundation. ★★.

Kelly, Thomas R. *A Testament of Devotion*. New York, 1941: Harper. ★★.

Kilby, Clyde S. *Tolkien and the Silmarillion*. Wheaton, Ill., 1975: Harold Shaw Press. ★.

The Koran. Of the English translations of the Koran, that of Pickthall was considered best by a man well qualified to judge, one who had perhaps a greater stake in understanding

Islam than any non-Muslim who ever lived: Mohandas Gandhi. *The Meaning of the Glorious Koran.* (Translated by M. M. Pickthall. New York, 1953: New American Library.) ★★★.

———. Since Gandhi's death, Abdullah Yusef Ali has provided a new edition, showing the Arabic text together with English translation and commentaries: *The Holy Qur'an.* (Lahore, 1977: Sr. Muhammad Ashraf.) ★★★.

———. *The Koran Interpreted.* A. J. Arberry. London, 1955: George Allen & Unwin. ★★★.

Kreeft, Peter. *Angels and Demons. Ignatius Press.* ★★.

———. *C.S. Lewis for the Third Millennium.* Ignatius Press. ★★.

———. *Heaven: The Heart's Deepest Longing.* Ignatius Press. ★★.

Lamb, George. *Brother Nicholas.* New York, 1955: Sheed & Ward. ★.

Laotse. *The Wisdom of Laotse.* Edited and translated by Lin Yutang. New York, 1958: Random House. ★★★.

———. See also Tao Te Ching.

Lecaro, Cardinal. *Methods of Mental Prayer.* London, 1957: Burns Oates. ★★★.

Lewis, C. S. *The Abolition of Man.* New York, 1972: Macmillan. ★.

———. *The Chronicles of Narnia.* 7 vols. New York, 1950: Macmillan. ★.

———. *The Discarded Image.* Cambridge University Press. ★★.

———. *The Four Loves.* Harcourt Brace. ★★.

———. *George MacDonald: An Anthology.* New York, 1987: Macmillan. ★★.

———. *God in the Dock: Essays on Theology and Ethics.* Grand Rapids, Mich., 1989: Eerdmans. ★★.

———. *The Great Divorce.* New York, 1973: Macmillan. ★.

———. *Mere Christianity.* New York, 1973: Macmillan. ★★.

———. *Miracles.* New York, 1973: Macmillan. ★★.

———. *Out of the Silent Planet.* New York, 1965: Macmillan. ★.

———. *Perelandra.* New York, 1973: Macmillan. ★.

———. *The Screwtape Letters.* New York, 1961: Macmillan. ★.

———. *Surprised by Joy.* Harcourt Brace. ★.

———. *That Hideous Strength.* New York, 1973: Macmillan. ★.

———. *Till We Have Faces.* Grand Rapids, Mich., 1974: Eerdmans. ★.

————. See also Peter Kreeft, A.N. Wilson.

The Life of Mary as Seen by the Mystics. Compiled by Raphael Brown. Rockford, Ill.: TAN. ★★.

Lin Yutang. *The Wisdom of China and India.* New York, 1942: Random House. ★★★.

Lings, Martin. *Mohammad.* Rochester, Vt., 1983: Inner Traditions. ★★.

Lu K'uan Yu. *The Secrets of Chinese Meditation.* Samuel Weiser. ★★★.

————. *Taoist Yoga.* Samuel Weiser. ★★★.

The Little Flowers of St. Francis. Translated by Raphael Brown. New York, 1958: Doubleday. ★.

MacDonald, George. *At the Back of the North Wind.* New York, 1989: Words of Wonder. ★.

————. *The Gifts of the Child Christ.* 2 vols. Grand Rapids, Mich., 1973: Eerdmans. ★.

————. *Phantastes* and *Lilith.* With an introduction by C. S. Lewis. Grand Rapids, Mich., 1964: Eerdmans. ★★.

————. *The Princess and Curdie.* New York, 1973: Penguin. ★.

————. *The Princess and the Goblin.* New York, 1973: Penguin. ★.

Machen, Arthur. *Tales of Horror and the Supernatural.* New York, 1948: Knopf. ★★.

Maharshi, Ramana. *The Collected Works of Maharshi.* Translated by Arthur Osborne. New York, 1972: Weiser. ★★.

————. *The Spiritual Teaching of Ramana Maharshi.* With an introduction by Carl G. Jung. Berkeley, Calif., 1972: Shambhala. ★★.

————. See also Arthur Osborne.

Maritain, Jacques. *Approaches to God.* New York, 1954: Harper. ★★.

————. *Saint Thomas and the Problem of Evil.* Milwaukee, 1942: Marquette University Press. ★★.

————. *Three Reformers: Luther, Descartes, Rousseau.* New York, 1970: Apollo. ★★.

Martin, Malachi. *The Decline and Fall of the Roman Church.* New York, 1981: Putnam. ★.

————. *Hostage to the Devil.* New York, 1979: Harper. ★.

————. *The Jesuits.* New York, 1987: Simon & Schuster. ★★.

————. *Rich Church, Poor Church.* New York, 1984: Putnam. ★.

———. *Vatican.* New York, 1986: Harper. ★.

Martin, P.W. *Experiment in Depth.* Boston, 1955: Routledge and Kegan Paul. ★★.

Mary of Agreda. *City of God.* 4 vols. Washington, N.J., 1971: Ave Maria Institute. ★★.

The Mathnawi of Jalálu'ddin Rumi. Edited and translated by Reynold A. Nicholson. London, 1926: Luyac. ★★★.

Mead, G.R.S. *Thrice Greatest Hermes.* A translation of the extant sermons and fragments of the Trismegistic literature. 3 volumes. London, 1949: Watkins. ★★★.

Merton, Thomas. *The Seven Storey Mountain.* New York, 1948: Doubleday. ★.

Miller, Basil. *George Muller: Man of Faith and Miracles.* Minneapolis, 1981: Bethany Fellowship. ★.

Mowrer, O. Hobart. *The Crisis in Psychiatry and Religion.* Princeton, 1961: Van Nostrand. ★★.

Muck, Otto. *The Secret of Atlantis.* New York: Times Books. ★★.

Muggeridge, Malcolm. *Something Beautiful for God.* San Francisco: Harper San Francisco. ★.

The Mysteries. Papers from the Eranos Yearbooks. Edited by Joseph Campbell. New York, 1955: Pantheon. ★★★.

Nicoll, Maurice. *Living Time.* Boston, 1984: Shambhala. ★★.

———. *The Mark.* Boston, 1987: Shambhala. ★★.

———. *The New Man.* New York, 1972: Penguin. ★★.

———. *Psychological Commentaries on the Teachings of Gurdjieff and Ouspensky.* 6 vols. Samuel Weiser. ★★★.

Nigg, Walter. *The Heretics.* New York, 1979: Knopf. ★.

———. *Warriors of God.* New York, 1972: Knopf. ★.

O'Brien, John A. *The Faith of Millions.* Huntington, Ind., 1974: Our Sunday Visitor. ★.

Osborne, Arthur. *The Incredible Sai Baba.* New York, 1972: Weiser. ★.

———. *Ramana Maharshi and the Path to Self-Knowledge.* New York, 1954: Weiser. ★★★.

———. *The Teachings of Ramana Maharshi.* New York, 1971: Weiser. ★★★.

Ouspensky, P.D. *The Fourth Way.* New York, 1971: Random House. ★★.

————. *In Search of the Miraculous.* New York, 1971: Harcourt, Brace, and World. ★★★.

————. *A New Model of the Universe.* New York, 1971: Random House. ★★★.

————. *The Psychology of Man's Possible Evolution.* New York, 1974: Random House. ★★.

————. *The Strange Life of Ivan Osokin.* New York, 1973: Penguin. ★★.

————. *Tertium Organum.* New York, 1970: Random House. ★★★.

Paracelsus. *Paracelsus: Selected Writings.* Edited by Jolande Jacobi. London, 1951: Routledge & Kegan Paul. ★★★.

————. See also Franz Hartmann.

Pardue, Austin. *Create and Make New.* New York, 1952: Harper. ★.

————. *Prayer Works.* New York, 1950: Morehouse-Gorham. ★.

Pascal, Blaise. *Thoughts: An Apology for Christianity.* Edited by Thomas S. Kepler. Cleveland, 1955: World. ★★.

————. *Pensées.* Translated by A. J. Krailsheimer. London, 1966: Penguin. ★★.

For study and interpretation:

————. *The Clue to Pascal.* By Emile Cailliet. Philadelphia, 1943: Westminster. ★★.

Patanjali. *How to Know God: The Yoga Aphorisms of Patanjali.* Translated by Prabhavananda and Isherwood. Hollywood, Calif., 1953: Vedanta Press. ★★★.

Phillips, D.B. *The Choice Is Always Ours.* Riudge, N.H., 1954: Richard H. Smith. ★★.

Philo. *Works.* 11 vols. Cambridge, Mass.: Harvard University Press. Loeb Classical Library. ★★★.

The Philokalia. *Writings from the Philokalia on Prayer of the Heart.* Translated by Kadloubovsky and Palmer. London, 1951: Faber & Faber. ★★★.

————. *Early Fathers from the Philokalia.* Translated by Kadloubovsky and Palmer. London, 1954: Faber & Faber. ★★★.

The Pilgrim. *The Way of a Pilgrim.* Translated by R. M. French. Harper San Francisco. ★.

Plato. *The Dialogues of Plato.* Translated by Benjamin Jowett. New York, 1953: Oxford. ★★★.

Plotinus. *The Enneads.* Translated by Stephen MacKenna. London, 1969: Faber & Faber. ★★★.

———. *The System of Plotinus.* By the editors of the "Shrine of Wisdom." London, 1924: Shrine of Wisdom. ★★★.

Poulain, A. *The Graces of Interior Prayer.* Translated by Lenora L. Yorke Smith. St. Louis, 1950: Herder. ★★★.

The Practice of the Presence of God. See Brother Lawrence.

Progoff, Ira. *The Death and Rebirth of Psychology.* New York, 1956: Julian Press. ★★.

Pythagoras. *The Golden Verses of Pythagoras.* Translated by Fabre d'Olivet. New York, 1975: Weiser. ★★.

The Quest of the Holy Grail. Translated by Pauline Matarasso. Harmondsworth, Middlesex, 1969: Penguin. ★★.

Radhakrishnan, S. *History of Philosophy, Eastern and Western.* 2 vols. London, 1952: George Allen & Unwin. ★★★.

———. *Recovery of Faith.* New York, 1955: Harper. ★★.

Ramakrishna, Sri. *The Gospel of Sri Ramakrishna.* By M. Translated by Swami Nikhilananda. New York, 1969: Ramakrishna-Vivekananda Center. ★★.

———. *Words of the Master.* Compiled by Swami Brahmananda. Calcutta, 1951: Udbodhan Office. ★★.

Ramayana. A telling of the story of the Ramayana in simple English prose, by Mrs. Shudha Mazumdar. Bombay, 1953: Gita Press. ★★★.

Read, David H. C. *The Christian Faith.* New York, 1956: Scribner. ★.

Reinhold, H. A. *The Soul Afire.* New York, 1944: Pantheon. ★★.

Richard of Saint-Victor. *Selected Writings on Contemplation.* New York: Harper. ★★★.

Robertson, A.T. *A Harmony of the Gospels.* New York, 1950: Harper. ★★★.

Rolle, Richard. *The Fire of Love.* New York, 1971: Penguin. ★★★.

Rosten, Leo. *A Guide to the Religions of America.* New York, 1955: Simon & Schuster. ★★.

Ruffin, C. Bernard. *Padre Pio: The True Story.* Our Sunday Visitor Press. ★★.

Sacred Sex. Edited by Thomas R. White. Hankins, N.Y., 1975: East

Ridge Press. ★★.

Schaer, Hans. *Religion and the Cure of Souls in Jung's Psychology.* New York, 1950: Pantheon. ★★★.

Scheffler, Johannes (Angelus Silesius). *The Cherubic Wanderer.* Translated by Willard R. Trask. New York, 1953: Pantheon. ★★.

Schimberg, Albert P. *The Story of Therese Neumann.* Folcroft, Pa., 1937: Folcroft. ★★.

Schmoger, The Very Rev. K. E. *The Life of Anna Catharina Emmerich.* Fresno, Calif., 1968: Maria Regina Guild. ★★.

Scholem, Gershom. *Major Trends in Jewish Mysticism.* New York, 1961: Schocken. ★★★.

Schroeder, Eric. *Muhammad's People.* Salt Lake City, 1955: Wheelright. ★★.

Schuon, Frithjof. *The Transcendent Unity of Religions.* New York, 1953: Pantheon. ★★★.

———. *Understanding Islam.* New York, 1972: Penguin. ★★★.

Schweitzer, Albert. *The World of Albert Schweitzer.* By Erica Anderson and Eugene Exman. New York, 1955: Harper. ★.

Scupoli, Lorenzo. *Unseen Warfare.* (*The Spiritual Combat* and *Path to Paradise* edited by Nicodemus of the Holy Mountain and revised by Theophan the Recluse.) Translated by Kadloubovsky and Palmer. Crestwood, N.Y., 1978: St. Vladimir's Seminary Press. ★★★.

Shankara. *The Crest-Jewel of Discrimination.* Translated by Prabhavananda and Isherwood. Hollywood, Calif., 1978: Vedanta Press. ★★★.

Sheean, Vincent. *Lead, Kindly Light.* New York, 1949: Random House. ★★.

Sheed, F.J. *Theology and Sanity.* New York, 1946: Sheed and Ward. ★★.

Shestov, Lev. *Athens and Jerusalem.* Translated and with an introduction by Bernard Martin. Athens, Ohio, 1966: Ohio University Press. ★★★.

Smith, Margaret. *Readings from the Mystics of Islam.* London, 1959: Luzac. ★★.

———. *The Way of the Mystics: The Early Christian Mystics and the Rise of the Sufis.* New York, 1978: Oxford. ★★.

Sorokin, Pitirim. *The American Sex Revolution.* New York, 1960:

Dutton. ★★.

———. *The Crisis of Our Age.* New York, 1957: Dutton. ★★.

———. *Forms and Techniques of Altruistic and Spiritual Growth.* Millwood, N.Y., 1954: Kraus Reprint Company. ★★★.

———. *The Ways and Power of Love.* Boston, 1954: Beacon. ★★.

Stevenson, Robert L. *Dr. Jekyll and Mr. Hyde.* New York, 1972: Dutton. ★★.

Strehlow, Dr. Wighard and Dr. Gottfried Hertzka. *Hildegard of Bingen's Medicine.* Bear & Co. ★★.

Strong, James. *Strong's Exhaustive Concordance of the Bible.* Hendrickson. ★★★.

Suso, Henry. *The Life of the Servant.* Translated by James M. Clarke. London, 1952: James M. Clarke & Co. ★★.

Suter, John Wallace, Jr. *The Book of English Collects.* New York, 1940: Harper. ★★.

Suzuki, D. T. *The Essence of Buddhism.* London, 1947: Buddhist Society. ★★★.

———. *Introduction to Zen Buddhism.* New York, 1964: Grove. ★★★.

———. *Manual of Zen Buddhism.* New York, 1960: Grove. ★★★.

———. *Mysticism: Christian and Buddhist.* New York, 1957: Macmillan. ★★★.

———. *Outlines of Mahayana Buddhism.* New York, 1963: Schocken. ★★★.

Szasz, Thomas. *The Myth of Mental Illness.* New York, 1974: Harper. ★.

Tanquerey, Adolphe. *The Spiritual Life.* New York, 1960: Desclee & Co. ★★★.

Tao Te Ching. (The Book of Tao.) By Lao Tse. *The Way and Its Power.* By Arthur Waley. London, 1943: George Allen & Unwin. ★★★.

———. *The Way of Life, Lao Tzu.* By R. B. Blakney. New York, 1955: New American Library. ★★★.

For study and interpretation:

———. *The Parting of the Way.* By Holmes Welch. Boston, 1957: Beacon. ★★★.

———. See also Laotse.

Tauler, John. *The Life and History of the Reverend Doctor John*

Tauler of Strasbourg: with Twenty-five of His Sermons. Translated by Susanna Winkworth. New York: Eaton & Mains. ★★.

Teresa of Avila, St. *Complete Works.* Edited by E. Allison Peers. 3 vols. New York, 1973: Doubleday. ★★★.

————. *The Life of Teresa of Jesus: The Autobiography of St. Teresa of Avila.* Translated by E. Allison Peers. New York, 1973: Doubleday. ★★★.

————. See also William Thomas Walsh.

Tertius. *The Chronicles of Brother Wolf.* City of Oxford, 1952: Mowbray. ★.

Theologia Germanica. Anonymous. Translated by Susanna Winkworth, revised according to the Bernhart version. Introduction by Joseph Bernhart. New York, 1949: Pantheon. ★★.

Thérèse of Lisieux, St. *The Autobiography of St. Thérèse of Lisieux: The Story of a Soul.* Translated by John Beevers. New York, 1957: Doubleday. ★★.

————. See also John Beevers; Guy Gaucher.

Tolkien, J. R. R. *The Hobbit.* New York, 1974: Ballantine. ★.

————. The Lord of the Rings Trilogy. *(The Fellowship of the Ring; The Two Towers; The Return of the King.)* New York, 1965: Ballantine. ★.

————. *The Silmarillion.* Boston, 1977: Houghton Mifflin. ★★.

————. See also Clyde S. Kilby.

Tolstoy, Leo. *What Men Live By.* New York: Peter Pauper Press. ★.

————. *Why Do Men Stupefy Themselves?* Hankins, N.Y., 1975: East Ridge Press. ★★.

The Torah. Philadelphia, 1962: Jewish Publication Society. ★★★.

Toynbee, Arnold. *A Study of History.* 12 vols. New York, 1954: Oxford. ★★★.

Traherne, Thomas. *Centuries.* Milton, Conn.: Morehouse Publishing. ★★★.

Trochu, Francis. *The Curé d'Ars.* Rockford, Ill., 1977: TAN. ★.

Twain, Mark. *Personal Recollections of Joan of Arc.* Hartford, Conn., 1980: The Stowe-Day Foundation. ★.

Underhill, Evelyn. *Mysticism.* New York: Dutton. ★★★.

————. *The Spiritual Life.* New York, 1936: Harper. ★★.

Upanishads. *The Principal Upanishads.* Translated and with commentary by S. Radhakrishnan. New York, 1953: Harper. ★★★.

―――. *The Ten Principal Upanishads.* Translated by Shree Purohit Swami and W. B. Yeats. London, 1938: Faber. ★★★.

―――. *The Thirteen Principal Upanishads.* Translated by R. E. Hume. London, 1931: Oxford. ★★★.

―――. *The Upanishads.* Translated and with commentary by Swami Nikhilananda. 3 vols. New York, 1956: Harper. ★★★.

―――. *The Upanishads, Breath of the Eternal.* Translated by Prabhavananda and Manchester. Hollywood, 1947: Vedanta Press. ★★★.

For interpretation and study:

―――. *Brahma-Sutras.* Translated and with commentary by Swami Vireswarananda. Mayvati, Almore, 1948: Advaita Ashrama. ★★★.

―――. *Self-Knowledge.* By Shankaracharya. Translated and with commentary by Swami Nikhilananda. New York, 1946: Ramakrishna-Vivekananda Center. ★★★.

Van Paassen, Pierre. *Visions Rise and Change.* New York, 1955: Dial. ★★.

Vedanta for the Western World. Edited by Christopher Isherwood. Hollywood, Calif., 1978: Vedanta Press. ★★.

Vett, Carl. *Dervish Diary.* Los Angeles, 1953: Knud K. Mogensen. ★★.

Vogl, Adalbert Albert. *Therese Neumann: Mystic and Stigmatist.* Rockford, Ill.: TAN. ★★.

Voss, Carl Herman. *The Universal God.* Cleveland, 1953: World. ★★.

Waite, A. E. *The Hidden Church of the Holy Graal.* London, 1909: Rebman. ★★★.

―――. *Lamps of Western Mysticism.* New York, 1923: Knopf. ★★★.

―――. *The Secret Doctrine in Israel.* New York: Occult Research Press. ★★.

―――. *The Secret Tradition in Alchemy.* New York, 1926: Knopf. ★★★.

Walsh, William Thomas. *Our Lady of Fatima.* New York, 1954: Doubleday. ★.

―――. *Saint Teresa of Avila.* Rockford, Ill., 1987: TAN. ★★.

Watts, Alan. *The Supreme Identity.* New York, 1972: Random

House. ★★★.

———. *The Way of Zen.* New York, 1974: Random House. ★★★.

The Way to Higher Consciousness. Edited by Meredith Murray. Hankins, N.Y., 1975: East Ridge Press. ★★.

Weatherhead, Leslie. *The Will of God.* Nashville, Tenn., 1975: Abingdon. ★.

West, John Anthony. *Serpent in the Sky: The Higher Wisdom of Ancient Egypt.* New York, 1979: Harper. ★★.

Wilhelm, Richard. *The Secret of the Golden Flower.* With commentary by C. G. Jung. New York, 1962: Harcourt, Brace, & World. ★★★.

———. *The I Ching.* Rendered into English by Cary F. Baynes. 2 vols. New York, 1950: Pantheon. ★★★.

William of St. Thierry. *On Contemplating God.* London, 1955: Mowbray.

Williams, Charles. *All Hallow's Eve.* New York, 1969: Avon. ★★.

———. *Descent into Hell.* Grand Rapids, Mich., 1973: Eerdmans. ★★.

———. *The Greater Trumps.* New York, 1969: Avon. ★★.

———. *Many Dimensions.* Grand Rapids, Mich., 1970: Eerdmans. ★★.

———. *The Place of the Lion.* Grand Rapids, Mich., 1973: Eerdmans. ★★.

———. *Shadows of Ecstasy.* Grand Rapids, Mich., 1973: Eerdmans. ★★.

———. *War in Heaven.* Grand Rapids, Mich., 1972: Eerdmans. ★★.

Wilson, A.N. *C.S. Lewis: A Biography.* New York: Ballantine. ★.

A Woman Clothed with the Sun. Edited by John J. Delaney. New York: Doubleday. ★.

The World's Great Religions. By the editors of *Life.* New York, 1957: Time Inc. ★★.

Wyszynski, Stefan Cardinal. *All You Who Labor.* Sophia Institute Press. ★★.

Zimmer, Heinrich. *Philosophies of India.* New York, 1951: Pantheon. ★★★.

The Zohar. *Zohar, the Book of Splendor* (selections). Edited by Gershom Scholem. New York, 1949: Schocken. ★★★.

———. *The Zohar* (the whole work). 5 vols. Translated by Sperling and Simon. London, 1949: Soncino Press. ★★★.

Special Book Listings

The following books are grouped according to the special purposes to which they are related; note text page references.

These groups of books do not constitute a suggested schedule or diet of reading; taken as such they might produce indigestion. Each group, rather, is a kind of book cafeteria from which you can select what suits your appetite. You are responsible for your own diet. Titles representing widely different viewpoints are included — orthodox and unorthodox, Western and Eastern, ancient and modern. This broad scope is indicated because of the variety of the spiritual needs of individuals today. It is assumed that from the cafeteria offering you will choose such books as may meet your particular requirements. It is assumed further that you will not confuse yourself with incompatible mixtures but will simply pass over books which do not fit your background, are out of phase with your spiritual orientation, or are outside the range of your present interests.

BOOKS RELEVANT TO THE WAY OF REASON
See pages 45-53.

Two books, one Protestant and one Catholic, are suggested as bridge books between philosophy and the more specifically theological viewpoints. The first is Elton Trueblood's *Philosophy of Religion*, an excellent outline and examination of the possibilities and difficulties of thinking one's way toward the reality of God.

The second is the beautifully disciplined and boiled-down study entitled *Approaches to God* by the great Catholic scholar Jacques Maritain. This little book covers the various philosophical approaches to God, with major emphasis naturally on a philosophy which is fundamental in Catholicism, that of St. Thomas Aquinas. If one wishes to take a deeper look in this area he can do so in *The Christian Philosophy of St. Thomas Aquinas* and in the *History of Christian Philosophy in the Middle Ages*, both by Etienne Gilson.

There are lots of kinds of theology, and we will put off some of them to another place: ascetical and mystical theology, for example, deal more with spiritual experience and with knowing and keeping the rules than with reasoning. But anyone who hopes to keep his own thinking about God on the track should get acquainted with at least the main outlines of formal theology.

An easy and interesting book of basic Catholic theology is F. J. Sheed's *Theology and Sanity*. A deeper book, bearing directly upon the question of God's reality, is *God: His Existence and His Nature* by the Dominican theologian Father Reginald Garrigou-Lagrange, a thorough exposition of the traditional proofs of God's existence and the knowledge of God's nature and attributes from the Catholic point of view. A Protestant theology is ably presented in Reinhold Niebuhr's famous book *The Nature and Destiny of Man*. Another outstanding Protestant theologian, Paul Tillich, in his *Systematic Theology* goes extensively into the question of the reality of God and discusses fully the place of reason in the quest of that reality. An Anglican exposition of sacred doctrine is provided in *Theological Outlines* by Francis J. Hall, a condensation of Professor Hall's classic ten-volume work.

An approach to God sometimes called "natural theology" develops out of the questions "Is there evidence in nature and in natural science for the existence of God? Can we see God in nature?" Gerald Heard presents a contemporary essay in natural theology in *Is God Evident?* Other books in this area are *Human Destiny* by Lecomte Du Nouy, *Man Does Not Stand Alone* by A. Cressy Morrison, and *The Imprisoned Splendour* by Raynor Johnson, particularly Part 1, entitled "The Data of Natural Science."

Reason may be used to seek evidence of God not only in nature and in science but also in history (a very important pursuit for Christians, whose religion is particularly historical). Gerald Heard follows this line of inquiry in *Is God in History?* See further *A Study of History* by Arnold J. Toynbee, *The End of the Modern World* by the Roman Catholic philosopher and theologian Romano Guardini, and *The Crisis of Our Age* by Pitirim A. Sorokin. Note also *The Dignity of Man*, an inquiry into the historic spiritual crisis of modern man by a former editor of *Fortune* magazine, the late Russell W. Davenport.

Finally, for those who wish to explore the nature of the divine Reality and man's place in it with an Eastern mind of universality, brilliance, and depth, *The Life Divine* by Sri Aurobindo is suggested.

BOOKS RELEVANT TO THE WAY OF FAITH
See pages 53-58

One of the most helpful of all books on faith is still Harry Emerson Fosdick's well-known and well-loved *The Meaning of Faith*. Arranged for daily reading over a twelve-week period, it covers the ground thoroughly from practical, inspirational, and rational viewpoints. The problem of faith and its renewal in the present human situation is explored on a world-wide scale by Sarvepalli Radhakrishnan in *Recovery of Faith*, a sharp pointing up of man's need for faith and the ways to its acquisition as taught and demonstrated in the great living faiths of Hinduism, Taoism, Judaism, Christianity, and others.

Faith, the spiritual reality, has a basic common meaning in all religions. But, in addition, "faith" as a system of belief or consent has different meanings in different religions, and you should make your choice of books with this condition in mind. For a Roman Catholic, for instance (as for the great majority of Christians of the past and present), faith is "a theological virtue by which our intellect is disposed to assent firmly to all the truths revealed by God . . ."* and also "a habit of mind by which eternal life is begun in us, in that it makes the mind assent to things which appear not . . ." (St. Thomas Aquinas' comment on St. Paul's statement that "faith is the substance of things to be hoped for, the evidence of things that appear not"†). So far the Catholic and

---

* *A Catholic Dictionary*, p.196.
† *Ibid.*

many other Christians could agree. But to the Catholic, "faith" also means "the sum of the truth taught by the Catholic religion." And "Catholic" here evidently means not simply "universal" and not Anglican and Eastern Orthodox and others who call themselves "Catholic" but specifically "Roman Catholic." "Faith," therefore, to a Roman Catholic, is belief in what the Roman Catholic Church teaches. *The* faith, in this view, *is* Roman Catholicism. For a succinct yet comprehensive presentation of what the Roman Catholic faith is, in both its general and its more particular sense, see *A Catholic Dictionary*. See also *The Faith of Millions* by Reverend John A. O'Brien.

To certain Evangelical Christian groups, "faith" means belief in the literal words of the Bible, literally understood. To Anglican and Eastern Orthodox Catholics, and to Protestants of various denominations likewise, "faith" has different and particular meanings in addition to its universal meaning of belief and trust in God.

There is a further particularity in which the word "faith" distinguishes a large part of Christianity from the rest of the God-seeking world: many Christian groups accept Jesus of Nazareth as the Messiah, the only Son of God, and the one incarnation of God. Other great world religious faiths — Judaism, Hinduism, Islam, and Buddhism, for example — do not share this viewpoint. So faith, as creedal or formal belief, has different meanings not only within Christianity but within the world-wide body of all those who believe in and seek to know the Supreme Reality.

The different shades of belief among the various Protestant denominations and other religions are described in the literature of each group, which is far too large for a listing to be attempted here. You can easily find the works you are interested in by contacting a minister, priest, or rabbi of the particular group whose faith you are studying. Among survey books in this area are *A Guide to the Religions of America,* edited by Leo Rosten, *Religion in the Twentieth Century* by Vergilius Ferm, and *The World's Great Religions* by the editors of *Life* magazine.

The following books, dealing with the faith from a broad Christian point of view, are by Protestant authors, but they treat the subject without provoking Protestant interdenominational issues or raising the Protestant-Catholic question: *Mere Christianity* by C. S. Lewis and *The Christian Faith* by David H. C. Read.

Finally, a particular modern view needs special attention. A movement of religious-psychological thought and practice has grown up around the fact that faith can produce increase in mental and physical well-being and success in daily undertakings and practical affairs. In this movement faith is emphasized as a means to some or all of these ends. Christian texts, such as Mark 11:24, are quoted in support of this view. Faith is cultivated by prayer, by optimistic attitudes ("positive thinking"), by disciplined affirmation of good and denials of evil, and by keeping watch over the mind so that desired thoughts are retained and undesired thoughts are rejected. In brief, this movement believes and demonstrates that man, by religious and psychological techniques, can influence his mind and outer circumstances for good. The movement can trace its origins to the work of Ralph Waldo Emerson, Phineas Parkhurst Quimby, and Thomas Troward.

It is recognized that certain of the groups within the pattern would not acknowledge their inclusion in any such over-all designation as a movement. The common denominators, however, are apparent. The term "movement" is used here for the sake of brevity, clarity, and convenience and not with any intention of grouping bodies which do not wish to be so grouped. The chief division within the movement are those which are known as New Thought Christian Science, Mental Science, Metaphysics, and the Unity School of Christianity. Many individuals who share the movement's views are not associated with these divisions but are members of regular Christian denominations. Dr. Peale, for example, one of the most influential spokesmen of the movement, is a minister of the Dutch Reformed Church.

These particular techniques in the application of faith, or "mental science," or "divine science" to the human problems of health and supply have become widely popular, especially in the United States. Obviously they fill a deeply felt need and often are genuinely effective. In some quarters, however, they have been regarded as serious distortions of the religious and psychological facts of life. A great contribution of these doctrines lies in their ability to correct and relieve people who are suffering from unfounded and obsessive pessimism. Difficulties arise, however, from the fact that when the teaching is not applied with understanding and discrimination, it tends to produce unfounded and obsessive optimism.

BOOKS RELEVANT TO THE WAY OF EXPERIENCE
See pages 58-73

There are many books which describe in detail the traditional three ways to God (purgation, illumination, union). Among the best of these are Evelyn Underhill's *Mysticism** and Father Garrigou-Lagrange's *The Three Ages of the Interior Life.* The follow-

---

* "Mysticism" is another one of those hot terms. It is a very old and universal concept, and no one studying empirical knowledge of God can afford to misunderstand it. Mysticism means experience of God. But the word has become muddled almost beyond recognition as our knowledge and valuation of spiritual experience have degenerated. Evelyn Underhill's book by that name is an excellent exposition of what mysticism really is. So also are the articles entitled "Mysticism" in the Encyclopaedia Britannica and in the Columbia Encyclopedia. At least look up and read these articles, so the next time you hear someone talking or writing as if a mystic were somebody with a crystal ball and a dunce cap you will be able to determine on whose head the dunce cap really belongs. See further *Mysticism in Religion* and *Christian Mysticism* by W. R. Inge.

Mysticism lies at the root of all religion. Aldous Huxley, in his introduction to the Bhagavad Gita, has written: "From this fact [that mystical knowledge is superior to the devotional practices which lead up to it] have arisen misunderstandings in plenty and a number of intellectual difficulties. Here, for example, is what Abbot John Chapman writes in one of his admirable *Spiritual Letters*: 'The problem of *reconciling* (not merely uniting) mysticism with Christianity is more difficult. The Abbot (Abbot Marmion) says that St. John of the Cross is like a sponge full of Christianity. You can squeeze it all out, and the full mystical theory remains. Consequently for fifteen years or so I hated St. John of the Cross and called him a Buddhist. I loved St. Teresa, and read her over and over again. She is first a Christian, and only secondarily a mystic. Then I found I had wasted fifteen years, so far as prayer was concerned.' And yet, he concludes, in spite of its 'Buddhistic' character, the practice of mysticism (or, to put it in other terms, the realization of the Perennial Philosophy) makes good Christians. He might have added that it also makes good Hindus, good Buddhists, good Taoists, good Moslems and good Jews."

ing books about the experience of God as reported in terms of the Western traditions are also suggested: *The Dialogues of Plato* (these works are usually read for their literary and philosophic interest, but actually they are full of references to experience of higher Reality; note particularly *The Republic,* Book VII, the story of the prisoners in the cave; *The Mysteries,* edited by Joseph Campbell (the Greek, Egyptian, and other mysteries were techniques for introducing their subjects into direct experience of spiritual Reality; note particularly "The Meaning of the Eleusinian Mysteries," pages 23, 24, 29, 30); *The Enneads of Plotinus* (writings of one who experienced God directly* and whose views deeply influenced Christian thought for many centuries).

Outstanding books by or about Western saints and mystics include: *The Confessions of St. Augustine; St. Francis of Assisi,* by G. K. Chesterton; *The Little Flowers of St. Francis of Assisi; The Treatise on Purgatory and the Dialogue* of St. Catherine of Genoa; *The Complete Works of St. Teresa of Jesus,* particularly in Vol. I, the *Life; The Life of the Servant,* an autobiography by Henry Suso; *St. Ignatius' Own Story,* a short, direct biography of St. Ignatius of Loyola; *Brother Nicholas,* a biography of Nicholas of Flüe, "Bruder Klaus," by George Lamb; *The Curé d'Ars,* a biography of an amazing man, the patron saint of priests, by Abbe Francis Trochu; *Storm of Glory* by John Beevers, the story of St. Thérèse of Lisieux; *The Life and Doctrines of Jacob Boehme* by Franz Hartmann.

The Miracle of Lourdes by Ruth Cranston and *The Voyage to Lourdes* by Alexis Carrel are books which touch upon special aspects of spiritual experience: charismatic healing, the apparition of persons in a supernatural state to human beings, unaccountable physical phenomena or miracles, stigmatization, and so on. Note also: *Miracles* by C. S. Lewis, *The Physical Phenomena of Mysticism* by Herbert Thurston, S.J., *The Story of Therese Neumann* (the life of a contemporary stigmatist) by A. P. Schimberg, and *Our Lady of Fatima* (an account of the appearance of "a Lady made wholly of

---

* "Four times, during the period I passed with him, he achieved this Term, by no latent fitness but by the ineffable Act. To this God, I also declare, I Porphyry, that in my sixty-eighth year I too was once admitted and entered into Union" (*Enneads,* Vol. 1, p. 24).

light" to three Portuguese shepherd children and the unaccountable solar phenomena witnessed by 70,000 people) by W. T. Walsh.

Experiment in Depth by P. W. Martin is a good introduction to spiritual experience from the standpoint of modern depth psychology, particularly the psychology of C. G. Jung. Freud's psychology basically is materialistic, mechanistic, and atheistic, and so he and his followers are bound by their most fundamental hypotheses not to understand spiritual experience as spiritual experience but rather as illness, superstition, or illusion (see *The Future of an Illusion* by Freud). Jung, on the other hand, is genuinely and profoundly open to and interested in the reality of religious and spiritual experience. See *Psychology and Religion: West and East* by C. G. Jung. For a criticism of Jung's religious views see *Eclipse of God* by Martin Buber (pp. 78-92 and 133-137).

Two modern survey books which cover the field of spiritual experience very thoroughly are *The Ways and Power of Love* and *Forms and Techniques of Altruistic and Spiritual Growth* by Pitirim A. Sorokin.

Insight into spiritual experience may be gained by exposing oneself to the witness of contemporaries who have had such experience. Four books by widely different modern witnesses are suggested: *The Seven Storey Mountain* by Thomas Merton, a young man who became a Trappist monk and priest; *You Are Greater Than You Know* by Lou Austin, a businessman who discovered he had a Partner; *Alcoholics Anonymous Comes of Age* by "Bill," the anonymous co-founder whose spiritual experience has led to the recovery of two million alcoholics; and *Release* by Starr Daily, the incorrigible criminal who was visited by Christ in prison and taught the way of freedom.

Anthologies offer a very practical and enjoyable way to study spiritual experience. The following are suggested: *The Perennial Philosophy* by Aldous Huxley, *The Choice Is Always Ours* by Dorothy Berkeley Phillips, *A Year of Grace* and *From Darkness to Light* by Victor Gollancz, and *The Soul Afire* by H. A. Reinhold.

Of special interest to the world of today is the spiritual experience of the Russian people. For a historical survey, including many writings and accounts of the lives of Russian theocentric saints, see *A Treasury of Russian Spirituality* edited by G. P.

Fedotov (note particularly the conversation of St. Seraphim of Sarov with Nicholas Motovilov, pp. 266-279, an interesting example of a theophany transmitted to one man by the power of another, an ability which Sri Ramakrishna also possessed). For an inquiry into the spiritual life of present-day Russia see *Visions Rise and Change* by Pierre Van Paassen.

The Eastern traditions of direct experience of God have much of interest, wisdom, and help to offer the seeker, whatever his religion. The literature of these traditions is very large. The following books would provide a rudimentary introduction to this great area of empirical knowledge: *How to Know God: The Yoga Aphorisms of Patanjali* translated by Prabhavananda and Isherwood; *The Gospel of Sri Ramakrishna* translated by Swami Nikhilananda; *The Essence of Buddhism* by D. T. Suzuki; *Tibet's Great Yogi, Milarepa* edited by W. Y. Evans-Wentz; *The Secret of the Golden Flower* translated by Richard Wilhelm. (The Eastern scriptures are of course most essential for an understanding of the matter in hand and should be consulted ahead of the books indicated immediately above.) Zen Buddhism, a strictly experiential school of spiritual awakening, has aroused increasing interest in the Western world. A good introduction is *The Way of Zen* by Alan Watts. See also *Introduction to Zen Buddhism* by D. T. Suzuki.

The experimental path to God has had an interesting history in Islam. Note *Readings from the Mystics of Islam* by Margaret Smith, *The Mathnawí of Jalálu'ddín Rúmí* edited by Reynold A. Nicholson, and *Muhammad's People* by Eric Schroeder.

Jewish experience of God is set forth in the Old Testament. For later developments see *Major Trends in Jewish Mysticism* by Gershom Scholem; *Tales of the Hasidim* and *The Legend of the Baal-Shem* by Martin Buber; *God in Search of Man* by Abraham J. Heschel; and *The Zohar*.

BOOKS RELEVANT TO THE PRACTICE OF PRAYER
See pages 133-181

Useful books on prayer cover a very wide range. One must be careful not to read too many different kinds at anywhere near the same time, and not to read deep books too soon. To do so can lead to either pride or confusion or both; or it can give you a bad taste for books which, taken in right time, would be wonderfully good for you. On the other hand certain people, without vanity or gagging, are able to get help from even the deepest sources (from Meister Eckhart, for instance) quite early in their work. As you must find your own way in the Way, so you must find your own books.

The following listing is arranged in four divisions. These are necessarily somewhat arbitrary, and experts on prayer might easily rank some of the books differently. Our purpose, however, is not scholarly but strictly practical. The present grouping can serve as a rough but functional guide by which you may select books according to your present condition and need. These books are listed not chronologically but in the estimated order of their usefulness and interest to a working prayer.

BEGINNERS' BOOKS

Prayer Works by Austin Pardue. Written in the simplest of language by the Episcopal Bishop of Pittsburgh, this is an excellent primer for anyone who wants to start prayer and really work at it, without getting into complications or intellectual problems right away.

Prayer by Dr. Alexis Carrel. A simple, powerful essay on prayer by a world-famous scientist, surgeon, and physiologist, "for those of little faith or none at all" as well as for more mature Christians.

The Meaning of Prayer by Harry Emerson Fosdick. Written back in 1915, this book remains to this day one of the classic practical introductions to prayer for the ordinary person. It is simple but thorough and quite complete in covering what you need to know in the first few years of work in prayer.

The Way of a Pilgrim. Anonymous. This book is discussed elsewhere (pages 166-177). but it must be included in any list of beginners' books on prayer, because it is the only introduction in Christian terms to one of the most powerful of all methods of prayer — a method which, for all its depth, is within the range of the rankest novice.

WORKING BOOKS

A Preface to Prayer by Gerald Heard. A penetrating working inquiry into the meaning and practice of low, middle, and high prayer, by a man who has devoted a lifetime to the search for such meaning.

How to Pray by Jean-Nicolas Grou. This book consists of the chapters on prayer from Père Grou's outstanding work, *The School of Jesus Christ*. A working outline of prayer based on the view that God alone teaches to pray, including discussions of various ways of prayer and a spiritual commentary on the Lord's Prayer.

Spiritual Letters by Dom John Chapman, O.S.B. These letters, written to individuals who were involved in specific problems in prayer, are a mine of skilled and sensitive counsel, particularly in abandonment and in those phases of prayer in which "dryness" and lack of consolation are encountered. Abbot Chapman was one of the most understanding of near-contemporary directors of prayer. He taught that "the simplest kind of prayer is best" and "the more you pray the better it goes."

The Way to Christ by Jacob Boehme. The famous collection of prayers and instruction in prayer by the God-illuminated shoemaker of Goerlitz, Germany, written in the years 1622-1623 and containing six tracts as follows: "Of True Repentance," "Of True Resignation," "Of Regeneration or the New Birth," "Of the Supersensual Life," "Dialogue Between an Enlightened and Unenlightened Soul," and "Of Divine Contemplation." Boehme is not for everyone, but those who can hear him find him a very great help.

Contemplative Prayer by Shirley C. Hughson, O.H.C. "The only object [of this book] is, in a humble way, to introduce souls who desire to love God to that higher, simplified mode of prayer which St. Francis de Sales calls contemplation, and which he describes as 'no other than a loving, simple and permanent attention of the spirit to divine things.'"

The Book of *English Collects* by John Wallace Suter, Jr. The collect is a peculiarly useful and powerful form of short prayer. "Often it consists of one sentence; usually it expresses a single main thought, which is either a petition or a thanksgiving." A few favorite collects committed to memory can serve as a backlog and working resource in the life of prayer. This book is an outstanding compilation of collects from traditional sources.

The Book of Common Prayer. The Episcopal Prayer Book is listed here for both particular and general reference. It is understood, of course, that each one will find the greatest usefulness in the Prayer Book or books of his own particular denomination. Prayer books are prime aids in the study and practice of communion with God, incorporating as they do the wisdom of great bodies of praying men and women over the centuries.

ADVANCED BOOKS

Holy Wisdom by Augustine Baker. The famous book of "directions for the prayer of contemplation" written by "a monk of the English Congregation of the Holy Order of St. Benedict" who lived from 1575 to 1641. It is one of the most complete, most thorough, most respected, and most useful of all works on prayer. Although it is certainly not a beginners' book, nevertheless many beginners are able to get real help from it. As in the case of all advanced books, *Holy Wisdom* should be used judiciously and if at all possible with experienced counsel. It is among the very greatest treasures in the whole field of the work of prayer.

The Cloud of Unknowing. Anonymous. This book is discussed elsewhere (pages 162-163). It is included here as a basic, lucid, powerful, and traditionally revered guide in a difficult and critical area of the soul's ascent to direct experience of God: the passage from sensible and mental images of any and all kinds into the tremendous realm beyond the senses and beyond the mind wherein lies the "cloud" which is the last veil between man and his Lord. Since in our time it is very widely assumed that there are no realms of consciousness beyond the mind, this book establishes a point of departure for a kind of inquiry and experiment much needed today if our psychology is ever to rise out of the artificial and strangulating limits it has set for itself.

The Scale of Perfection by Walter Hilton. A gentle, charming, wise, and incisive survey of the ladder of prayer. Not much is known of Hilton beyond what his works reveal. He may have been a Carthusian monk, although it seems more probable that he was an Augustinian canon. However that may be, he "occupies a central position in the small group of English medieval mystics, being third in time of its four outstanding personalities." (The other three are Richard Rolle, Julian of Norwich, and the unknown author of *The Cloud.*)

The Graces of Interior Prayer by A. Poulain, S.J. Possibly this is the greatest work of its particular kind on prayer. It is a comprehensive, technical, detailed, meticulous, scholarly, and at the same time deeply understanding and inspired treatise on the many aspects of mystical prayer. It is exactly the kind of book which most beginners, and certainly those with any tendency toward spiritual ambition or pride, should leave strictly alone. Also it is not for anyone who is unable or unwilling to study. But for those in whom experience of God actually is developing, it may serve as an invaluable source of knowledge.

Methods of Mental Prayer by Cardinal Lecaro. Like Poulain's book listed above, this is a technical, scholarly, and in a certain sense scientific work on prayer. It is concerned with method, degree, and structure in various Roman Catholic schools of mental prayer since the sixteenth century. It includes extensive and very helpful schemata of Ignatian, Salesian, Sulpician, and Carmelite prayer and of the prayer of St. Alphonsus and St. John Baptist de le Salle. The value of such a work as this is obvious for one whose conscious contact with God has been made and is developing, and who wishes to be guided not only by inspiration but by the most careful mental and rational use of traditional resources. For anyone else the dangers and difficulties of so highly intellectualized and strictly formalized an approach are also obvious.

The Complete Works of St. Teresa of Jesus. St. Teresa (of Avila) was a person who combined tremendous experience in prayer with great insight into her own states and encounters in divine communion and with a talent for expression. She deals particularly with techniques, problems, and stages of prayer in "The Way of Perfection" and "Interior Castle," both in Vol. II of *The Complete Works*.

The Ascent of Mount Sion by Bernardino de Laredo. This was the book upon which St. Teresa of Jesus leaned for help during the most critical years of her spiritual life. It is a systematic but heart-centered guide to the union of the soul with God. Bernardino de Laredo was a Spanish physician of the sixteenth century who became a lay brother in the Franciscan order.

On Contemplating God by William of St. Thierry. A short, beautiful, and intellectually limpid treatise on the deepest love of God, by a Benedictine contemplative by whom St. Bernard was influenced. This is a first translation of a twelfth-century manuscript which is a mirror of profound simplicity in the prayer of transforming love.

Of Cleaving to God by St. Albert the Great. St. Albert for his own use made this compilation, as he calls it, from the thought of such authorities in prayer as Cassian, St. Bernard, and St. Thomas Aquinas. It is an explorer's and guide's book on prayer which pays particular attention to abandonment and clinging to God in all the circumstances of life, in and out of the set periods of prayer. Strict and demanding but uncomplicated, warm, and genial.

Letters of Spiritual Direction by Bossuet. This brief collection of letters reflects the mastery of a man so evolved and so skilled in the inner life that he expresses his insight in terms of great simplicity. Although this is certainly an advanced book, it seems to me that many beginners might be able to use it as well as those who have been working for some years. Bossuet, who was tutor to the Dauphin at the time of Louis XIV, knew the life of prayer in juxtaposition to the life of this world as few men do, and his letters show this knowledge wonderfully.

On Prayer by J. P. de Caussade, S.J. Those who are looking for the fire and joy of Père de Caussade's writings on abandonment will not find them in this book. Its usefulness lies in another direction. It is a careful, restrained, and balanced study of a question which greatly disturbed the time in which it occurred, the so-called quietist controversy. Anyone hoping to understand the prayer life of European Christianity in the past several hundred years should inform himself as to what "quietism" is (and is not) and why it became so hard an issue. Caussade's work, subtitled "spiritual instructions on the various states of prayer according to Bossuet, Bishop of Meaux," seems to me an excellent presentation of the viewpoints of those who opposed the quietists. For the viewpoints of the quietists themselves, see *The Life of Madame Guyon* by Thomas C. Upham and *The Spiritual Guide* by Michael de Molinos.

A Testament of Devotion by Thomas Kelly. This is not only a book that people who are new to prayer might find helpful; it is a beginners' book par excellence. Nevertheless I have included it here among advanced books because that is where, in my opinion it belongs. The gift of communication which enabled this beloved Quaker to convey his knowledge of God in terms nearly everyone can understand and accept should not be permitted to blind us to the height and depth of Thomas Kelly's place in the spiritual life. I believe that his book is directly comparable to *The Practice of the Presence of God* in that its beauty and its simplicity serve both to reveal and to conceal a master's experience and a master's way of prayer. Remember that most of the writings which comprise this short book represent the latter few years of Kelly's life, a period following a long time of hard work and struggle in prayer. In these years just before his death, he broke through into the singing, all-embracing, keen-seeing, seldom-interrupted love of God which is so powerfully and tenderly mediated in his *Testament*. For beginners, for old-timers, for all — here is great fare, and nothing to worry about by way of reservations, unless your heart is still so hard that the very exuberance and lyric quality of this man's song of God is unassimilable to you.

DEEP-WATER BOOKS

Enneads of Plotinus. "It is the secret of the power of Plotinus that in him the mystic's impulse to the finding of his own Soul and the scientific impulse to criticize and understand experience are so completely united" *(The System* of *Plotinus,* Shrine of Wisdom ed.). Plotinus is what Meister Eckhart would call a "heathen authority." He was a native of Egypt (born in A.D. 205) of unknown race. He had direct, personal, experimental knowledge of the ineffable and unutterable heights of communion with God, and he had real genius in communicating, so far as is possible in words, what he knew. He is both very deep and very balanced, very sane. His influence upon the history of thought, and upon Christian experience of God in the centuries following his death, is incalculable.

The Mystical Theology of Dionysius the Areopagite. (See also *The Celestial Hierarchies* and *The Divine Names.*) Here is a man writing obviously (particularly in *The Mystical Theology*) from direct experience, who stands as the fountainhead, the first and probably the greatest single influence, of the whole stream of Christian experiential knowledge of God, after the apostles and Jesus Christ himself. Again and again he probes the (to human eyes) dark and terrible threshold of God's very Being and man's experience of that Being. And he plunges beyond the level of Being into kinds of knowledge of God in which words, including the word "knowledge," simply collapse in any of their usual senses and can be used only negatively, and doubly and triply negatively. This is very far from a speculative or a semantic exercise; it is what happens to the human tongue and the human mind when they have quite literally exceeded themselves. It is what happens when God and man have entered into a relationship (which is no longer "relationship") beyond all telling. And yet something *can* be told, and Dionysius has told it in a way that has nourished and inspired Christian Godseekers, the greatest and the least, ever since. Who he was is entirely unknown. He writes obviously under a pseudonym (that of St. Dionysius, St. Paul's Athenian convert), and his work was done probably some time around the end of the fifth century.

The Philokalia. A very large compilation of writings of the Fathers and the greatest saints and mystics of the Eastern Christian Church, from the third to the fourteenth centuries. Books of extracts from *The Philokalia* are now available, as noted and discussed on page 170. This basic work is listed here because it must be considered among any essential grouping of great charts of the deepest waters of prayer. The actual experience and the inspired expression of that experience among the Eastern Christian masters is of such authenticity, clarity, and power that it cannot very well be ignored by anyone who hopes to enter these waters, or who finds himself even now, by God's leading, drawn into them.

Selected Writings of Richard of Saint-Victor. Richard is the one whom Dante described as "more than a man" in his relationship to God. He is a disciplined and profoundly experienced teacher of contemplative prayer. He is outstanding, and in his era perhaps unique, in his knowledge of the psychological aspects of deep prayer. Contemplatives of all times owe a great debt to him who first showed clearly the reasons for the infirmities and difficulties which accompany the understanding of these things. Richard often is studied from the standpoint of his influence upon later currents and schools of Christian mysticism, but our interest in him here is as a great, sound, and currently available guide in experimental knowledge of God.

On the Song of Songs by St. Bernard. The relationship of the soul to God changes (from the soul's standpoint) at various stage of the regenerate life — from that of an outcast rebel, profligate scorner — to that of a servant — to that of a friend — to that of a child — and finally, highest and most intimate of all, to that of a spouse. God as bridegroom of the soul is not merely a pious or poetic thought; it is a fiery and hair-raising truth at the very summit of the spiritual life. The recognition of this truth is universal; you will find it in the Old Testament (particularly in the Song of Songs), the New Testament, in the teaching of the Sufis, the Baal Shem Tov, John of the Cross, John of Ruysbroeck, and very widely elsewhere. Among the greatest of the traditional interpreters of this relationship is St. Bernard of Clairvaux. Nothing but confusion can come from a merely curious reading of his writings on the subject. But if you are beginning to come alive to the reality of the Supreme Person, and if you are being inwardly drawn to understand the awful mystery of his true relationship to your own soul, you may read St. Bernard *On the Song of Songs* with profit.

Before this area of knowledge can be touched with real insight, the intelligence first must have been purged of such sick notions as that which sees in mystical union a deviated or "sublimated" sexuality. The ignorant pruriency represented in such an attitude is very widespread and even naively respected and taught today, and it is not healed by argument. It is seen through only when the soul finally is beginning to open to the radiant and penetrating Truth.

Meister Eckhart, a modern translation, by Raymond Blakney. At first respected and beloved, and then mistrusted and rejected, in his own time (1260-1328), Meister Eckhart is one of the most deeply God-experienced and God-inspired of all Christian teachers after Christ himself. Meister Eckhart was that rare kind of man, a great scholar, a consummate and technically disciplined thinker, who at the same time was God-saturated and God-intoxicated. This condition led to a head-on encounter with the authorities of that day, but it also left one of the great intellectual and mystical teaching legacies of all time. It is said very truly that "Eckhart now emerges as a pivotal figure in the making of the modern religious mind." And Raymond Blakney writes of the enigmatic Dominican of Cologne: "It was in his doctrine of God that Meister Eckhart went beyond the tolerance of his time and perhaps beyond the capacity of ours . . . certainly be lifted Christianity above any parochial conception and revealed its inner relation to the great, universal spiritual movements which have found expression in many forms. . . ."

Eckhart's teaching was estimated as dangerous in his own era, and perhaps those who so regarded it were not all knaves. Maybe it was dangerous, and maybe it still is. His doctrine later was abused, and it still may be abused. But if you have got your feet on the ground, if you are working seriously in prayer, and if you are open to teaching of great originality, great boldness and sweep, great depth, and utter authenticity, Meister Eckhart is a man whose acquaintance you should make.

The Spiritual Espousals by John of Ruysbroeck. Spiritual history is full of key men named John. This one was the greatest of the Flemish mystics, born in the little village of Ruysbroeck, between Hal and Brussels, in 1293. In his long and lovely lifetime of eighty-eight years be became one of the earth's most lucid teachers of the spiritual espousals and the spiritual marriage. From the viewpoint of clarity he is perhaps even greater than St. Bernard and St. John of the Cross in this regard. His first biographer, Pomerius, describes him as "a simple, quiet, rather shabby-looking person who went about the streets of Brussels with his mind lifted up to God." John of Ruysbroeck is noted above all for his direct experience in mystical communion, and then for his shrewd common sense, his great intellectual power well based in profound intellectual humility, and his transparent genius in logical, sane, methodical exposition of the deepest and highest experience of the soul in the Uncreated Light. His writings are distinguished by their order, balance, and symmetry. He was a homely, humble, wise, and kind man who loved the forest and the birds. Indeed, he lived in the forest for a long time, and he wrote in the forest, under a beloved lime tree. This tender and heavenly man was at the same time a surgically ruthless exposer of the vagaries of the "Brethren of the Free Spirit" and other false twists in the spiritual life of his time. His very purity and sanctity are obstacles to reading him in some cases; but otherwise he is a wonderful friend and guide.

Complete Works of St. John of the Cross. (Note particularly "The Ascent of Mount Carmel" in Vol. I and "The Living Flame of Love" in Vol. 11.) Juan de Yepes was born in Fontiveros, near Avila, in old Castile, in 1542. He spent all of his adult life in a strict monastic order, and he died at the age of forty-nine. He was later called St. John of the Cross. He understood communion with God as few men ever have, and he taught what he knew with a master's skill. His teaching technique ranges from bold and ecstatic poetry of immense depth and beauty to the most meticulous and manysided prose. He is strictly for work, not for entertainment. He may be helpful to beginners, but they must be serious, well-balanced, and not-easily-discouraged beginners, because this man wades right in where the going is tough, and he does not admit any pious prettiness before the true beauty is touched.

John's beginners must already have reached some kind of

end. Before you come to John of the Cross you must be, within your capacity, given up to God. He assumes that much, and he shows you where the path goes from there. He is particularly noted for his teaching of the "dark nights" (of the senses, of the soul, and of the spirit) through which the soul passes in her journey toward the Spouse, "the living Flame of Love."

Like Meister Eckhart, and no doubt for some of the same reasons, John of the Cross heavily strained the tolerance of his contemporaries, by whom he was imprisoned and disgraced. His works, however, have survived to establish him as among the greatest and soundest teachers of all ages and "Doctor of the Church Universal."

May we close with a practical note: the record (as given by Bucke) of John's escape from prison:

"When his imprisonment was drawing to its close, he heard our Lord say to him, as it were out of the soft light that was around him, 'John, I am here; be not afraid; I will set thee free.'

"A few moments later, while making his escape from the prison of the monastery, it is said he had a repetition of the experience as follows:

"He saw a powerful light, out of which came a voice, 'Follow me.' He followed, and the light moved before him toward the wall which was on the bank, and then, he knew not how, he found himself on the summit of it without effort or fatigue. He descended into the street, and then the light vanished. So brilliant was it, that . . . his eyes were weak, as if he had been looking at the sun in its strength."

May our Lord and Savior thus set us all free. And may the Truth nourish and keep us forever. Amen.

Appendix A

Examples of Spiritual Experience in Holy Scripture

ADAM: And they heard the voice of the Lord God walking in the garden in the cool of the day: . . . And the Lord God called unto Adam, and said unto him, Where art thou? And he said, I heard thy voice in the garden [Gen. 3:8–10].

ENOCH: And Enoch walked with God: and he was not; for God took him [Gen. 5:24].

ABRAHAM: And when Abram was ninety years old and nine, the Lord appeared to Abram, and said unto him, I am the Almighty God; walk before me, and be thou perfect. . . . And Abram fell on his face: And God talked with him [Gen. 17:1, 3].

JACOB: And the Lord appeared unto him [Jacob] the same night, and said, I am the God of Abraham thy father: fear not, for I am with thee [Gen. 26:24].

MOSES: God called unto him out of the midst of the bush, and said, Moses, Moses. And he said, Here am I [Exod. 3:4]. And the Lord told Moses, I will grant this request of thine; such favor thou hast with me, thou, my familiar friend [Exod. 33:17]. [The books of Exodus, Leviticus, and Numbers are full of extended direct conversations between God and Moses. Here is a mortal man whose entire adult life is one long series of experiences of God.]

SAMUEL: And the Lord came, and stood, and called as at other times, Samuel, Samuel. Then Samuel answered, Speak; for thy servant heareth [I Sam. 3:10].

DAVID: [A Psalm of David, when he was in the wilderness of Judah]: O God, thou art my God; early will I seek thee: my soul thirsteth for thee, my flesh longeth for thee in a dry and thirsty land, where no water is; to see thy power and thy glory, so as I have seen thee in the sanctuary [Ps. 63:1-2]. [Large parts of the Book of Psalms bear witness to the hunger for spiritual experience and to the experience itself.]

ELIJAH: And Elijah took his mantle, and wrapped it together, and smote the waters, and they were divided hither and thither, so that they two went over on dry ground. And it came to pass, when they were gone over, that Elijah said to Elisha, Ask what I shall do for thee, before I be taken away from thee. And Elisha said, I pray thee, let a double portion of thy spirit be upon me. And he said, Thou hast asked a hard thing: nevertheless, if thou see me when I am taken from thee, it shall be so unto thee; but if not, it shall not be so. And it came to pass, as they still went on, and talked, that, behold, there appeared a chariot of fire, and horses of fire, and parted them both asunder; and Elijah went up by a whirlwind into heaven. And Elisha saw it, and he cried, My father, my father, the chariot of Israel, and the horsemen thereof. And he saw him no more: and he took hold of his own clothes, and rent them in two pieces [II Kings 2:8-12].

ISAIAH: In the year that king Uzziah died I saw also the Lord sitting upon a throne, high and lifted up, and his train filled the temple. . . . Then said I, Woe is me for . . . I am a man of unclean lips, and I dwell in the midst of a people of unclean lips: for mine eyes have seen the King, the Lord of hosts. . . . Also I heard the voice of the Lord, saying, Whom shall I send, and who will go for us? Then said I, Here am I; send me [Isa. 6: 1, 5, 8].

DANIEL: I [Daniel] saw in the night visions, and, behold, one like the Son of man came with the clouds of heaven, and came to the Ancient of days ...[Dan. 7:13]. [The Book of Daniel is full of preternatural experience. Some of it is plain historical miracle, as in the episodes of the lion's den and the handwriting on the wall and the three men in the fiery furnace, and much of it is visionary material which is hard to understand but which is important particularly because of Christ's references to it.]

JESUS: And Jesus, when he was baptized, went up straightway out of the water: and, lo, the heavens were opened unto him, and he saw the Spirit of God descending like a dove, and lighting upon him: And lo a voice from heaven, saying, This is my beloved Son, in whom I am well pleased [Matt. 3:16-17].

PETER, JAMES, JOHN: And after six days Jesus taketh Peter, James, and John his brother, and bringeth them up into an high mountain apart, And was transfigured before them: and his face did shine as the sun, and his raiment was white as the light [Matt 17:1-2].

APOSTLES AND DISCIPLES: For I delivered unto you first of all that which I also received, how that Christ died for our sins according to the scriptures; And that he was buried, and that he rose again the third day according to the scriptures: And that he was seen of Cephas, then of the twelve: After that, he was seen of above five hundred brethren at once; of whom the greater part remain unto this present, but some are fallen asleep. After that, he was seen of James; then of all the apostles. And last of all he was seen of me also, as of one born out of due time [I Cor. 15: 3-8].

PAUL: And it came to pass, that, as I made my journey, and was come nigh unto Damascus about noon, suddenly there shone from heaven a great light around about me. And I fell unto the ground, and heard a voice saying unto me, Saul, Saul, why persecutest thou me? And I answered, Who art thou, Lord? And he said unto me, I am Jesus of Nazareth, whom thou persecutest [Acts 22:6-8].

APOSTLES AND DISCIPLES: And when the day of Pentecost was fully come, they were all with one accord in one place. And suddenly there came a sound from heaven as of a rushing mighty wind, and it filled all the house where they were sitting.

And there appeared unto them cloven tongues like as of fire, and it sat upon each of them. And they were all filled with the Holy Ghost, and began to speak with other tongues, as the Spirit gave them utterance [Acts 2:1-4].

JOHN: I was in the Spirit on the Lord's day, and heard behind me a great voice, as of a trumpet, . . . And I turned to see the voice that spake with me. And being turned, I saw seven golden candlesticks; And in the midst of the seven candlesticks one like unto the Son of man, clothed with a garment to the foot, and girt about the paps with a golden girdle. His head and his hairs were white like wool, as white as snow; and his eyes were as a flame of fire; . . . and his countenance was as the sun shineth in his strength. And when I saw him, I fell at his feet as dead. And he laid his right hand upon me, saying unto me, Fear not; I am the first and the last [Rev. 1:10, 12-14, 16-17].

Appendix B

The All Addicts Anonymous
Way of Life

With the coming of AA (Alcoholics Anonymous), millions of alcoholics, otherwise hopeless, have found their way back to sanity. But there is far greater lifesaving power in the principles of AA than has yet been widely recognized, because what is involved is *the practice of the ethical and spiritual principles common to all mankind,* and applicable to all mankind.

The original Program of Alcoholics Anonymous consisted of the Four Absolutes of the Oxford Group, later formulated by AA as the Twelve Step Program. The Absolutes were the foundation on which the Steps were built. This original Program was a world-shaker. This is the Program by which co-founders Bill Wilson and Dr. Bob Smith got sober — by which the famous first hundred AAs recovered — by which the whole movement was launched, in the United States and Canada, and worldwide.

Over the years, as it turns out, a remarkable discovery has been made. It has been found that these original AA principles are equally effective in producing recoveries not only from addictive drinking but also from many other forms of addictive behavior, including both the substance addictions and the mental addictions. Consequently it is now possible to have one Program which works equally well for all addicts and all addictions, and especially for the many persons who are fighting more than one addiction at the same time.

And so the original Four Absolutes, the original Twelve Steps, and the original commentary on the Steps — as adapted for all addicts and all addictions — are now called the All Addicts Anonymous Program.

The Four Absolutes
as adapted for all addicts and all addictions

Note well: the Four Absolutes are the time-tested moral and ethical code of the All Addicts Anonymous Program. The Four Absolutes, in one form or another, have actually been the foundation of the moral and spiritual life of mankind in all ages and in all civilizations —

1. Absolute honesty — no lying, no cheating, no stealing. In a word, in all your affairs, simply and absolutely no falsehood.
2. Absolute purity — purity of mind, purity of body, purity of the emotions, purity of heart, sexual purity.
3. Absolute unselfishness — seeking what is right and true ahead of what I want, in every situation.
4. Absolute love — loving God with all your heart, all your soul, all your mind, and all your strength, and your neighbor as yourself.

The Twelve Steps of Alcoholics Anonymous
as adapted for all addicts and all addictions

The Twelve Steps are a lifeline for alcohol addicts, many of whom — lacking opportunity to contact an AA group — have recovered by the mere knowledge and application of these twelve principles. It is impossible to exaggerate the importance of the Twelve Steps of Alcoholics Anonymous, not only for alcoholics, but for all other addicts.

Adapted versions of the Twelve Steps have been used by non-alcoholics for many years — by the Al-Anon Family Groups, Alateen, Neurotics Anonymous, Narcotics Anonymous, Gamblers Anonymous, Overeaters Anonymous, Sexaholics Anonymous, and many others. The original version of the Steps, for use by alcoholics only, may be found in the Big Book, *Alcoholics Anonymous* (New York,

1976: Alcoholics Anonymous World Services, Inc.).

The Twelve Steps as adapted for use in the All Addicts Anonymous Program can be used by any addict —

1. We admitted we were powerless over our addictions, that our lives had become unmanageable.

2. Came to believe that a Power greater than ourselves could restore us to sanity.

3. Made a decision to turn our will and our lives over to the care of God as we understood him.

4. Made a searching and fearless moral inventory of ourselves.

5. Admitted to God, to ourselves, and to another human being the exact nature of our wrongs.

6. Were entirely ready to have God remove all these defects of character.

7. Humbly asked him to remove our shortcomings.

8. Made a list of all persons we had harmed and became willing to make amends to them all.

9. Made direct amends to such people wherever possible, except when to do so would injure them or others.

10. Continued to take personal inventory and when we were wrong promptly admitted it.

11. Sought through prayer and meditation to improve our conscious contact with God as we understood him, praying only for knowledge of his will for us and the power to carry that out.

12. Having had a spiritual awakening as the result of these Steps, we tried to carry this message to other addicts, and to practice these principles in all our affairs.

The Ten Points
as adapted for all addicts and all addictions

Chapter five of the book *Alcoholics Anonymous* has always been a faithful guide for people who want to practice the Twelve Step Program. The following Ten Points are a summary of the lifesaving directions given in chapter five, and currently used in the All Addicts Anonymous Program —

1. *Completely give yourself* to this simple Program.
2. Practice *rigorous honesty.*
3. Be *willing to go to any lengths* to recover.
4. Be *fearless and thorough* in your practice of the principles.
5. Realize that there is *no easier, softer way.*
6. *Let go of your old ideas absolutely.*
7. Recognize that *half measures will not work.*
8. *Ask God's protection and care* with complete abandon.
9. *Be willing to grow* along spiritual lines.
10. Accept the following pertinent ideas as proved by All Addicts Anonymous experience:
    (a) that *you cannot manage your own life;*
    (b) that probably *no human power can restore you to sanity;*
    (c) that *God can and will* if sought.

The All Addicts Anonymous Program is a thoroughly tested and proven answer to addiction — but its healing power extends very far beyond that sphere. All Addicts Anonymous experience proves that *any addict* — drunk, drug addict, resenter, smoker, crazy eater, crazy gambler, fornicator, masturbator, depressive, worrier, liar — can attain spiritual awakening, self-control, sanity, peace, and joy if he or she will go to sufficient lengths in adopting the Four Absolutes, the Twelve Steps, and the Ten Points as a way of life.

How to Get Going on the
All Addicts Anonymous Way of Life

If you are in real trouble — if you are addicted to alcohol, drugs, tobacco, food, sex, worry, resentment, lying, depression, or anxiety — if you want to recover, and if you are willing to accept and act on suggestions from people who themselves have recovered - the outlook for you is good. Do not let anybody tell you that recovery from addiction is impossible, or unusual. Millions of addicts have recovered — fully, beautifully, and permanently.

The people who clutter up the addictive scene and make it seem like a big deal are the addicts (all of us, at one stage of the game) who do not really want to recover and who are still horsing around with the situation and mainly playing games. When you reach the point of wanting to recover and becoming willing to do what recovered addicts tell you to do, the battle is more than half won.

In the beginning of your recovery you are so weak physically and so bombed out mentally that you are easily confused and easily put off. Therefore you have to make "first things first" a rule and stick to it.

The first thing you do is to learn the *first principles of recovery* from someone who knows them and practices them, and to begin to practice them yourself. If you approach them with a little humility, they are not hard to understand, and it is not an impossible task to follow them. These principles (and the company of the people who practice them) are your lifeline. You simply cannot afford to argue about them. You merely have to *do* them, one day at a time.

The way to recovery begins with a few simple, uncomplicated first principles, which come to you as suggestions. Maybe you will not like some of these recommendations, but the thing to remember is that they work, and none of them should be left out. The whole problem is to *hang on* while you are coming out of the woods, and these suggestions tell you what (and what not) to hang on to.

Hang on to God

The first source of help to which an addict needs to turn — first in the order of time and first in the order of importance — is God. This is not a matter of religion or philosophy but simply a matter of fact. It is the power of God which enables addicts to recover. Without that power, there are very few recoveries.

Now there are a lot of different opinions about God, but we are not talking about God as an opinion but as a living power. You have to remember that you are an addict, not a professor. Do not waste time theorizing about God. What you do is *get in touch* with God by the simple and direct means of talking to

God, that is, by plain, old, ordinary prayer. Every nitwit knows how to pray; the knack here is to *do it.* No preliminary ducking or bobbing is necessary. Just do it.

Do not waste energy debating about God. Take God as a *possibility* — a working hypothesis. Make the experiment of getting in touch. This comes ahead of everything else, and anybody can do it. You can do it. Millions of alcoholics and drug addicts (many of them atheists) have made this experiment and proved to themselves that there *is* a Power greater than themselves who responds and gives real, practical, effective help when called on. All real recovery begins here. It makes no difference whether you are a believer or not. If you are not, start by praying to the God you don't believe in. Just park your objections for a while, and *do it* as an experiment.

Hang on to the truth

You connect with God by means of the truth. And you connect with the truth by stopping lying. All addicts are liars. Please do not resent this. It is just a statement of fact. Some of us lie in gross ways, some in subtle ways; but all of us are ferocious liars.

As a starter, stop lying to yourself about your addicted condition. Stop pretending it is better than it is. You are in the grip of a disease which is a vicious killer, and you cannot do anything about it — not by yourself and not with the best scientific, psychiatric, or medical help in the world. Addiction is usually incurable except through spiritual conversion. Face that fact, and your chances for recovery are good. Ignore it, and your chances are practically nil.

Next, stop lying to get out of jams or to smooth off the rough edges of life. Don't lie for the sake of peace; don't lie when common sense invites you to do so; don't lie to cover up your past; don't lie on job applications, expense accounts, or tax returns; don't lie to your boss; don't lie to your husband or wife. Just don't lie. When you fail in this resolve (as you will), admit it promptly. And don't indulge failure; that is, don't fail any oftener than you have to.

This policy of non-lying takes real courage if you have a messy past, as most of us do. It feels like it is going to cause problems for you, rather than solve them. But in actual practice it is a lifesaver and a life-transformer. Try it, and you will find that non-lying simplifies life and makes it easier to deal with. And it does something else of greatest importance: When you take truth-telling seriously, you put yourself in direct touch with God. God *is* truth, and throughout the day every decision you make to be honest opens you up to the healing light of his presence. This is not just a pretty thought; it is something real, like electricity, only alive. Work for the truth, as best you can, and the living Truth — God — will work for you. He will give you the strength which you yourself lack, the strength to take the next step.

Hang on to total abstinence

One day at a time, stay away from alcohol, drugs, smokes, or whatever it is that you are addicted to. *Total* abstinence is the key. That means *none* — not even a little bit, not even one or two. (In the case of alcohol addiction, drug addiction, tobacco addiction, and coffee addiction, stopping is achieved by a program of total abstinence. In the case of food addiction and sex addiction, stopping is achieved by faithful adherence to a program of limited use.)

One day at a time, with the help of God and the truth, *you can do it.* It is the first drink or pill or shot or cigarette to which you must say no. One day at a time, stay away from the first drink or drug or whatever, and you will never have to worry about all those disastrous ones that follow. "One day at a time" is not a trick with words; it is a thoroughly practical, well-proven formula for success. No addict can face the prospect of a whole lifetime of total abstinence. It seems too big an order. But *any* of us, with God's help, can stay away from the first drink, the first pill, the first shot, the first cigarette, or whatever, *for twenty-four hours.* Do not underestimate the power of this principle.

Hang on to your recovering brothers and sisters

You cannot recover alone. It is a deadly mistake to think that you can. In our times God has chosen to speak to addicts through brothers and sisters who are ahead of them on the road to freedom. These are the people who can show you how to recover. Find them. Learn from them. Work with them. Join their group, and go to their meetings. If you cannot locate a group, do what the pioneers in this field did: dig up a couple of people who are also looking for recovery, and start your own group. Go to meetings — practice the Four Absolutes, the Twelve Steps, and the Ten Points in all of your affairs, one day at a time — work with others as you go. It really is that simple.

Working with a group is necessary; you cannot sustain a recovery without it. But the group is not God; it is only a vehicle through which God works. It is the principles that communicate the power. Recovery begins with getting in touch with God. *He* gives us the courage to get honest; *he* gives us the strength to stay away from the first drink or pill or shot or cigarette or whatever, one day at a time; and *he* puts us in touch with the people we need to work with.

At the same time, do not misuse trust in God as an excuse to avoid people, or to try to get around any of the other factors in the basic equation. Hanging on to God, hanging on to honesty, staying away from alcohol or drugs (or whatever your addictive substance is), and working with your recovering brothers and sisters — these constitute the formula for recovery, and they go together. You cannot work successfully with any of them unless you are working with all of them. By doing these few simple things, literally millions of previously desperate and hopeless men and women have had their lives, their sanity, and their strength restored through the All Addicts Anonymous way of life.

Appendix C

The Greatest Books

First in interest for most Western men and women is the Bible. The word "bible" means simply "book." The Bible is "the Book" (although really it is a collection of books). The Christian faith is based upon the Old and New Testaments of the Bible. The New Testament is a group of writings about Jesus of Nazareth, the Christ, and his disciples. It consists of the Gospels, which tell of the life and teachings of Jesus and describe his death by crucifixion, his resurrection, and his ascension; the Acts of the Apostles, an account of the activities of the first followers of Christ Jesus; the Epistles, letters of counsel and doctrine written by Paul, James, Jude, Peter, and John; and a concluding prophetic book, the Revelation of John.

The Old Testament contains books that are held sacred in both Christianity and Judaism. These books deal with the Creation, the story of Israel in Egypt and the deliverance, the Law and the Prophets, Psalms and Proverbs, stories like Ruth and Esther, and great psychological and spiritual treatises like Job and Ecclesiastes.

The effect of the Bible upon mankind is quite incalculable. It has inspired Christianity and Judaism directly, and Islam indirectly, and the influence of the peoples of these faiths upon the rest of the world has been enormous. It is impossible to interpret the Bible's impact upon humanity in terms other than those of an immense spiritual power and a very great and critical revelation of Truth.

The Bible is the written wellspring of the spirituality of the Western world. To read the Bible, if only a little bit, daily and to meditate upon its message would seem to be a minimum discipline for anyone who hopes to understand the soul of Western man. For us who are Western men, it would be the minimum for a beginning in self-knowledge as well as in God knowledge.

After the Bible, the most influential book in the world is the Koran. It is the book upon which is founded the faith of Islam, one of the most widespread of the religions, embracing about one eighth of the world's population, distributed mostly in North Africa, the Middle East, and Asia. The Koran, which means "the reading," provides the canon of faith in the Islamic world, and also the textbook of ritual and the principles of civil law.

Islam means "submission to God," and a follower of this faith is called a Muslim, "one who submits." Muhammad is the Prophet of Islam, and it was to him, over thirteen hundred years ago, that God, in Muslim belief, made the revelations that are embodied in the Koran.

This book is held in great veneration throughout the Muslim world. It is described as "the glorious Koran, that inimitable symphony, the very sounds of which move men to tears and ecstasy." Pickthall, in introducing his translation, makes the point that the Koran truly exists only in Arabic, that it cannot in fact be translated, and that his "translation" is really only an attempt to present the meaning of the Koran, and perhaps some of its charm, in English.

The Koran was given to Muhammad on various occasions when he was in a condition of ecstasy. The following account of his first illuminative experience is condensed (with some rearrangement) from Washington Irving's *Life of Muhammad* as quoted by Bucke.

> He was passing, as was his wont, the month of Ramadan in the cavern, endeavoring by fasting, prayer, and solitary meditation to elevate his thoughts to the contemplation of divine truth. It was on the night called by the Arabs Al Kadar, the Divine Decree. As Muhammad, in the silent watches of the night, lay

wrapped in his mantle, he heard a voice calling him. As he uncovered his head, a flood of light broke upon him of such intolerable splendor that he swooned. On regaining his senses he beheld an angel in human form, who, approaching from a distance, displayed a silken cloth covered with written characters. "Read!" said the angel. "I know not how to read!" replied Muhammad. "Read!" repeated the angel. "I cannot read!" said Muhammad. The voice, more terrible now, commanded: "Read! In the name of the Lord, who has created all things; who created man from a clot. Read, in the name of the Most High, who taught man the use of the pen; who sheds on his soul the ray of knowledge and teaches him what before he knew not."

Whereupon Muhammad instantly felt his understanding illumined with celestial light and read what was written on the cloth, which contained the decree of God, as afterward promulgated in the Koran.

India has been a deeply God-centered land since prehistoric times and is rich in sacred writings. Two works stand out as most honored and cherished in Hindu hearts generally, and these same two have been found helpful to Western seekers. First are the Upanishads, and the second is the Bhagavad Gita, although not necessarily in that order of importance. It would be very hard to say which should come first. The Upanishads are the older, so we shall consider them before the Gita.

The Upanishads are part of the Vedas, the part which deals with knowledge of God, as distinct from parts which deal with works: rules of conduct, sacrifice, ritual, and so on. The Vedas are the oldest scriptures of India; conservative Western scholars think they go back to about 1200 B.C., but Indian authorities put their origin very much earlier, perhaps as early as the fifth millennium before Christ.

The Upanishads, as part of the Vedas, share the prestige of the Vedas. In the Hindu view, the Vedas are eternal, without beginning. Their author is no man or men but the Lord himself. It is not, of course, the words of the Vedas which are thought to be eternal but the spiritual knowledge which the words express.

The Upanishads were actually put into writing for the first time a few hundred years before the time of Buddha (563-483 B.C.). But it must be remembered that these were sacred teachings before they were sacred writings; they were transmitted by word of mouth for many centuries before they were recorded. They were sung, chanted, spoken from sage to king, from husband to wife, from teacher to pupil, through a long line of illumined souls before they were written down.

If the Upanishads embody eternal knowledge, who were the men who penetrated to that knowledge and expressed it in terms that other men might hope to understand? They were the *rishis,* the seers who dwelt in the forests of ancient India. Their lives were devoted to the one great concern of knowing by experience (not just knowing about) the Supreme Reality immanent and transcendent in themselves and in the world around them, the Reality which has been called God in all generations but which these researchers most often call the Atman, usually translated as "the Self."

In the Upanishads the Self is not merely the exterior personal self of man, not just the phenomenal ego, but the Divinity pervading the universe and all things in it, including man. The essential Reality in man (Atman) and the essential Reality in the universe (Brahman) are identical. Both are One, and that One is the Self. And the great message of the Upanishads is *tat tvam asi,* "That art thou." This will seem blasphemous only if we make the error of taking "thou" to be merely the phenomenal ego. "That art thou" and "I and my Father are one" are equivalent statements. Both may be shocking statements for any man to make. (A certain Person, it will be recalled, so shocked his fellow men by taking this position that they executed him.) But the shock arises only if we mistake the surface ego or the mere body-mind for the true being of man. Here we are in deep water certainly, but these are depths which no man ultimately may hope to avoid.

The Upanishads say over and over again that the Self can be known. To know it is not easy, but it is possible, and life can never make sense until the Self *is* known. "Only when men shall roll up the sky like a hide will there be an end to misery, unless God has first been known," says the Svetasvatara Upanishad. Again and again the sharpest distinction is drawn between knowing *about* the Self and actually *knowing* the Self by transforming identification with it. This unitive knowledge is held up as the great aim of human life, failing which all other aims without exception are bitterly futile.

The Bhagavad Gita is a great spiritual poem which has been called "the Sermon on the Mount of Hinduism." The present value of the Bhagavad Gita is by no means confined to India and Indians. More and more Westerners are discovering that the Gita is an explicit and practical textbook on the technique of seeking God while working in the world. If you are sincerely pursuing truth, and if at the same time your duty places you in the midst of worldly obligations, you will find in the Gita a series of inspired instructions addressed directly to your problem. The central message is this: surrender your life to God; put God first; then do your duty whatever it is, but without attachment to the fruits of action; work, but surrender the results of work to God; work, but without desire for reward.

The divine teacher of the Gita recognizes that this is easy to say and hard to do. So he goes on to tell just how, in spite of difficulties, it can be done. Even so, it is easy to misunderstand the Gita's basic teaching; it is a common error, for example, to suppose that surrender of the fruits of action means that there will be no fruits. This is far from the truth. Hear what Gandhi says: "Again let no one consider renunciation to mean want of fruit for the renouncer. The Gita reading does not warrant such a meaning. Renunciation means absence of hankering after fruit. As a matter of fact, he who renounces reaps a thousandfold. The renunciation of the Gita is the acid test of faith. He who is ever brooding over results often loses nerve in the performance of his duty. He becomes impatient and then gives vent to anger and begins to do unworthy things; he jumps from action to action, never remaining faithful to any."

Chinese moral and social philosophy is summed up in the gentle wisdom of the scholarly sage Confucius. But the deepest essence of Chinese spirituality is expressed in a little book of 5,000 characters written 2,500 years ago. It is the Book of Tao, or the Tao Te Ching, traditionally said to have been composed by Lao Tse, who was born about 571 B.C. and whose name when translated means "ancient youth." He was a contemporary of Confucius and of the Buddha.

Very little is known about Lao Tse, and that little is in dispute among scholars. Ssu-ma Ch'ien says that Lao Tse was Keeper of the Imperial Archives or a sort of librarian at the Chou court. Legend says that he disappeared in middle life, although it is reported that he lived to a great age after his disappearance. He is said to have written the Book of Tao in a few hours to please a frontier guard as he was crossing the border on his way to retirement.

Some estimate of the importance of the Tao Te Ching may be made from Lin Yutang's evaluation of it: "If there is one book in the whole of Oriental literature which one should read above all others, it is, in my opinion, Lao Tse's Book of Tao. If there is one book that can claim to interpret for us the spirit of the Orient, or that is necessary to the understanding of characteristic Chinese behavior, including literally 'the ways that are dark,' it is the Book of Tao. For Lao Tse's book contains the first enunciated philosophy of camouflage in the world; it teaches the wisdom of appearing foolish, the success of appearing to fail, the strength of weakness and the advantage of lying low, the benefit of yielding to your adversary and the futility of contention for power. It accounts in fact for any mellowness that may be seen in Chinese social and individual behavior. . . . It is one of the profoundest books in the world's philosophy."

The word "Tao" is variously translated as "the way" — "a means" — "a doctrine" — "a principle." But it is more than these, much more. It is the ultimate Reality in which all attributes are united. According to Kuan Tsu, Tao is "that by losing of which men die; by getting of which men live. Whatever is done without it fails; whatever is done by means of it, succeeds." It is the harmony of things, the way the universe works. It is, in fact, God. And therefore it is essentially indescribable and unutterable. "The Tao that can be told of is not the Absolute Tao." These are the first words of the Tao Te Ching.

The Book of Tao is full of paradoxes, and one wonders in the first place how the material came to be articulated at all, for "he who knows does not speak, and he who speaks does not know." And one hesitates to praise the book, for "true words are not fine-sounding; fine-sounding words are not true."

Among all the world's sacred writings, the Book of Tao stands out as gentle, motherly, profound, with a haunting nostalgia for a beatitude long forgotten yet ever at hand, resplendent with hints of the spiritual gold still buried in every man and indeed in every thing, and withal full of a strange sense of humor, a smile just starting — as if behind the enigma, behind the mystery and terror of human life, someone were gently laughing.

The reward for even a little knowledge of Buddhism is great, but it is not easy to achieve. Some of the difficulties are in Buddhism itself (which is logical and unsentimental, endlessly explicit, humorous, and very stern — all at the same time). And some of the difficulties we make ourselves. Ignorance of Buddhism is very thick today, and contempt for Buddhism is therefore common. Mention the Buddha and wearily, inevitably, you evoke a remark about Buddhists contemplating their navels, or a somewhat more serious but equally ignorant remark to the effect that the Buddha was an atheist This atheist business, however, is a good point of entry into Buddhist teaching. If ever a man knew God, it was the Buddha. Yet he patiently and flatly refused to talk about God all through a long lifetime of teaching. Why? Possibly because he saw with the clarity of perfect enlightenment how people hypnotize themselves and deceive themselves with words, particularly with key words like "God," and how talk about God lulls us into the pathetic assurance that we know something about God when we are actually in the darkest and deadliest ignorance of God.

Buddhism is shock treatment for conventional religious attitudes, for lazy piety, for pretense and deceit, for the "good" folks whose hypocrisy is lethal to the spiritual life but doesn't smell quite bad enough to be found out. (Christ, you will recall, also spanked this section of the human bottom with a very heavy hand.)

The man who became the Buddha was an Indian prince, born in 563 B.C., and known among Buddhists as Gautama Sakyamuni. He was intelligent, handsome, strong, and otherwise naturally well favored. He married happily at sixteen and spent his early manhood in comfort and luxury. At the age of twenty-nine, however, the bitter facts of worldly life had become so apparent to him that he renounced his family ties, left home, and retired to the forest, seeking Truth. After experimenting with extreme asceticism, he saw that the answer did not lie in that direction, and he thereafter developed his own way, later taught as the Middle Path. He finally attained full awakening and perfect enlightenment under the famous Bo tree, and thus he became a Tathagata: one who "has thus gone" — the last in a long line of Buddhas or Awakened Ones. He was thirty-five at the time of his Great Awakening and was at first reluctant to teach. Subsequently, however (he died at eighty), he was persuaded to teach a great deal, and from his influence have sprung streams of spirituality which to this day continue to water a large part of the earth.

A good example of Buddhist scripture for a newcomer to sample is the Dhammapada. Although its authorship and date are in dispute among scholars, it is quite certain that the words of the Dhammapada actually represent the teachings of the Buddha himself. It is a masterpiece of spiritual instruction and exhortation, a brilliant summary of the condition of unregenerate mankind, and a ringing call to snap out of the nightmare of ordinary life and to set out upon the journey to freedom and joy.

Buddhist sacred writings are divided generally into two groups: Theravadin (Pali) and Mahayana (Sanskrit), representing the two great divisions which have occurred in Buddhism. (Zen is a division of Mahayana. For Zen reading references see Suzuki listings in the bibliography.) Selections from Sanskrit, Pali, Chinese, and Tibetan sources will be found in *A Buddhist Bible,* edited by Dwight Goddard.

Appendix D

The Relationship of the
Higher and Lower Selves

As in all experience which goes deeper than the sensual nature, actual experience of the Higher and lower selves can be reported in verbal terms only under difficulty and with some very necessary qualifications. The following observations are from an anonymous source, a contemporary who has had experiential knowledge of the two selves over a period of eighteen years. These notes are not easy reading, but they are perhaps as easy as possible, and the points made are essential to an understanding of this great facet of spiritual life:

> The concept of the two selves in man is a working view of great practical utility and real validity for the God-seeking personal man. As one enters more deeply into the truth, however, it is recognized that the distinctions made are not finally acceptable. From the standpoint of the personal consciousness, yes: in each individual man there is a Greater Self and a lesser. But *in the truth* it is seen that *there is only One Self.* Infinite distinctions continually occur in him, but they do not divide him; indeed, they really do not affect or modify him in any way whatsoever. How this can be, it is impossible to say; but one must say that it is so.
>
> The Reality is One-imperishably, unutterably, serenely, and eternally One. Here in the One — and here alone — is peace, security, fulfillment. To seek these things outside the One is simply an impossible quest, and it can end in a kind of madness. The One is what everyone hungers for,

however ignorantly, and strives for, however blindly. The One is triumph, rest, refreshment, father and mother — *home*.

The Higher and lower selves always must be remembered in terms of the One Self; otherwise, while saving one from ignorant confinement in the concept of the merely personal, the idea of two selves leads into an invalid and harmful separatism. In the mysteries of Islam, the Cosmic or Higher Self and the individual self are shown as concentric circles, with the Ka'Ba (the point of identity and realization, the One), in the center. This is a very true figure (but only from the viewpoint of awakened awareness).

More from the angle of the personal consciousness, it can be said that a single ray from the Higher Self illuminates, inspires, and vivifies the heart, and the personal man arises from this root. The personal self is a development along one of the rays of the Higher Self.

A single ray from the Cosmic or Higher Self pours steadily into the core of the human heart. This is the source of the individual human life, consciousness, and power. The unripe ego refracts the pure light into the human manifestation, with all its imperfections. But God dwells, in the spark of pure light, in the heart of everyone, quite literally. And he waits calmly until the central spark flares out and begins to seek its Source.

And yet always and again we must come back to this: although the personal self stands in relation to the Cosmic Self as planet to sun, there are not, in full truth, two selves, but One. The One is *not the opposite* of the many. The One *contains* the many. The Infinite is not opposed to the finite. The Infinite embraces, includes, *makes possible* the finite. The personal self is discrete, and at the same time in identity with the Higher Self (which in turn is in identity with the One Self). Maybe it can be said more plainly, but I don't know how. The truth is simple enough, but the dualistic mind creaks and groans in trying to penetrate to it.

I sometimes feel ashamed when I have dared to speak or write about these matters. One feels a need to speak or write, but it seems impossible to do it adequately, let alone well. It makes the things of the truth seem ponderous and difficult-cold and remote-abstract and obscure. Whereas in reality they are light, genial, benign, easy, gracious-vivid, alive, warm, intimate, immediate-clear, bright, sparkling, crisp, definite.

The human faculty of speech is a wonderful thing, but it needs to undergo a transmutation, perhaps of fire, before it is fit to touch even the skirts of God's holy truth. Anyone who comes near to that truth must find himself crying out with old Isaiah, "I am a man of unclean lips. . . :'

Appendix E

Group Experience Using
Invitation to a Great Experiment
as a Work Book

Some years ago in Kansas City a small group of people came together and decided to meet once a week to study and to work in a certain direction. They were looking for something more than "success" in life. They were looking for meaning. They were looking for the Way to God. This group was followed by another, and then another, until more than two dozen such groups had formed. Some of the people in them were prosperous and "successful," some were not. Some were basically happy but somehow dissatisfied. Some were unhappy and in mental and emotional trouble. Some were Christians, some Jews, some agnostics and atheists. The book they used was *Invitation to a Great Experiment* (first published as *First Questions on the Life of the Spirit*). Their experience, as told by Donald L. Campbell, may help you in your own group work:

It is easy to start a study group whose purpose is the improvement of the spiritual life of its members. It is like, say, starting a bird-watching group. Someone who is interested in the subject calls together some like-minded people; they decide on time, place, and agenda; and off they go.

Keeping a spiritual life group going, however, is something else. It is not easy. When I first came to Kansas City, I attempted to repeat an experience I had had with prayer groups for men in Chicago.

Back there, a few of us, all members of the same church, had started a group, and in short order, by chain reaction, there were any number of similar groups going great guns. This experience convinced me that all you needed was a few people interested in advancing their inner lives and a place to meet.

So I started a prayer group in Kansas City. I expected a quick pick-up and another chain reaction like the one in Chicago. But what we got was a bust. I still don't know why that group fizzled out, but I look back now and wonder if it was not all for the best, since the experience taught me that something more was needed than just spiritually hungry people. You need a recipe book, if I can call it that — a chart, a blueprint, a program. And if you want some real action in your group, this recipe book, or chart, or blueprint, needs to do the exact opposite of putting people to sleep. It needs to challenge their customary ideas down to the ground, rattle all their comfortable assumptions until they hurt.

I found such a blueprint some years ago, in a book by Tom Powers called *First Questions on the Life o f the Spirit*. The book has a new title now, *Invitation to a Great Experiment*. The book had an effect on me when I first read it that is best described by a current expression (that nobody was using then): it turned me on. I found that I wanted to tell as many people as I could about it, and I bought numerous copies and gave them to friends.

There is no book, of course, that will have the same impact on everyone who reads it, but it has been my experience that *Great Experiment* turns on a higher percentage of genuinely, spiritually hungry people than any other book I know of. In fact the only hungry people I know of that it turns off are those who feel they must screen all new ideas about God and the spiritual life through a creedal "sifter." If something does not dovetail perfectly with the "credentia" they are already used to, they cannot deal with it.

Before we get into the "how-to" of starting a group, I'd like to mention one more reason why *Invitation to a Great Experiment* seems to me such a good book to use in working with groups: it does not require the group's members to be religiously all-of-a-kind, or very advanced in whatever religion (if any) they may belong to. I've been in groups with Presbyterian and Congregational ministers, Jews, agnostics, spiritual mongrels of all kinds, people in trouble, people who are Doing All Right, Bible experts, behavioral science fans, and everything in between. Uniformly the wise and humble discover that they are not so wise or so humble as they thought.

We have launched our groups with as few as a half-dozen or so members. On the first night a new group assembles, the leader explains the purpose of the group, describes its format, and gives people a general idea of what to expect. Here, not necessarily in order of importance, are points we learned to cover in this first organizing session:

1. We made it very clear at the outset that the goal of the group is to help each other come to know God the way we know another person. Of course God is not *merely* another person. But *Great Experiment's* author emphasizes that knowledge of God is a *personal* relationship. The group will be working toward an awareness of God that is like awareness of another person. They should expect to talk to and be talked to, to love and be loved. These are kinds of communication persons have with persons. They are not the experiences of persons with abstract concepts or ideas or forces.

2. We stressed that there would be *work* involved. Not just studying the book but putting its "recipes" to the test. The aim is to build new habits, a new style of life. That takes at least as much effort as making money.

3. We always suggested to members of the group that they would not know for sure whether this kind of work was for them for at least three months. They ought to be prepared to stick with it that long if they start at all. (To cover the book's contents takes about two years of once-weekly sessions.)

4. We advised our groups to expect some pain in the stages of self-discovery, as well as relief and joy from the whiffs of reality that will come to each member as he shares his search with the others. Being part of a group venture into the spiritual life is like having six or eight other people standing around you, each holding a mirror for you to look into. They will help you see as-

pects of yourself you never saw before. That's why we need to work in a group. To see ourselves. And, finally, to love and accept ourselves and others.

5. We had our leaders make known their own stands, their individual "bias." Are you, as leader, starting out as agnostic, humanist, confessed Christian, or what? The group has a right to know.

6. We would agree on the length of our meetings. By far the most successful format for Great Experiment groups in our experience at Kansas City was weekly meetings of at least ninety minutes. An hour is just not long enough. Semimonthly or monthly get-togethers are not frequent enough to keep the fire going under the boiler.

7. We established time and place for meetings. The majority of our groups have met evenings, but we have had some fine morning groups when the members couldn't find a common evening time. A businessmen's group meets at 6:30 in a broker's office here every Friday morning.

A church room, business-office conference room, and private living room have all been used successfully. The drawback to using people's houses is that family and phone distractions can keep the host or hostess from really being present in the group all the time.

8. We discussed the following two approaches to the structure of our groups at the outset, and decided what our group policies would be:

a. Did we want to have a single leader for the whole two-year term, or did we want leadership to rotate in the group? By far the majority of Kansas City groups had a single leader, a person who calls the group into being, leads each session, and is the group's "irreducible minimum." The group can count on his regular presence and enthusiasm.

It is possible to rotate leadership among the group members every week, or to alternate every month or so. Spreading the experience of leadership is a good thing, but the danger is — and it is a real one — that too much diffusion of leadership will weaken the whole group's grasp on the subject matter.

b. Were our groups to be open or closed to new members after they started (say, after five or six weeks)? Here our experiences were pretty well divided. Four or five people who have led our groups have preferred open membership, so that the group could welcome a new seeker at any point in the group's life. I personally have preferred the closed-membership plan, because it allows the group's members to trust each other in sharing deep feelings much sooner than they are apt to if new people keep joining the group.

How to take care of the seeker who wants to join a group after yours is well started? We always tell him to stand by, and send out the word among our "community" (all the people who have been in our group in the past) to find out how many interested people everyone knows about who could make up a new group. So far, we have never failed, in eight years, to rally a new group and find a leader when just one serious, hungry soul said, "I'd like to take the journey toward God in this way."

9. We made plain that there were no preconditions for membership in the group, but the group's size ought to be limited. We have found that the maximum should be ten or twelve. If more came, we split up into two groups of seven or eight.

It is a great advantage, by the way, if an abrasive person joins up — someone who is not amiable, agreeable, optimistic, amenable, and conforming. Someone with the capacity to bug others often makes a good mirror-holder. He may have problems himself, of course, if he can't see the truth because he gets caught on the "bugging for bugging's sake" tack; but then it will be his turn to look in the mirror!

10. We made clear in our first meeting whether the group was free-lance or sponsored. A free-lance group is simply a group of adults meeting on their own. A sponsored group is part of the program of some church or other institution. Most of our groups have not been sponsored by any institution, although many do use church facilities. Our Kansas City groups mush-

roomed because individuals got turned on, not because "adult-study-group program committees" thought it would be a successful new "class."

I think the foregoing ten points cover most things prospective members will want to know starting out. The really important thing anyone who is acting as the organizer needs to remember is that if he is serious, God is already at work and will keep him from falling. If it is God's will that this group come into being, one's own inexperience or ineptitude won't hurt its chances.

In this as in everything else, there is no real substitute for experience. If you decide to start such a group, start it, and learn as you go. I predict you will see remarkable changes in people. And the changes will begin right away. The first thing in the book is the challenge to become rigorously honest, and this hits most of us where it hurts. It did me. I remember well the feelings of resentment I had when I read:

> The fact is that you have to be crudely, brutally, mercilessly honest with yourself even to make a pass at knowledge of God. Every man thinks he is an exception, and no man is. Unless you put yourself on the honesty carpet with the rest of the spiritual small boys, this flight never gets off the ground. (I hear you crying, and I am full of sympathy. In fact I am crying with you. This is my problem, too. The only comfort I can think of is that we all have so much company.)

Of course what happened was that the words "Every man thinks he is an exception to the rule . . . that to even make a pass at knowledge of God you must be mercilessly, brutally honest" did speak sharply to me. I did want to believe that I was the exception, that I had always been honest and that no discipline in the direction of honesty was necessary to lead me to personal knowledge of God.

I found out how wrong I was.

The hard challenges in *Invitation to a Great Experiment* were balanced, however, by new resources in our group work for support and comfort. There was the help — the real love — of others. And above all, we discovered that when you take God seriously enough to begin really doing some of the disciplines outlined in the book, God will already have been there ahead of you. His spirit becomes your guide, companion, enabler, and comforter, as well as the ultimate goal you seek. He leads you to the manna, and he is the manna.

Index

Abandonment; *see* Surrender to God

Addiction, recovery from, 231-238

Adultery and fornication, contraindicated, 81-82, 136

Adversary (Monkey, *Shaitan, Mephiztophel*), 13, 30, 33, 50, 63-64, 124, 135, 143-145, 149

Ahriman and Lucifer, 144

Alcoholics Anonymous, 8, 16, 231-234

Alive, spiritually, 106-110, 132

All Addicts Anonymous way of life, 8, 231-238

Asleep, spiritually, 94, 106-119, 142

Atheism, 45, 45-46n.*, 138

Attachment; *see* Concupiscence; *see also* Bhagavad Gita (for non-attachment)

Attention, 112, 113, 114, 174, Prayer of, 178-180

Aurobindo, Sri, 209

Austin, Lou, 214

Avalokitesvara, 170, 170n.*, 173

Avesta, 38

Awake, spiritually, 106-111

Awakening (conversion), 66-70, 80, 158,

Awareness of God, sustained, 92, 93

Baal Shem Tov, 223

Baker, Augustine, 218

Bar Hebraeus, 62

Beevers, John, 213

Benedictines, the, 16

Benoit, Hubert, 114, 115n.*

Bhagavad Gita, 40, 79, 83, 99-100, 185 (bibliog.), 212n.*, 241, 243-244

Bhakti (devotion), 169n.†, 178

Bible, 38-40, 45n.*, 183, 185-187 (bibliog.) and spiritual experience, 60, 227-230

Bible reading, 38-40

Blakney, Raymond, 224

Body, physical, 41-43, 101 position of, in prayer, 153-155 spiritual, 102-103

Boehme, Jacob, 124, 213, 217

Boisen, Anton, 71n.*

Book of Changes, 38, 51-52

Book of Common Prayer, The, 39, 218

Book of English Collects, The, 217-*218*

Book of Tao (Tao Te Ching), 40, 244-245

Books, bibliography, 183-206
  as helps in spiritual life, 30-41, 47, 64-65
  special listings, 207-226

Brahmananda, 58, 61, 170-171

Breathing; *see* Prayer

Brianchaninov, Bishop Ignatius, 170, 175

Buber, Martin, 61, 98, 214, 215

Bucke, R. M., 31, 31n*

Buddha, 78, 112, 116, 170n.*, 245-246

Buddhism, 3, 112, 161, 170n.*, 210, 212n.*, 215, 245-247
  Zen, 112, 215, 247

Buddhist Bible, A, 56, 83, 247

Buddhist Guiding Principles, 83-84

Campbell, Donald L., 253

Carrel, Alexis, 213, 216

Chaitanya, 70n.*

Chapman, Dom John, O. S. B., 175, 212n.*, 217

Chesterton, G. K., ii, 213

Christ, and Christ Jesus, 3, 21, 27, 38, 40, 42, 55, 69, 73, 97, 101-106, 108, 110, 112, 115, 125, 129 164, 210, 214, 222

Christianity, Christian religion, 3-4, 51, 66n.*, 99, 130, 166, 209-211, 221, 222, 224

Eastern Orthodox, 85, 113, 165, 165n.*, 169, 179, 210, 223-224

Christians, 3-4, 164, 168, 169, 212n.*
  and books, 39-40

Christian Science, 211

Cleckley, Hervey, M. D., 13n.*

Cloud of Unknowing, The, 162-163, 218-219

Collin, Rodney, 80

Concupiscence (craving, attachment), 85

Confucius, 244

Conversation with God, 90-93

Conversion; *see* Awakening

Coomaraswamy, Ananda K., 102

Cosmic Consciousness; *see* Mysticism

Cranston, Ruth, 213

Craving; *see* Concupiscence

Cross, the, 103, 142

Cure d'Ars, 213

Daily, Starr, 214

Davenport, Russell, 209

Dead, spiritually, 106-107, 132

Death, of the ego, 101-102
  and resurrection of Jesus, 102

Decalogue, the, 81

De Caussade, J.P, 33, 145-149, 220-221

De Laredo, Bernardino, 220

Desert Fathers, the, 16, 169, 173

Dhammapada, The, 246-247
Dionysius the Areopagite, 36, 66n.*, 161n.*, 222
Divine Comedy, The, 36
Do Nouy, Lecomte, 208
Durant, Will and Ariel, 51

Eckhart, Meister, 36, 98, 216, 224, 226
Ego, and egotism, 65-66, 85, 96-106, 119, 134, 144, 181
Emerson, Ralph Waldo, 211
Essenes, 16
Evil, 129
Evola, 112
Exman, Eugene, 47n.*
Experience, books about, 212-215
  and psychosis, 59, 70n.*
  spiritual, 58-73

Faith, as help in spiritual life, 53-58, 63
  books about, 209-212
Fénelon, 79
Ferm, Vergilius, 210
First Questions on the Life of the Spirit, 253, 254
Fischer, Louis, 21
Fosdick, Harry Emerson, 209, 216
Four Absolutes, 231, 232, 234
Fox, George, 70n.*
Freud, Sigmund, 214

Gamblers Anonymous, 8, 232

Gandhi, M. K., 21, 83, 99, 168, 176
Garrigou-Lagrange, Father Reginald, 91-92, 208, 212
Gautama Sakyamundi; see Buddha
Gilson, Etienne, 208
God, existence, and reality of, 3, 7-11, 41, 69, 88
  grace of, 148
  knowledge of, 20, 25, 26, 30, 45, 78, 126-128, 221-226
  the Way and ways to, 76-80
  will of, 123-132, 147
Gollancz, Victor, 214
Gospel According to St. John, The, 21
Grace, of God, *see* God; Prayer of, 178-181
Gregoreite (wake up! watch!), 82, 108-109, 115, 11 117
Grou, Jean-Nicolas, 148n.*, 163-165, 217
Groups, spiritual or growth, 7-8, 143-144, 231-238, 253-259
Guardini, Romano, 209
Gurdjieff, G. I., 79, 80, 112, 116-118, 117n.* 128

Hall, Francis J., 208
Hartmann, Franz, 213
Healing, 119, 176
Heard, Gerald, 95-96, 208, 217
Heart, the, 177
Heschel, Abraham J., 112, 215
Hesychast tradition, 16, 165, 169, 216, 222-223

Hilton, Walter, 219
Hinduism, 3, 168, 173, 209, 210, 243
Honesty, 10-17, 21, 22, 46-47, 49, 66, 68, 80, 83, 111, 124, 137, 161, 236-237
absolute, 16, 232
Householder (man or woman in the world), 76-80, 88, 150
Hughson, Shirley C., O. H. C., 85, 217
Humility, 15, 20, 49
Huxley, Aldous, 127n.*, 212n.*, 214

I Ching; *see* Book of Changes
Identity, one's own, "Who am I?", 43, 43n.*; *see also* Self
Illumination, 65, 67, 212
"Illuminism," 66, 123n.*
Inge, W R., 212n.*
Islam, 3, 70n.*, 168n.*, 210, 215, 240-241

James, William, 59
John of Ruysbroeck, 223, 224-225
Johnson, Raynor C., 208
Judaism, 112, 210, 215
Jung, C. G., ii, 51-52, 51n.*, 71-72, 214,

Kant, Immanuel, 46n.*, 49
Karma yoga, 79
Kavanah (attentiveness to God), 112

Kelly, Thomas, 36, 221
Koran, 196-197 (bibliog.), 240-241
Krishna, 115

Lamb, George, 213
Lao Tse, 78, 244
Lawrence, Brother, 88-96, 183,
Learning, 17-18, 21, 27
Lecaro, Cardinal, 219
Lewis, C.S., 73, 131, 213
Yutang, Lin, 244
Love, 45, 133-137, 162, 178
absolute, 232
and truth, 14
Lying, 10-13
contra-indicated, 81, 82, 136

MacDonald, George, 73
Maharshi, Bhagavan Sri Ramana, 35-36, 43, 43n.*, 170
Mantram, 168, 173
Maritain, Jacques, 207
Marmion, Abbot, 212n.*
Martin, P.W., 214
Materialism, 49, 130
Meditation, 178
Mental Science, 211
Mephiz-Tophel; see Adversary
Merton, Thomas, 214
Metanoia ("repent," change your mind, change your state), 81-82, 111
Metaphysics, 211
Miracles, 213

Monkey; *see* Adversary

Moral disciplines, pre-yogic, 83

Morals, moral clean-up, 135-137

Morrison, A. Cressy, 208

Moses, 69

Muhammad, 70n.*, 240-241

Murder, contra-indicated, 81-83

Mysteries, the, 213

Mysticism, mystical insight, 161, 212-213, 212n.*, 221-226

Myth of the Cave, The, 213

Narcotics Anonymous, 8, 232

Neumann, Theresa, 78, 213

Neurotics Anonymous, 8, 232

New Thought, 211

Nicephorus the Solitary, 113-114

Nicholas of Flue, 213

Nicoll, Maurice, 80, 111-112, 116-118

Niebuhr, Reinhold, 208

O'Brien, Rev. John A., 210

Osborne, Arthur, 43n.*

Ouspensky, P.D., 1, 79-80, 112

Overeaters Anonymous, 8, 232

Oxford Group, 16, 232

Pardue, Bishop Austin, 11, 177, 216

Pascal, 31

Patanjali, The Yoga Aphorisms of 85, 171-172, 215

Peale, Norman Vincent, 211

People, as helps in spiritual life, 2, 7-8, 21, 23-30, 47-48, 65

Phillips, Dorothy Berkeley, 214

Philo Judaeus, 36

Philokalia, The, 27, 36, 113-114, 169-170, 222-223,

Pilgrim, the, 166-167, 169, 173, 177, 216

Pilgrim Continues His Way, The, 166

Plato, 46n.*, 213

Plotinus, 36, 213, 221-222

Positive thinking, 211

Poulain, A., 219

Prabhavananda, 83, 85, 170-171, 174, 215

Practice of abandonment, the; *see* Surrender to God

Practice of continuous prayer, the, 163-177, 179

Practice of ego-reduction, the, 96-106

Practice of penetrating the cloud, the, 149-163, 181

Practice of the Presence of God, the, 88-96, 105, 114, 114n.*, 119, 148, 177

Practice of watching, the, 106-119, 148, 177

commanded by Christ, 82, 105, 108-109

Praos ("meek," trained, tractable), 82

Prayer, 103, 106, 119, 133-140, 149-181

and the body, 153-155

books about, 215-226

and breathing, 155-156

commanded by Christ, 82, 164

continuous, 163-177
of Jesus, 163, 164-165, 167, 173-177
"making the mind blank," in, 160-161
map of, 178
place of, 152
time of, 149-152
and visions, 158
Protestants and faith, 210-211
Psychic phenomena, 158-159
Psychopathic personalities, 13
Purgation, 67, 137, 212
Purity, absolute, 232
Questions, as helps in spiritual life, 1, 2
Quietism, 221
Quimby, Phineas Parkhurst, 211

Radhakrishnan, Sarvepalli, 209
Rama, 78, 168, 168n.†, 173
Ramakrishna, Sri, 34, 70n*, 78, 101, 170, 215
Ramanama, 168, 170, 176
Ramayana of Tulasidas, 166n.†
Read, David H.C., 211
Reason, as help in spiritual life, 45-53, 56-58, 61-62
books about, 207-209
Recollection of God, 89, 90-91; *see also* Remembering
Recovery from addiction, 231-238
Remembering, importance of, 142-144, 179; *see also* Recollection

Rheinhold, H. A., 214
Richard of St. Victor, 223
Roman Catholics, and faith, 209-210
Rosten, Leo, 210
Rules, of spiritual life, 80-85, 88
Rumi Jalaluddin, 36, 215

St. Albert the Great, 220
St. Anselm, 46n.*
St. Augustine, 31, 49, 213
St. Bernard, 65, 220, 223, 225
St. Catherine of Genoa, 213
St. Francis de Sales, 78-79
St. Francis of Assisi, 70n.*, 78, 213
St. Gregory of Sinai, 57
St. Ignatius of Loyola, 213
St. Isaac, 113-114
St. John of the Cross, 36, 159, 212n.*, 225-226
St. John of the Ladder, 113
St. Paul, 70n.*, 102, 209
St. Seraphim of Sarov, 215
St. Simeon, 113
St. Teresa of Jesus, 212n.*, 213, 219-220
St. Thomas Aquinas, 46n.*, 49, 53, 208, 209, 220
Satori (sudden awakening), 112
Schaer, Hans, 71-72
Schimberg, A.P, 213
Scholem, Gershom, 215
Schroeder, Eric, 215
Schuon, Frithjof, 169
Schweitzer, and rational thought, 47n.*

Scupoli, Lorenzo, 85
Secret of the Golden Flower, The, 215
Self, the Higher and the lower, 102-105, 249-251
Shaitan; see Adversary
Shankaracharya, 36, 62
Sheean, Vincent, 21
Sheed, F.J., 208
Sin, the seven capital sins, 84
Sincerity, 17, 66
Smith, Margaret, 215
Song of Songs, The, 223-224
Sorokin, Pitirim, A., 209, 214
Stealing, contra-indicated, 81, 83
Suffering (pain, loss, sickness, accidents), as helps in spiritual life, 82, 83, 138-139, 141-142, 176
Sufis, 223
Surrender to God (abandonment), 83, 106,
    practice of, 140-149, 177, 181
Suso, Henry, 213
Suzuki, D.T., 215

Tanquerey, Adolphe, 85
Tao Te Ching; *see* Book of Tao
Tauler, John, 158
Theologica Germanica, 105, 160
Theology, books about, 208
Therapeutae, 16
Thurston, Herbert, 213
Tibet's Great Yogi, Milarepa, 215
Tillich, Paul, 208
Toynbee, Arnold J., 209

Treasury of Russian Spirituality, A, 214-215
Trochu, Abbe Francis, 213
Troward, Thomas, 211
Trueblood, Elton, 207
Truth, 11, 13, 21, 27-28, 68, 80, 82, 83, 85, 124-125, 129, 158, 160, 181, 226, 236-237
Twelve Steps, The, 232-233

Underhill, Evelyn, 212
Union with God, 67-68, 212, 221-226
Unity School of Christianity, 211
Unselfishness, absolute, 232
Upanishads, 11, 40, 43n.*, 102, 241-243

Van Paassen, Pierre, 215
Vedas, the, 241-242
Virtue (holy power), 136

Waite, A. E., 60-61, 69
Walsh, W.T., 214
Watching; see Practice of watching
Watts, Alan, 215
Way of a Pilgrim, The, 166-167, 169, 173, 177, 216
Weatherhead, Leslie, 129, 130
William of St. Thierry, 220
Work, necessity of, 18-21, 42, 80, 85
    place of, 41-43